Edith Jemima Simcox

Natural Law

An Essay in Ethics

Edith Jemima Simcox

Natural Law
An Essay in Ethics

ISBN/EAN: 9783337232603

Printed in Europe, USA, Canada, Australia, Japan

Cover: Foto ©Suzi / pixelio.de

More available books at **www.hansebooks.com**

THE
ENGLISH AND FOREIGN
PHILOSOPHICAL LIBRARY.

VOLUME IV.

Ballantyne Press
BALLANTYNE, HANSON AND CO.
EDINBURGH AND LONDON

NATURAL LAW.

An Essay in Ethics.

BY

EDITH SIMCOX.

LONDON:
TRÜBNER & CO., LUDGATE HILL.
1877.

IF truth be at all within the reach of human capacity, 'tis certain it must lie very deep and abstruse; and to hope we shall arrive at it without pains, while the greatest geniuses have failed with the utmost pains, must certainly be esteemed sufficiently vain and presumptuous. I pretend to no such advantage in the philosophy I am going to unfold, and would esteem it a strong presumption against it were it so very easy and obvious.

HUME'S *Treatise of Human Nature.*

CONTENTS.

I.

NATURAL LAW.

	PAGE
Query, Whether human acts and feelings are subject to law in the same sense as the modifications of unconscious natural objects?	3
Human feeling presumably so subject as itself a product of physical laws	4
Human will so subject unless human nature is essentially unknowable	5
The nature of a thing = the laws of its manifestations . .	5
Definition of law	6
Accidental uniformities not to be called a law . . .	7
True laws state the relations between things which are made constant by otherwise fixed properties in the things related .	8
The laws imposed on the human will = the dictates of the sum of efficient motives	11
The laws of nature obeyed involuntarily and unconsciously; positive law by deliberate acts of will	12
Query, Whether positive law presupposes a lawgiver? . .	13
The essence of subjection to law consists in the general necessity of voluntary obedience to certain commands . . .	14
The real uniformities of human conduct conditioned by the nature of the agent, by his relations with other men, and by his relations to things in general	15

II.

CUSTOMARY AND POSITIVE LAW.

Positive law deals with the constant relations of men to each other following from their nature as men	19
Query, Have these relations any common quality? . . .	19
Most general natural law that society could not subsist without law, *i.e.*, if all volitions were incalculably unstable . . .	20

Customary law = a record of the habitual performance, by men of the same kind, of actions of the same kind, similar causes producing similar effects till some of the conditions vary . 21

Consciousness of constraint, the characteristic of positive law : acts that "have to be done," without desire, in obedience to external pressure voluntarily submitted to . . . 22

Custom passes into law when uniform practices cease to be instinctive, and men become conscious of the generality of an usage as a motive for conforming to it, or a deterrent from its breach 24

When customs have become divergent, the will of the community expresses itself through a special official organ . . . 25

Influence of political centralisation on legislation . . . 27

Distinction between legislation and government . . . 28

Differentiation of sovereign and subject 29

Law requires the co-operation of two natures, tendencies, or wills, *i.e.*, the subject's consent 30

Natural history of primitive potentates, the patriarch and the chief 31

Law formulates the real relations *inter se* of the subjects of law . 37

Whence the feeling that natural constancies of relation "ought" to be maintained ? 38

Distinction between fact and law 41

Law only gives the rule of life for the normal man . . . 43

Distinction between *jus* and *justa*. We ask, both, What is justice? and What kind of actions are just ? 46

Natural selection of possibilities in the direction of equity . . 48

Littré and Kant 51

Justice = the best general rule practically applicable . . 52

No standard of right or justice except the real tendency of the kind to its own good 54

The only "natural right" of individuals what the common good requires them to have 59

Metaphysical theories of the source of legal obligation . . 62

III.

MORALITY.

Sense of obligation = consciousness of causation . . . 75

Habit not a motive 77

Difficulty of separating the practical and speculative side of moral problems 78

Duty always conceived as relative to a person owning the obligation 79

Human feelings conditioned by natural facts, and not conversely 83

Divergent theories of obligation, theistic, sentimental, and utilitarian 85

Right being relative to the conscience, what is the good commonly thought right or moral ? 86

CONTENTS.

	PAGE
Three kinds of good : natural good, or full healthy life	87
Sensible good, or pleasure	90
Moral good, or the pursuit of natural good through obstacles which make the pursuit self-conscious	98
Such obstacles threefold	99
Utilitarianism fails to motive evolution, or to explain the cases in which sensible and natural good do not coincide	101
Natural necessity of self-denial	107
A morality of some kind—or formula of obligation, imposed by the nature of the agent in its fixed relations with the surrounding medium—exists necessarily, whatever the nature of its actual injunctions	117
The tendencies commonly called moral, those which conduce to the natural good of the kind	119
A kind could not subsist with essentially self-destructive tendencies	121
The sacrifice of the natural good of individuals only liable to become moral because men are members of a social body, so that their natural perfection includes the discharge of social functions, in the manner most conducive to the natural perfection of the whole	126

IV.

RELIGION.

The natural history of emotion	133
Comparative authority of feeling and reason	135
All human knowledge, belief, and perception natural, because all received through the natural faculties of man	136
Men find themselves affected by forces that are Not-man, and do not at once conceive any of these to be unconscious	139
Ceremonial observances associated with religion	141
Religious feeling first a reaction under the apprehension of uncontrollable power	142
Then under an apprehension of the moral influences of the Not-self on man	144
Agnosticism and the Cultus of the Unknowable	147
The metaphysics of ignorance	151
Personification of the imagined cause of a felt impression	154
Arbitrary grouping of events by each several centre of consciousness	156
Emotional vicissitudes explained in the same way as material incidents	158
Historical idolatries	165
Dualism	168
Pantheism	169

CONTENTS.

	PAGE
Mystical and natural love and worship	171
Comte : Humanity great, but not supreme	178
The religious sentiment one of complete dynamic acquiescence	182
Religious "conversion" of the will to such acquiescence in the real tendency of all that is	183
"Conviction of sin"	185
Naturalistic piety and its limits	190
Whether the religious sentiment is equally reasonable in all ages	193
Piety most rational when human aspirations after the Best possible find themselves most nearly in harmony with the spontaneous course of things	196
Atheistical religion	198
Rational faith only belief in the reality and trust in the power of goodness	200
Discrepancy between, even, lawful wishes and powers	205

V.

THE NATURAL HISTORY OF ALTRUISM.

Retrospect	211
The "sufficient reason" for moral conduct naturally identified with the standard of morality	215
The standard of Conscience	216
Of Utility	217
Of Perfection	218
Action instinctive or rational	220
Instinctive action disinterested as often as not	221
Power of acting develops more freely than power of enjoying	223
Power of acting with or upon other men craves exercise as it develops	226
The natural history of Altruism	228
Social discords accidental	232
Social wisdom and virtue consist mainly in harmonising the tendencies that exist, not in bringing them all into conformity with some outer standard	234
The general law of social duty enforced by penal sanctions, the force of which upon the human will is due to the same tendencies which caused the law to be proclaimed	239

VI.

THE NATURAL SANCTIONS OF MORALITY.

Causes and effects inseparable, so the dislike felt for the natural consequences of an immoral act, otherwise attractive, acts as a sanction of the law against it 245

CONTENTS.

The natural law against murder and theft	246
Against inconstancy	247
Against suicide	252
The natural history of charity	254
The pleasures of vice	258
Waste of moral force in the exercises of false religion	260
Doctrine of remission of sins an immoral evasion of the stringency of the natural sanction that no accomplished act can be undone	261
Remorse, the consciousness of having acted against the true nature	265
Human will gives voice and effect to human nature	271

VII.

SOCIAL AND INDIVIDUAL PERFECTION.

The best possible attainment, at any given period, a question of fact	275
Various types of specific excellence only comparable when tried by the standard of social serviceableness	278
Mutual dependence of the ruling few and the subservient many	280
Alternative vocations: politics, industrialism, art, science, philanthropy	280
Political ideals: postulates; that progress is normal and privilege unjust: definition of social progress	282
Danger of social disorganisation comes not from the fact of social development, but from its partial and unequal extent	283
Popular and providential theories of the function of government	284
Differentiation of social functions; self-willed service honourable and compulsory obedience base	288
Natural ability privileged to render the most honourable services	289
But beneficial services must be accepted as well as proffered, and so far the leaders of society are at the mercy of their followers	292
Growing complexity of the social ideal which makes the obligations of individuals less clear and notorious	295
The ideal in legislation neither more nor less attainable than the ideal in government	300
Legal rights of property subject to the common interest	302
Effect on proprietary rights of an absolute physical limitation of supply in the case of any commodity in demand, *e.g.*, land	304
The waiving of anti-social rights a step towards the formation of improved social custom which may in time rank as law	307
Organisation of public services	308
Theory of the production and distribution of wealth	309
Natural *versus* competitive value: cost and utility the essential elements	310
Third element in the price of labour: the *Wille zum Leben* of the vendor	311

CONTENTS.

	PAGE
Personal motives not always forthcoming to urge every one to the end generally most desirable	315
Inexpedient to interfere with the accidental consequences of unequal natural ability	317
Desirable to substitute a rational estimate of value for the fluctuating competitive price	318
Partition of the "unearned increment" of social wealth	318
Natural value not diminished by increased production, nor real purchasing power	323
Honorary services the natural price of unearned wealth	325
The ideal state on all points practically unattainable; query, Whether the best possible be an approach to the unattainable?	326
Demand that ethical theories shall carry with them their application to the practical emergencies which concern us	327
The duty of individuals traced out by the social and the personal ideal conjointly	328
Temporary, reluctant and conditional exaltation of the philanthropic reformer	331
Æsthetic emotion	335
Positive truth	337
Moral diffidence of a critical introspective age	339
The asceticism of secular fastidiousness	341
No real antagonism possible between the claims of social duty and individual perfection	344
Specialisation of function among individuals usually a gain, but increasing differentiation of classes a loss, if it extends beyond an external division of labour to a radical contrast of nature	346
Personal completeness a condition of the best action, however highly specialised	347

VIII.

CONCLUSIONS.

Pro and Con 352

CORRIGENDA.

Page 65, line 6 from bottom, *for* "things in themselves," *read* "things bad in themselves."

Page 187, line 14 from top, *for* "inconsistence," *read* "inconsistent."

I.
NATURAL LAW.

"Plerique qui de affectibus et hominum vivendi ratione scripserunt, videntur non de rebus naturalibus, quæ communes naturæ leges sequuntur, sed de rebus, quæ extra naturam sunt agere."—SPINOZA.

Query, whether human acts and feelings are subject to law in the same sense as the modifications of unconscious natural objects?—Human feeling presumably so subject as itself a product of physical laws—Human will so subject unless human nature is essentially unknowable—The nature of a thing equals the laws of its manifestations—Definition of law—Accidental uniformities not to be called a law—True laws state the relations between things which are made constant by otherwise fixed properties in the things related—Two things acting on each other modify each other in a given fixed way, but one does not impose the necessary modification on the other, it follows necessarily from the nature of both—The laws imposed on the human will equal the dictates of the sum of efficient motives—The laws of nature obeyed involuntarily and unconsciously; positive law by deliberate acts of will—Query, whether law presupposes a lawgiver?—The essentials of a law generality and obeyableness—The general rules which men find it natural and necessary to obey, regulate their actions and feelings towards each other, and their feelings towards the fixed immaterial conditions of their moral and intellectual life.

I.

NATURAL LAW.

ANY inquiry into the conditions of human existence takes for granted that something exists.

By the existence of a thing we understand only a real power of producing and undergoing modification; and as, by human consciousness of existence, we understand only the power of perceiving modifications produced or suffered by the conscious subject and other real things, it is evident that speculation concerning human existence can only be concerned with the perceivable modifications suffered or produced by human beings.

The shortest way of stating a case is always the most abstract. No simple word, to which we attach clear and ready images, will serve to describe both sides of the phenomena of life. We may speak of modifications, or change and the consciousness of change; but, saving a few metaphysicians, every one will object that change presupposes the existence of things that change; and there is no easily intelligible formula for the fact that it is only by changes in ourselves that we discern the existence of change, or changing things, beyond ourselves.

The provinces of natural science and moral philosophy touch in the problem : Whether the modifications of which human beings are conscious in themselves are subject to law in the same sense in which the modifications of unconscious natural objects are so subject, and whether they may become in the same way matter for positive, exact knowledge ?

If consciousness is to be trusted—or in other words, if

the changes of which we are conscious in ourselves are in any way a faithful reflection or counterpart of the changing relations among other objective existences—one-half of our life, that of passive perception, will be as completely and knowably subject to law as the orderly natural phenomena that we perceive. If, further, the human mind is made, as the human body is made, of that which it feeds on and assimilates, its long course of orderly perception will grow—must have grown long since—into an organic habit of knowledge, a set of mental predispositions, answering to the most general set of outward impressions.

As the animal eye is made by the action of the light which it perceives upon specially organised matter, so the animal mind is made by the perceptions it registers through a still higher development of the vital mechanism. This natural continuity, or congruity between thought and things, fixes the objective place of man, the knowing and feeling, in the order of nature, the knowable and sensible. But man is not merely a passive register of natural phenomena. No natural force is more active and prolific than the human will, and we cannot venture, as yet, to take for granted that the actions and mental passions of men stand in as constant relations to their nature and circumstances as their physical feelings and mental perceptions.

Human consciousness is beyond doubt a something distinct and unique, but it is still an open question whether we are to class mental processes on one side and every other natural phenomenon on the other, or whether we should look on man as only the chief and most interesting among the many marvellous products of natural evolution. The question is one of vital importance, because all the other objects of natural knowledge have points of contact amongst themselves; the history of most is in a sense continuous, and each object of knowledge stands in definite, knowable relations to other objects. If man were the only exception to this universal rule, either his own nature must be essentially unknowable, or his life must be subject to determination by some extra-natural, unknowable force. But before resorting to such an hypothesis we should satisfy ourselves that the simple view which regards man as a part of the natural order wherein he lives is unsustainable.

By the nature of a thing we understand the classes of actions (or sufferances) constantly characteristic of it under given circumstances, *i.e.*, the laws it follows; and our knowledge of everything, from men to molecules, is coextensive with our knowledge of the rules, or laws, according to which they suffer and act, or cause and undergo modification. It would appear, therefore, that unless human acts and sufferances are subject to law in the same sense as the regular modifications of natural objects, they cannot become matter of knowledge. In other words, knowledge is orderly, and unless human life is orderly, mankind is doomed to self-ignorance.

The difficulty is to frame a definition of law which shall include the laws of nature, as conceived by men of science; the laws of human nature, as conceived by philosophers and moralists; and "laws properly so called," or the laws of human society, as conceived by jurists and politicians. It is not by accident that common speech uses but one and the same word to characterise the methods of gravitating bodies, of scrupulous consciences, and of suitors in a civil court. But common speech is inexact, and its rough and ready classifications need to be tested. Specialists at one extreme call every recurring fact that they observe a law, and specialists at the other extreme deny the name to the most elaborate statement of fixed derivative relations, unless the fixity is secured by the fiat of a personal lawgiver; and if both these schools err on the side of restriction, the broader customary use of the word is too vague and fluctuating for scientific purposes.

Of all the classical definitions which have been hazarded

of the idea of law, perhaps that of Montesquieu approaches most nearly to the desired comprehensiveness; and it has the additional merit of taking nothing for granted save the assumption implied in all reasoning, that the data for reasoning exist—*i.e.*, that things have definite, knowable natures. "Les loix," says the French philosopher, "sont les rapports nécessaires qui dérivent de la nature des choses." That is to say, two things acting on each other, modify each other in a given fixed way, but one does not impose the necessary modification on the other, it follows necessarily from the nature of both, as thus related. The definition may be faulty, as well as the arguments in which the conception recurs; but the first step towards clear thinking is to know what we mean by the chief terms used, and in the following pages the reader is requested always to understand by the term law—"*a statement of constant relations posited by the nature of things.*"

That there may be constant or apparently constant relations, the statement of which is not properly called a law, most scientific observers admit. The statement of absolute stability or absolute change in a single thing out of relation to every other, if it could be formulated, would not constitute a law, unless the changes repeated themselves in a fixed order, and even then the statement of the constant relations observed amongst the changes would not be held to constitute a true, or necessary—only an empirical—law. An empirical law (or generalisation) states an observed order in the modifications produced or suffered by a given thing, which order, after repeated observations, is provisionally assumed to be constant; but the constancy is not considered to be demonstrated, or the possibility of exceptions to the law excluded, until that one constant relation has been connected with, or explained by, or deduced from, those other known constancies of relation which form, taken together, what we know as the nature of the thing under investigation; or until unbroken experience of the recurring constancy causes it to be included in the simple definition, or description of the nature of the thing itself.

Coexistences, however uniform, do not make a law unless the coexisting phenomena are traceable to a common cause; for it is not a part of the nature of one thing that other quite different things should exist in such and such proportions in the same universe with it. A body of laws declaring the relations between contemporary effects of independent causes would only be conceivable if the first elements of all things had been arranged in cosmic regularity preparatory to the evolution of an absolutely orderly system. A true law of nature enables us to predict with certainty what will happen under given circumstances to any specimen of the class of substances to which the law applies. Mere averages which give a general summary of results, without distinguishing the causes that produce them, do not give a true law, because it is impossible to predict from them, except approximately and in the gross.

It would be scarcely a caricature of the way in which some so-called statistical and historical "laws" are ascertained, if we were to mark the rate of motion of a number of glaciers in different parts of the world, and then strike an average and call the result the "law of glacial motion;" or if we noted the order and rapidity with which places with a "season" fill and empty, and then supposed ourselves to have discovered a "law" of fashionable migration. When there is no permanent connection in nature between the various sources of the conditions necessary to the observed result, the result itself is, properly speaking, accidental or contingent, and predictions respecting its recurrence or reproduction must be conditional on the incalculable persistence of stable relations amongst those causes which we call ultimate because we do not know their constant antecedents, or whether they have any.

The only scientific laws to which we can easily ascribe a logical or metaphysical necessity, comparable to that of the truths of geometry, are those which presuppose certain other fixities of relation. Thus an observed regularity in the movement of light or sound is rationally called a law of optics or acoustics when it has been connected with a broader physical law of motion in general. Given such a law, each new observation concerning the motion of bodies must be either an example of the law, or an exception to it, and the original law, though itself only empirical, acquires new force when it has been found that new cases always illustrate and confirm its truth, and that the assumption that it will be found true in each case that arises is never found to mislead in practice. The laws, then, which we think of as necessary, that is to say, of actual universal cogency, are either such as state a constancy of relations amongst relations, or those which state a simple relation from which it has been found possible to draw inferences respecting other facts and relations that admit and receive subsequent verification.

In no other way can we be assured that the constancy of relations is not accidental, but really posited by the nature of the things of which we wish to know the laws: or, if the distinction between the nature of a thing and the laws of its nature appears trivial, in no other way can we have experience of the existence of different kinds of things. But if we take from science the tolerably elementary fact that distinguishable kinds of things do exist, we soon find a point of contact with the jurists; for, as is generally allowed, we do not know things in themselves, and when we distinguish an object as being of a certain kind, we do not predicate anything concerning its essence, only concerning what may be called its actions, its manifestations, the modifications which it is capable of producing or suffering.

Now the orthodox lawyer's definition of a law is "a command binding to actions of a class;" and it would therefore seem that the only difference between a true positive law and a law of nature is that the latter declares, instead of commanding, what class of actions will, under given conditions, certainly be performed (or suffered) by the subject of the law. But the wisdom of our ancestors, as evidenced in etymology, does not favour the modern assumption that it was essential to a law to be imposed, or laid down, by word of mouth or writing, by a personal legislator; it was enough for it to be imposed or "put;" and the observed relations of the natural world may, with perfect propriety, be spoken of as "posited" by the nature of the things which are, as a fact, related thus and not otherwise, and which would, we take for granted, be differently related if they themselves were different, since difference and resemblance are but words by which we express the real or apparent relations of things.

The ridicule cast by Austin upon "Ulpian's law of nature" may be explained by the strong and perfectly well-founded feeling of lawyers, that consciousness of constraint or recognition of authority is an essential element in the obedience paid to human law as such. The conception of Nature, as a lawgiver, instructing all the members of the animal world in their respective rights and duties, is sufficiently fantastical; but it is not certain, though the words will bear that interpretation, that the *jus quod natura omnia animalia docuit* was regarded by the later Roman jurists in the light in which no naturalist would regard it now, as a law imposed upon things by the will of a metaphysical providence, called Nature, exterior to themselves. And if the Nature that imposes the law is only the nature of the beings subject to it, Ulpian and Montesquieu are at one; and so far from being self-evidently in the wrong, against those who recognise no other source of law than external arbitrary will associated with power—they may be credited with penetration in advance of their age, for having made their conception of the animal life of men and beasts serve as a connecting link between their knowledge of the inanimate world and their conception of the purely human, rational life of man.

If we regard the laws observed by natural objects as the record of their specific nature as manifested under given known conditions, it is evident that the presence of the conditions is essential both to our knowledge of the law and to its actual observance by the thing. All sugar will dissolve in tea, but as long as it is dry it does not dissolve: the liquid in which it may be immersed does not bestow upon it the property of solubility, but if we could suppose a lump of sugar to be conscious, it would not unnaturally conclude the necessity, under which it found itself, of dissolving, to be imposed upon it by the first cup of tea in which it was placed. The inference is sound, with one important qualification, which the sugar is scarcely in a position to make. The tea dissolves it on condition of its being sugar, and not, for instance, rock-crystal; but to effect the result—of dissolution to the sugar and sweetening to the tea—it is not enough for the sugar to be sugar, unless the tea is tea, and not, for instance, frozen mercury; one of these substances cannot be said to impose upon the other the law which regulates their relations, yet the existence and nature of each is the *sine quâ non* of a particular compulsion exercised upon the other.

Now, though the consciousness of constraint exercised by an external power is a part of the idea of laws properly so called, we do not find that their binding force depends upon their being set, or laid down as expressions of the lawgiver's will, as human or divine "commands." It belongs at least as much to the idea of a law that it shall be generally obeyed as that it shall be authoritatively imposed, and it is misleading to insist on one of these elements to the exclusion of the other.

Supposing that human conduct follows knowable laws, or exhibits perceptible constancies of relation, it is still an open question whether the necessary constancy is imposed from without or from within, or whether it arises, as in the case of natural law, from the juxtaposition of certain influences and certain susceptibilities. Or, to state the problem in another form, it is still an open question, how far it is possible to compare the unconscious regularity of nature with the conscious uniformities of human conduct produced by the presence of permanent motives and virtually permanent susceptibility to motives.

The conditions of life are so multiform and human character so various that we do not easily discern the laws of human life in society. The individual does not survey the circumstances of his own and others' life from a vantage-ground which might enable him to see the method according to which he and they act and forbear under the inevitable pressure. The limited experience attainable only suffices to make it seem desirable that certain classes of action should be regularly performed, and others omitted, and to secure this needful measure of regularity, the law commands and enforces its commands with penalties. But we cannot conclude from this that the law, or its organ, is the ultimate source of the actual constancy of human conduct in social relations.

Men are compelled by circumstances to desire a more orderly life than they attain spontaneously; they are beset by dangers, moral and physical, against which they spontaneously *strive* to protect themselves by rule; and it is for us to choose whether we shall say that the necessity for the rule is imposed by the circumstances which make men desire it, or by those qualities of their nature which make them desire it under the given circumstances. The new element of consciousness gives rise to the idea of the law (or objective regularity of things) as addressed to the will, which is moved by the real action of external forces in favour of uniformity. But, at any given moment, the only true lawgiver, in Austin's sense, the only source of the compulsion to which the will submits, is to be found in the impersonal sum of efficient motives; though in practice we may also look on the rule which men in general, on the whole, desire to have enforced, as compelling the conduct of the few who wish to break it, either from native perversity of will or peculiar temptation of circumstances.

The law, in so far as it is the creation of human will and choice, expresses the permanent, average will of the generality, but their will is determined by natural conditions of possibility as well as of inclination. It is the formula for the most desirable—or the most desired—conduct attainable. Positive law, then, is a command binding to actions of a class, necessarily performed, or sought to be performed, by the community under actual conditions: while natural law is the formula for the classes of modifications made necessary to natural objects by their own nature and the other fixed conditions of real existence. In the case of natural law the compulsion and the obedience are of the same involuntary kind; in the case of positive law both compulsion and obedience are of the same voluntary, deliberate kind. The debateable land of confusion and controversy therefore extends no further than the area of questions relating to the normal subjection of man, as a voluntary, conscious, responsible agent, to the natural forces, which we do not believe to be conscious, voluntary, or responsible agents.

Much thinking, theological and otherwise, starts with the assumption that no such intelligible relation of constraint as belongs to the human feeling of lawful government can subsist between man that wills and the impassive tendencies of nature. The most popular explanation of the order of the natural world, and man's place therein, ascribes the existence and nature of everything that is to an act of will on the part of a personal First Cause; and it is supposed that man can only feel bound to obey the laws which express a personal will—the will of some conscious subject like himself, *i.e.*, in practice—man is only bound by the laws of nature in so far as they express the will of God.

The adherents of this view would think it little short of blasphemous to seek materials for a clear and adequate conception of *how* the will of a person can cause anything to come into existence out of nothing. We are supposed to know by moral and intellectual assurance *that* God is, and the name by which He is acknowledged bears with it the association of a great *What* unknowable by finite faculties. And it is no harder to imagine a will creating the properties of acts and relations than it is to imagine the same will creating real substances.

The theological faith and feeling in its entirety commands so much respect and sympathy that we may consider ourselves fortunate in not having to take sacred names in vain in discussing this conception of law, which postulates a personal first cause—outside the law and its subject—of the obligatoriness of the law. Hobbes, who regards the Sovereign as a miniature Deity, and Austin, who regards the Deity as a magnified legislator, both apply to purely human relations a similar theory of personal will as the source of legal compulsion, and it will be sufficient if we can show its inadequacy to explain even the superficial uniformities of conduct enforced by the rods and axes of political authority.

Any one can "call spirits from the vasty deep," but to constitute an act of sovereignty over the spirits, they must be prepared to come "when you do call for them." The intention of a ruler, his mere will that such an act be done or forborne, does not of itself control, or even materially influence, the will of the person to whom the command is addressed. The will of another person may be accepted as a rule of conduct either from affection, or because it is deliberately judged to be wiser and better than the subject will, or because it is conceived to possess an irresistible strength, the thought of which paralyses, so to speak, the power or the will to disobey. But for either of these conditions to be fulfilled, it is not enough that the legislator be good, wise, or strong, unless the subject is also affectionate, reasonably modest, and comparatively weak. Austin and his school are therefore driven to the *petitio principii* involved in defining law as the command of a "political superior," meaning by political superior simply some one whose commands are *de facto* binding. All attempts to analyse the origin, source, or nature of political superiority are obliged to represent it as relative to the political inferiors on whom the laws are imposed, and whose nature is therefore an indispensable condition to the binding force of the law. We can only escape from this circle by admitting that two parties are concerned in the making of every law, or rather that law is made when, and only when, the wills of the two parties consent and meet in one.

The two essentials of a law are that the relation which it formulates should be constant, and that it should be the result of constant qualities in the things related. Everything that exists is, in a certain sense, a lawgiver, imposing fixed and necessary modifications upon every other thing which comes in contact with it. The bodily life of man is subject to the despotic sway of fixed natural conditions, formulated in the laws of nutrition, respiration, and general hygiene. But though it is the peculiarity of human consciousness to bring, as it were, into a focus many far-fetched rays of influence, these general facts are not felt to control the particular volitions of a man, or thought of as addressed to his whole personality. He lives his own life as he chooses subject to the natural laws of life in general. Pantheists, for instance, do not conceive the universe as playing the legislator to its inmates; and one of the many points of variance between theologians and naturalists is that the latter do not enter into the ideal synthesis of human egotism, which imagines all the rays of influence, that meet in the focus of consciousness, to have this convergence for their final cause, and to spring from some remote invisible centre of will, resolved to bring them all to bear at last upon the subject centre of consciousness. Men are certainly subject to the law of gravitation, but they do not look on weight as one of the

NATURAL LAW. 15

forces by which their lives are ruled; it concerns their existence as bodies, not their consciousness as men; and we may add to the definition of the laws of human life that the relation formulated must make itself felt by the conscious subject as affecting his volitions.

Law, according to our definition, supposes a personal subject of the law, whether it supposes a personal lawgiver or not; and it is open to us to investigate the necessary relations of man to society and the natural world, in so far as their nature and his are knowable, without prejudice to the metaphysical question, by what right or power the relations became necessary, *i.e.*, whether or no natural laws are of supernatural imposition.

In other words, we may have a theory of the subjective necessities of man, of the influences which he feels to act irresistibly and steadily upon his moral and intellectual nature, without personifying the influences, or conceiving them to be the expression of a will as personal as his own. We may, however, and we naturally do, classify the laws to which men are subject, or the permanent conditions under which they will, according to the various objects whose constant relations to man are stated in the laws. Law, morality, and religion, as generally conceived, state the constant necessities, or stable modifications of human conduct, imposed on man by his various objective relations. Law states the compulsion exercised on his will by other human wills; morality states the compulsion exercised on him by his own nature in relation (mainly) to these other wills; and religion deals with the compulsion exercised on man by the strongest general influences of the universe, what Mr. Arnold calls the Not-Ourselves. Positive law gives a rule for the overt acts of men; moral law gives a rule for the will, and includes the intention as well as the act; and religion, or the law of spiritual liberty, gives a rule for the inclinations, and includes the feelings and wishes as well as the will and deed. All these laws, without forfeiting their scientific character as "a statement of constant relations posited by the nature of things," may be variously conceived, according as the subject of the law apprehends the rule imposed upon and accepted by its will as primarily imposed by its own nature, or by the nature of something else; the necessity really arises from the relation between the two natures, but as man is only directly conscious of his own side of the relation, he naturally, and not untruly, classifies his obligations according to the manner in which he is affected by them, and the degree to which he is conscious of the affection.

If the objective pressure resulting in these uniformities is real, natural, and constant, human life is not lawless, and the nature and working of the pressure exercised upon the human will from all these points will be knowable. If there is no such real, natural, and knowable pressure, it is time that we cleared our minds from the haze of antique prejudice, and enjoyed the melancholy satisfaction of knowing universal licentiousness to be the natural lot of men. No positive construction is possible until we have got rid of the confused ideas and phraseology of credulous scepticism and half-hearted faith. In any case let us have the courage of our convictions, and distrust most of all the formulæ which promise to reward our quest for truth by stranding us at a secure halting-place between two opinions.

II.

CUSTOMARY AND POSITIVE LAW.

"Dans ces choses, voulez-vous savoir si les désirs de chacun sont légitimes ? Examinez les désirs de tous."—MONTESQUIEU.

"Si l'unité de composition a sa cause primitive dans la limitation des substances matérielles qui portent la vie, l'unité de plan a sa cause dans les prédéterminations ou lois qui règlent cette même vie. Avec des matériaux identiques et des lois impérieuses de manifestation, il est impossible qu'il n'y ait pas unité de composition et unité de plan ou de plans."—LITTRÉ.

Positive law deals with the constant relations of men to each other following from their nature as men—Query, Have these relations any common quality?—Most general natural law that society could not subsist without law, *i.e.*, if all volitions were incalculably unstable—Customary law equals the performance by men of the same kind of actions of the same kind, similar causes producing similar effects till some of the conditions vary —Consciousness of constraint the characteristic of positive law: acts that "have to be done" without desire, in obedience to external constraint voluntarily submitted to—Custom passes into law when uniform practices cease to be instinctive and men become conscious of the generality of a usage as a motive for conforming to it, or a deterrent from its breach—When customs have become divergent, the will of the community expresses itself through a special organ or authorised exponent of law—Distinction between legislation and government—Differentiation of sovereign and subject—Law requires the co-operation of two natures, tendencies, or wills, *i.e.*, at some stage the subject's consent. The efficiency of sanctions depends on the disposition of the subject towards the evil threatened—Natural history of primitive potentates, the patriarch and the chief—Law formulates the real relations *inter se* of the subjects of law—Whence the feeling that natural constancies of relation "ought" to be maintained?—We ask ourselves not only What is justice? but also What kind of actions are just?—Justice the best general rule practically applicable—Natural selection of possibilities in the direction of equity—No standard of right or justice except the real tendency of the kind to what it conceives as its good: (the only "natural right" of individuals what the common good requires them to have)—Metaphysical theories of the source of legal obligation.

II.

CUSTOMARY AND POSITIVE LAW.

THE passage from the abstract to the concrete is the *pons asinorum* of speculation. We have put forward a theory of the nature and force of natural laws which ought to correspond to the facts of contemporary observation and history. The theory is symmetrical; remains to be seen if it is true.

To begin at the beginning: Are the fixed rules concerning the relations of men to each other, observed in real communities, such as follow from the nature of men, or are they arbitrary inventions? Is the distinction between customary and positive law in any way inconsistent with the substantial naturalness of both? Can we trace the evolution of civil and criminal laws, of historical reality, from the play of intelligible human qualities in the necessary relations of civil society? Can we instance any of the constant relations between man and man which follow from the nature of men associated in communities? And, finally, granting that the provisions of custom or civil law are in the main natural, can we explain the peculiar sentiment which, in this case, recognises the natural as obligatory, and yet persists in imagining some other test or condition of true obligatoriness than the bare fact of natural reality?

Perhaps the most general statement possible of a relation following necessarily from the real nature of man is this, that human society cannot subsist without law, not necessarily present to consciousness as such, but still generally observed. The grounds of this necessity are easily seen. After the automatic regularity with which men, like other animals, provide for the satisfaction of their bodily needs and appetites, conscious intelligence comes into play. The first condition of rational life is the stability of nature; for the scope of reason lies in the adjustment of means to ends, and action with a view to ends would be impossible if its calculated effects were always liable to be disturbed or frustrated by incalculable foreign influences. And what is true of the dealings of men with the natural world, applies equally to men in social relation with those of their own kind.

The first condition of society is mutual confidence, and unless there is such a thing as human nature, unless, that is to say, man possesses certain substantially fixed class characteristics, individual men would be unable to shape for themselves any course of conduct in which they might have to depend on the assistance or neutrality of beings acting without law—even if we could suppose it possible for lawless impulse to conceive a rational and orderly plan. As a fact, of course, we know that man has a specific character as clearly marked as that of any other organism, animal or vegetable. Certain kinds of action are natural to men, and nearly the first use to which they put their intelligence is to conceive the ends of such actions as their own cause, the motive force or impulse that causes them to be done. Granted, then, that men act from motives, if their action is in any way regular or calculable, this must proceed from persistency in the determining conditions, the force of the motives must be in the main stable, not varying at random either in the same man at different times or amongst different men under the same circumstances.

A natural constancy in the instinctive, customary actions of men is a preliminary step towards the resolved constancy (called law) of their actions in relation to each other. Other things being equal, the same actions will be natural to the different members of a simple, primitive community, in which, probably, even diversity of race is unknown; but if the same action is naturally performed together by different persons, that circumstance alone modifies its nature. Joint action suggests the possibility of concerted action, and discourages or discredits isolated action. The habit is formed, not only of doing certain things, but of seeing every one else do them, and one person who does differently jars on the established sense of fitness in the rest. Originally, men act together in certain ways, led by common sympathies and interests, but their union brings fresh necessities with it: established social relations, by making life slightly more complicated, suggest, while they restrain, fresh personal impulses; the nature of an indifferent action is modified by its joint performance becoming customary, as that of an indifferent omission is modified when it comes to appear as a departure from established usage.

As Sir Henry Maine says: "It is of the very essence of custom, and this indeed chiefly explains its strength, that men do not clearly distinguish between their actions and their duties—what they ought to do is what they always have done, and they do it;" not, however, distinctly "because" they always have, but rather for the same reason, so long as it continues to apply, that they did before. Among savages "ce qui ne se fait pas" includes the illegal, the wrong, and the ridiculous, and to this day we are not much nearer a reason why we should not do what is illegal, wrong, or absurd, than the intuition that we had better not.

Primitive custom, which exists before either law or morality, consists in doing what every one else does; but so far as every one readily and naturally does the same things, it is not by conscious voluntary submission to an external rule, but from a common internal impulse, which may be called necessary, since it is effective as well as natural. Law does not originate in a conspiracy of the community to coerce the individual, any more than in a conspiracy of the individual to coerce the community; and while the association is wholly voluntary, that is, based on common, identical inclination, there is no need for positive legislation to enjoin practices which are followed as of course.

The consciousness of law as a constraining power fixing the classes of action to be performed by the subject is not primitive, nor indeed would it be possible for it to arise before the constraint referred to had become present to consciousness. The habit, however, of doing thus or thus (like everybody else) creates a secondary, subjective disposition to go on doing so, which is, of course, in its nature conscious, and felt as a restraint upon the natural liberty of absolute indifference. Primitive morality, or the idea that certain things *must* be done (those, namely, which *are* done by the tribe or family), is the offspring partly of deficient imagination, partly of the fact that the original action has become habitual as well as natural, whence a secondary, artificial difficulty is felt in substituting any other kind of action, till motives of a new class have come fully into force. The majority, after feeling the same kind of original impulse, experience the same kind of difficulty in ceasing to act upon it in particular cases while its general force subsists, and the same necessity for ceasing if a change in the conditions makes the old act uneasy or undesirable. The mere cessation of an old motive does not give a feeling of obligation unless a habit formed under its influence survives the change of circumstances which makes its maintenance useless or inconvenient; but if a present motive for acting in one way comes into collision with the formed habit of acting in another, obedience to the habit, if it proves the strongest, is attended by a consciousness of necessity, legal, moral, or religious, that may be quite independent of reason or expediency, as we find, in fact, that meaningless ceremonial observances are among the first to be associated with the idea of moral obligation or duty. And when this first kind of constraint becomes present to consciousness, all who feel themselves bound by it, agree spontaneously in saying, "We" (not yet "*I*") "must do thus and thus:" in other words, custom and morality are identified, and made to sanction each other's ordinances.

We are, however, at present less concerned with the foundations of morality than with the foundations of positive law, with duty than with obligation. The history of society is the history of relations, between individuals and groups, whose conduct and attitude towards each other is liable to be modified by the fact that they are conscious of the relation, and liable to affections of pleasure and pain in connection with that consciousness, which supply new motives for the maintenance or modification of the relation. The stability of the relations between the various members of a community is proportioned to its simplicity. These relations, considered objectively, while it occurs to no one to modify them, or to conceive them as modifiable, form the *status* of individuals, who are classified naturally by their own acquiescence in the position allotted to them by circumstances. Early law, as is now generally admitted, rests on status, not contract; it begins by consecrating or affirming that which already is, for facts precede reasoning, even from immediate self-interest.

The explanation of this apparently irrational, impulsive origin of the "Social Compact" becomes clear, if we consider that contract—a deliberate engagement to do or to forbear on certain conditions or for certain considerations —implies the distinct conception of two independent, voluntary actions, and the possibility of performing either, neither, or both; conceptions which, it need hardly be said, will not be formed until experience, that is, previous action, has furnished material for them. The only social law which seems to be laid down without appeal by the nature of man is the necessity for some law; but the addition of new facts, the growth of impulses or appetites not absolutely essential to the nature of man as such, produces new, still stable relations, forming the matter of more particular legislation. But relations must be real, must exist, before their regularity can be observed and accepted as imperative. Law, as the record of facts, is posterior to the facts themselves; which may be illustrated by the rather singular suggestion of Comte, that society must constitute itself somehow, unscientifically, *tant bien que mal*, before social science can exist—can have a subject, a patient, to treat.

This peculiarity must be allowed to mark a natural distinction between the laws of physical science and human legislation. Human law proclaims not only a conditioned uniformity, but a self-conscious uniformity, and a true law might be defined as the passing into consciousness of a fixed natural relation or effective tendency. The transition from a society based on status and ruled by unbroken custom, to one based on contract and ruled by positive law, is that from relations *de facto*—or of practically unquestioned validity—to relations *de jure*—or of validity that is affirmed against questioners; and it is made by the growing consciousness of the relation as *binding* as well as *existing*. Custom, in becoming conscious, adds a legal necessity to itself, but the new necessity is only subjective, and adds nothing to the antecedent uniformity.

Law, properly so called, does not innovate or create, and this natural limitation to the power of making quite random experiments in legislation applies as much to a single sovereign or lawgiver as to an autonomous community. It is at this point that the Naturalistic theory of law (as it may be called) diverges from the political or arbitrary theory represented by Hobbes and Austin. The dictates of custom, as we have seen, may come to be associated with feelings of compulsion to all appearance like those which secure obedience to laws properly so called, and if a body of customary law happens to be written down, or fixed in a sacred metrical tradition, its text has a force indistinguishable from that of any imperial code. But it is a fact, apparently in favour of the other side of the argument, that most ancient codes of law profess to have been made, or proclaimed by some one mythical sage, king or priest; and though we cannot, on the faith of such traditions, altogether accept the personal theory of legislation, we may at least admit that law differs from custom in possessing, and requiring, always some definite, authorised organ.

The need for an authoritative exposition of the law of the land arises at nearly the same stage of social progress as the centralisation of political power, and one of the earliest functions of government is the administration of law. But, as Sir Henry Maine has pointed out, there are many absolute political rulers who never legislate, and whose edicts, even though enjoining actions of a class, cannot be mistaken for laws. Austin held that generality in a command was enough to constitute it a law, while we should distinguish, even in cases where the sovereign is his own legislator, between laws, or the regulation of existing relations, and simple precepts or general commands. We know as a fact that customary law was in many instances full grown before political organisation had passed its infancy, while the political organisation of a military despot has never resulted in the establishment of a system of law where the subject population had no fixed civil relations to perpetuate; but the simultaneous crystallisation of legal and political authority led not unnaturally to the mistake of treating the narrower phenomenon as naturally subsidiary to the wider. Every independent community had a government which enforced its laws, and as anarchy was a synonym for lawlessness, legislation was made a synonym for government.

In speaking of the rise of law, we are after all generalising from a comparatively small number of historical cases, and the illustration that lies nearest us will serve as well as any other to show how far the growth of a central authority may further the growth of a body of national law upon the foundation of popular custom. The outlines of the real supply the best boundary against the hypothetical, and the parallel development of English Common Law and the power of the Crown under our early kings supplies more intelligible and authentic grounds for speculation than the legends of Deiokes, Lykurgus, or Numa.

"Consuetudo," says Lord Coke, "is one of the main triangles of the lawes of England; those lawes being divided into common law, statute law, and custom." The common law is—or rather in those days of its departed glory was—the general custom of the kingdom, as distinguished from that of single cities or manors; and its authority only ceased to be sufficient as well as supreme, as the mass of the inhabitants of the kingdom ceased, from a variety of causes, to live habitually in such a way that the *same* custom could serve to regulate all their civil and social relations; or, in other words, when social and civil distinctions and relations became too numerous for all the members of the community to know familiarly and remember the rules and precedents according to which their intercourse with each other was to be carried on, under all the conditions actually liable to arise.

The chief difference between a custom and a law is that the followers of a custom consciously make their actual practice the standard of right or obligation, while positive law is the utterance of an embodied authority enjoining something which the subject does not know or imagine that he would have done without the injunction. Law is —ideally—the expression of what *would* be the general will if the self-consciousness of the community could be suddenly sublimated and intensified, so as to become at once aware of all its own strongest impulses, and of the adjustments and limitations necessary for reconciling and harmonising their indulgence. Only, as the organ by which the community expresses this will is itself subject to concrete human infirmities—of timidity, self-interest, or stupidity—statutes are no more infallible than custom is omniscient, and to secure a tolerable practical approach towards the ideal, the intelligence of the community needs to be consciously turned towards the consideration of its own real organic needs and wishes, which the legislature may otherwise ignore, for want of a sufficiently present sense of their material force. Good customs, when they exist, are patent to sense; good laws, when they are possible, demand a higher intellectual intuition, discerning not merely facts but relations.

The Norman Conquest helped to precipitate the transition from the régime of custom to that of law in England, by multiplying class interests and usages. Political inequalities are one source of social differentiation, and it is the development of social differences that causes relations to multiply, and—with the multiplication of cross relations—the chance of collision between distinct, if not necessarily opposing interests. Local or national custom may be strong enough to control the erratic or rebellious impulses of individuals, but a class having common interests not identical with those of the rest of the community may form a custom of its own, incompatible with older customary rights and privileges. If the appetites or interests of individuals come into collision, they either fight out their quarrel or compromise it, as it were instinctively; but when the conflict is between the interests or usages of sets of persons, instead of individuals, the power of automatic adjustment or adaptation breaks down, and the scattered motives to mutual concession existing in nature have to be summed up and brought home to the consciousness of all alike in the official sanction of a law. The growing want of some central authority—such as the king and his officers of justice—to decide between "bad customs" and those that were good, lawful, and binding, contributed as much as any directly political cause to the strengthening of the royal prerogative that went on under the "English Justinian" and his immediate followers and predecessors; the lawful power of the Crown and Legislature increased the more because there was no avowable *class* interests concerned in resisting it, while every dawning custom that could claim to be innocent or advantageous was eager to receive its sanction.

In the same way, in most historical nations, the making of good laws became an important part of government, and a necessary step towards the welding into one of an artificially large and heterogeneous community. But cases also abound of sovereigns who have been content with the exercise of purely political authority, and have not attempted to regulate the relations of their subjects among themselves. Perhaps it is too much to say that such sovereigns do not legislate at all, since their general commands define the duties of the subject to the prince; at the same time, however, it is clear that they do not specify the permanent relations between the two, or the gift of a "constitution" would not be so long coveted and so reluctantly accorded: they decree from time to time what taxes the subject shall pay, and what military service he shall render, and they may restrict his private liberty to an indefinite extent to suit the prince's pleasure or whim. These enactments are even less general than our statutes, and these, though included under the general head of laws, have ever had less sanctity, to the true legal mind, than the ancient common law, since one statute may be repealed by another, and many are avowedly of only temporary force and interest.

The distinction, then, is by no means unreal or formal between laws that state permanent natural relations and develop their logical corollaries, and other enactments of political authority. In an absolute government the only true law is that which affirms the despotic constitution of the state, and this is as far as any other law from being of purely arbitrary imposition; it formulates the necessary relations between an arbitrary sovereign and a servile population, but the law does not make the population servile—it must find them so.

The differentiation of a primitive community into tyrants and slaves is just as double-sided as any other social development, and the historical steps in the process refuse to be summed up in the simple generalisation which makes all law and government alike the mere expression of *force majeure*, the will of the strongest. The most obvious difficulty in the way of supposing law to be made by the arbitrary will of individuals, is that no merely natural difference between the powers of men living in patriarchal or barbarian simplicity is sufficient to enable individuals to terrorise, or control, the wills of the community; while an artificial or conventional superiority, that is to say, one based on wealth, or popularity, or family *prestige*, has to be built up gradually, and with the consent or assistance of those whose subsequent obedience to the power they have helped to found, is assumed by the arbitrary theory to be naturally reluctant and only extorted by force.

It will scarcely be maintained that human societies subsist without law till such time as they have succeeded in educating a tyrant (benevolent or otherwise), and in providing him with friends, ministers, and servants in such force as to make the mere announcement of his will an imposing motive; and it is in this gradual process, of the consolidation of political authority, that we shall find the real antecedent of the phenomenon called sovereignty —and not in a generic difference between the one and the many. The one will be obeyed if his subjects believe in his power of compelling obedience, but even so their obedience is determined by their opinion about his authority, as the real extent of that authority is determined by their readiness to acquiesce or not in its exercise.

Of course at this point the doctrine of sanctions is introduced. It is not the will or opinion of the subject, we are told, but the power of the ruler to inflict punishment, that gives the commands of the latter their binding and constraining force. This, however, does not diminish the original difficulty. A simple expression of will by one man to another is a motive, though a slight one, for compliance, when the act enjoined is either indifferent or agreeable; other things being equal, children and adults generally do unthinkingly as they are told, either because they do not care to disoblige a fellow-creature without motive, or because, when personal desires are in equilibrium, the slightest touch from without suffices to turn the scale; but if other things are not equal, and compliance is thoroughly repugnant to the will of the person upon whom a command is laid, the effective force of any sanction, even capital punishment or eternal damnation, depends not on the intrinsic gravity of the threatened evil, but upon the disposition of the subject; his private opinion or judgment respecting the comparative disadvantages of obedience and the consequences of rebellion. If the alternative is to fall down and worship the golden image which Nebuchadnezzar the king has set up, or to be cast into the burning fiery furnace, there is no true compulsion, even though the obstinate monotheist should not be saved from death by a miracle. An irksome law enforced by sanctions will only be generally obeyed if the punishment attached to its non-observance is one which a majority of the subject population thinks a more serious evil than the original evil of obedience; but the lawgiver, as such, has no influence upon the opinion to which his laws owe their force. To complete the idea of command, we must have that of obedience, which, however reached or produced, implies consent.

In point of fact, however, neither law nor government depend mainly on the penalties which they proclaim for offences; obedience is the rule, and rebellion the exception, or it would cease to be rebellion, and succeed to the vacant seat of power. The earliest examples of quasi-political authority that we meet with in the domain of fact may be reduced to two: the power of the patriarch over his household, and the power of the chief over his tribe. This power is sustained in both cases alike by the possession of wealth by the political superior; but this wealth is not, as in later times, received by the chief or father as tribute from his inferiors; his power is coextensive with his will and ability to feed dependants; and at the earliest possible moment at which we find social inequalities beginning, we find the difference between man and man to consist only in slightly greater or less power of accumulating wealth, associated with greater or less disposition to call the accumulation "*mine*"—even if the only use of it is to be given away.

The earliest road to possession is, no doubt, by the primitive process of "taking," and the power of taking is the first to inspire general respect; but it is sometimes argued that property has originally to be defended, as well as acquired by force, and that, unless he is prepared to do so, the early chief, or strong man, will be despoiled of his gains by his fellow-tribesmen. There is some confusion of the natural order in this view, for the tribe has made no step towards political unity, if it does not even respect its chief, and, except as a unit, it cannot act together, while, by the hypothesis, no single individual within it has greater power of "taking" than the chief. It is felt to be more profitable to let him take as he can and share as he chooses than to scramble once for his takings; and the weakest members of the community have most inducement to let the partition of the lion's share be made on some other principle than that of a free fight among the jackals.

But in this discussion of possible alternatives, we take too little account of the profoundly unimaginative temper of primitive man. When he has but lately, by a mental effort, raised himself to the conception of a right of property in things extending beyond their momentary use, he cannot all at once contradict himself. The invention of a possessive case has a meaning or not; if a horse or cow is thought of as "belonging to A," it is *ex vi termini* thought of as not available to B for annexation by the same natural process as unappropriated goods. The conception is not easy, and in some of the Pacific islands it is only reached by the help of a metaphysical or religious artifice; to appropriate a thing, it must be proclaimed "taboo" to the rest of the world; and in Tonga especially, the system is said to serve all the purposes of police, apparently because the idea "we must not touch this," finds easier acceptance than any statement of the reason why—namely, that somebody else has claimed or captured it first. In any case, we find together with the first existence of private property, a spontaneous recognition of its existence by others than the owner—at once the condition and guarantee of the ownership, as the obedience of the subject is the condition and guarantee of the more immaterial possession, political power.

Taking the possession of wealth—whether measured in food, shells, skins, wives, slaves, or other live stock—as the first source of social inequality, we have to consider how this possession tends to found or strengthen the authority, within either the family or the tribe, of the owner of the wealth. In the least advanced, polygamous societies, where wives are the chief article of property, the man who has most wives is also best able to maintain those he has, because he has most command of labour, but his authority in the tribe is not increased in proportion to the increase of his social dignity; he has still no hold upon his fellow-tribesmen or adult sons, except by his personal qualities and a larger supply of exchangeable daughters. If his wealth takes the form of implements, and his stores of food are in excess of his own requirements, a tacit understanding generally exists as to the mode in which they are to be got rid of. Wealth is the source of dignity, but the proof of wealth is its distribution, and the candidate for popularity and honour must reduce himself periodically to poverty, by giving feasts to his neighbours, with the assurance that his credit will be lost as soon as he becomes unable to repeat the process.

This primitive exploitation of the strong by the weak is sufficiently illustrated by the experience of European travellers in Africa. Livingstone in one of his earlier journeys expressly complains of the hardship of having, after a day's march, to go in search of game, while his followers rested, and when he had shot anything, having to return to the camp to summon them to bring it home, he being *ex officio* the bread (or rather meat) winner of the band. His influence was strictly proportioned to his usefulness, and though, by using all the authority his previous usefulness had won, he could, on an emergency, secure obedience to his recommendations for a time, unless their utility became promptly apparent, a passive mutiny, against which there was no remedy, became inevitable. The savage chief, like the patriarch, first acquires ascendency and then thinks of utilising it for his own advantage; the subject class, on the contrary—consisting of those who, by accepting passively a present benefit, begin to contract the habit of letting their fate be determined for them by other forces than their own will and energy—by the time the habit has become fully formed have become ready in their turn for exploitation, of which the fruit is longer in coming back to their descendants in the shape of a general social gain.

In communities dependent on human labour only, if the division of classes is carried further than the simple distinction of master and servant, the next source of social subordination seems to be afforded by the ascendency of one class or profession—practically, of course, that of the warrior class—over the rest. In all these societies the chief is not a political authority unless there are already existing social grades, of which his authority is not the source. The explanation seems to be, that the accumulation of wealth on a scale to give one person authority over the whole community, in virtue of his wealth alone—is impossible without domestic animals; and that among communities in which the accumulation of wealth by the royal road of pasturage is excluded, difference of skill or employment—*i.e.*, caste—is the source of more real and important distinctions than inequality of wealth. Political authority, of the most tyrannous kind, may exist in such communities, but the habit of submission to it is formed gradually, at least records of its existence in very different stages of its formation may be met with among kindred populations, and as all these social processes are substantially rational, under the given conditions, we are not likely to be far wrong in ascribing ordinary human motives for each transition.

Slaves taken in war supply a servile class, as soon as the custom is abandoned of marrying the women, adopting the children, and putting the warriors of the vanquished to death. Slaves have little to do in the absence of arts and industries, but as soon as a choice exists, the slaves will be habitually employed, and their children after them, in the least honourable and remunerative of needful pursuits. Certain skilled arts may become hereditary in free families, but war continues to be *par excellence* the honourable art. In all these cases the authority of the chief seems to depend upon a more or less strictly hereditary precedence in a dominant class or caste. The chief is followed in battle because of his ability to lead; and in time of peace he can command, within variable limits, the services of the lower classes, who believe in the superior dignity of the pursuit which they do not follow. The habit of joint tribal action for purposes of common interest is easily extended, and rude palaces and other public works are erected at the summons of the chief (who thus acquires a nucleus of immoveable property) as readily as communal huts and fishing-dams. Primitive despotic monarchies, of all sizes and dates, have more in common with bodies of this type than with the patriarchal family, and in fact we find that the power of the chieftain, if it exists at all, develops apart from the organisation of the family, whenever it is impossible for one family alone to represent, or collect, enough wealth to give political authority over the community at large to its chief member.

The organisation of the patriarchal family, after a pattern of solid durability fit for imitation on a large scale in the state, seems to have begun with the power and will of the patriarch to assert the substantially identical nature of his dominion over all that was his, wife, children, slaves, and domestic animals, as well as chattels, acquired, manufactured, or inherited. The tie was still property rather than descent; if a man owned several wives as slaves, their children were his by ownership more certainly than by paternity. If he had dwelling around him and under his protection, in virtually the same position as his own sons, both slaves and clients, or voluntary dependants, the children of these two classes would cease to be distinguished, the only exception being made in favour of the eldest son, or son of the favourite wife, who would inherit unimpaired the whole burden and privilege of paternal power. If the patriarch is rich enough to have many children, they make him powerful as well, by multiplying his dependants, so that poor men from a distance are glad to be received amongst them, and render the same services in exchange for the same protection. And it is observable that in proportion as the utility of these followers increases, the responsibility of the head diminishes, for the burden of rearing children for his service is thrown upon the actual parent, while the gain is reserved for the patriarch who nominally represents the community, and really represents the fruit of its sacrifices and docility.

Communities in which families are organised on the patriarchal pattern may be subdivided into those consisting of fathers who are equal landowners (*i.e.*, where the "village system" is developed), and those in which great inequalities of wealth are made possible by the possession of cattle.

The chief develops into the despot, or military leader and king; the father into the aristocrat or free citizen—as Plato makes the first laws consist of various sets of family custom, harmonised by heads of houses. In all early communities customary law has the same kind of history, and only varies in its matter according to the nature of the interests it is chiefly called on to regulate, *e.g.*, the conditions of land-tenure, of pasturage, or of marketing and commerce and mechanical industries.

But the political circumstances of the community—what we may call its international relations—react on the form of government, and frequently serve as a motive with the subject class, to strengthen the hands of the central authority, even though such accession of strength is likely to be used against themselves. The dramatic scene between the prophet Samuel and the children of Israel asking for a king, is true in the spirit if not in the letter, and if a free people can be plausibly represented as desiring a king like the other nations, *a fortiori* may the nations where kings grew up spontaneously be supposed to obey them, on the whole, voluntarily. But when the state has acquired a central organ of power, capable of legislating as well as governing, the natural limitations on arbitrary law-making already referred to, begin to apply. The art of government lies in determining which, out òf several courses that the subject can be induced to take, shall be taken, in matters concerning the interests of the state as a whole or the ruler as an individual. That of legislation consists in determining which, out of a similar variety of alternative courses, shall be habitually adopted by the subjects in matters mainly concerning their private, non-political interests. The sovereign, once installed as such, may govern as he pleases, provided he does not command anything radically inconsistent with the true nature of the subject population; and he may legislate as he pleases, subject to the same limitation; but as, in practice, more human interests are concerned in the laws of a civilised country than in its government, bad laws betray themselves more easily than bad government, and as the selfish gain of the prince is less direct, the administration of law is more often neglected than perverted under evil rulers. The bad laws which a bad sovereign might wish to make, in nine cases out of ten would simply fall wide of the national practice and have no effect at all, and it is to this fact, rather than to the essential wisdom of sovereigns by the divine right of establishment, that the substantial disinterestedness of all considerable systems of law is owing. The few exceptional cases in which a well-meaning ruler attempts to introduce positive reforms by way of legislation, rather confirm than invalidate the rule of the natural separation between the functions of law and government, for the success of such attempts has always been conditional on the presence of real progressive tendencies among the people, only needing to be developed and directed.

Every digression into the precincts of history confirms our original thesis, that law cannot be made by arbitrary will without reference to the subject of law; and we must add to the definition of a law, besides generality in the command, that the command be one which, in the nature of things, can and will be generally obeyed. The substance or provisions of any law are therefore necessarily limited by the nature of the subject, the real relations of which—natural, social, moral, or political—it is in fact the function of law to enumerate. Law may state the necessary relations of sovereign and subject, posited by the nature of both, when they have differentiated themselves; or it may describe the normal relations of men in their various other characters, as equal citizens, as proprietors, acquiring, using, and inheriting wealth, as master and servant, husband and wife, or as entering together into free contracts not extending to the general status.

But the question whether, in the dealings of men with

each other, there are any perceivable constancies of relation which can be traced to permanent qualities of their nature, even supposing it to be answered in the affirmative, still leaves half of the problem untouched; for we have further to account for the fact that the mere statement of these constant relations (supposing them to exist and to be formulated in positive law) acquires a kind of sacredness, a binding force, so that men do not see in law the record of what *is* done, but variously, a statement of what *ought* to be done, and a precept as to what *must* be done. The mere existence of such constancies of relation is not a reason, much less a motive constraining the will to submit to the restrictions they impose; yet in positive law we see, as it were, the constancy reflected upon, and its maintenance resolved: and we distinctly do not find that this feeling depends upon associations of pain or disgrace consequent on breach of the law, since it is only when the law corresponds to the set of popular will and feeling that its breach can be permanently so visited.

It is true of law, as Adam Smith says of morality, that it teaches men to try particular actions by general rules expressive of their permanent disposition with regard to acts; but he does not explain why people think they *ought* to feel merely what they usually do. No doubt they verify their sentiments by an unconscious reference to the natural sentiments of an ideal "impartial spectator" or their own unimpassioned judgment; but the fact that a precept is of general application does not seem by itself to add in any metaphysical way to its inherent force or obligatoriness. The dictates of positive morality or custom are felt to have the force of law whenever the moral or customary motive is recognised as properly dominant *as a rule*. To obey a law is to act in accordance with it, and "actions of a class" are not performed without some constant cause or motive. The *vera causa* of regularity in the action is regularity in the motive, and the regularity with which men seek to reduce their actions to rule has its cause in the constant pressure of an orderly system of things in favour of systematic adjustment, concert, and co-operation amongst persons.

The cause or reason why human societies are governed by law is, that beings of the same kind in the same circumstances act in substantially the same way; this is true of gases, earths, and vegetables, and the conduct of men may be expected, in the same way, to have ascertainable common qualities or tendencies, all the more so from its being rational, that is to say, deliberately planned with a view to attaining the end of the spontaneous tendency. Natural causes might thus explain the origin of law and social order, but the secondary, self-conscious desire for the observance of law and the maintenance of order finds its motive or explanation neither directly in nature nor in reason, but in the special feeling of subjection to a constant pressure of motive in certain fixed directions; the motive is not only felt, but it is felt as always there, laying its injunctions on the will, and acquiescence in its power grows into a habit. Volitions are regular because— and in so far as—the constant conditions under which men will are regular; but consciousness of voluntary regularity is virtual obedience to law, and the conscious love of regularity implies a kind of piety or loyalty towards the conditions which secure it, so that in practice respect for law always means respect for the laws that are.

The readiness of society to put all its available resources at the service of the law, to enforce or sanction its observance, springs from more obvious grounds of self-interest, and is connected with the natural impulse of men towards rational action, *i.e.*, action in pursuit of ends, which implies the adjustment of means to anticipated effects, or, in other words, calculation. Regulated volitions can be calculated upon, and therefore, by an elementary necessity, the individual will desires for itself, and all kindred wills, the recognition and acceptance of whatever fixed conditions are necessary for the free indulgence of its impulses.

This conclusion coincides substantially with Kant's conception of *jus*, or law in general, as the sum of conditions under which a general law of freedom can harmonise the arbitrary will of one man with the arbitrary will of all, or, in other words, a statement of the conditions under which social life, as men actually desire to lead it, is possible. Law, or *jus*, or the existence of binding rules of conduct, depends then upon the fact that human life is "conditioned," and this is so truly natural a necessity that men are not conscious of a legal or moral obligation to have laws; on the contrary, the necessity is often spoken of as a sign of depravity: "Law is not made for the righteous man, but for the lawless and disobedient;" or, in the words of a writer of the last century, "Society is made by our needs, and government by our wickedness." The positive laws, which men do feel bound to obey, state the particular necessities imposed by social life, not—what they could by no means enforce—the duty of association in general, or the necessity for a law-abiding habit of mind. Similarly we cannot deduce the various moral obligations of men from a general law in favour of the existence of duties, or their religious emotions from the abstract desirableness of having feelings towards the Not-self. We can only enumerate the obligations actually felt, classify them according to their apparent source, and then, by a counter-synthesis, bring out the common quality of all the different kinds of obligation owned by the human will.

The question, which naturally comes into existence first, law or morality, is happily not of much importance, since it is certain that both exist, either together or separately, before the distinction between them is reflected upon. A vague sense of obligation is felt and acted upon before the source or the authority of the constraining power is even analysed, much less disputed; but the fact that human laws can be disputed, or, as we say, disobeyed, seems to point to a real difference in kind between them and the few true scientific laws which we conceive to be altogether infallible and inevitable. To know the nature of an inanimate object is to know all the "classes of actions" which things of the kind certainly perform under all discoverable conditions. To say, therefore, that man can disobey the laws of his own nature is to deny that he *has* a nature; not merely to doubt the possibility of discovering constancies of relation among his multifarious powers and appetites, but to deny that such constancies are real. Marcus Aurelius says, "Only to the rational animal is it given to follow voluntarily what happens, but simply to follow is a necessity imposed on all." Is it, on the contrary, given to the rational animal alone voluntarily *not* to follow what happens?

Stated in this way, the question answers itself; there must be some ambiguity about any use of the word law that can lead logically to the supposition that the only being that ever acts consciously by rule is the only being naturally incapable of acting by fixed and certain rules. The ambiguity would perhaps disappear if we could import into science the lawyer's distinction between the law and the facts of a case, or at least what one legal authority distinguishes as the rational and the historical element in law. Men must stand in some constant relations to each other, but *what* the relations shall be is not a matter for reason or law, but of fact and observation; only, when certain relations are an established fact, other secondary, derivative laws, or statements of relation, are necessarily limited to consistency with the broad first principles already laid down.

All positive law has the same practical authority, as in the natural world all occurrences are in one sense equally necessary; but there is a difference between the necessity of a rule established by an historical exercise of the legislative will and one reached by deduction from conclusions previously admitted; the latter necessity is logical, and the only one that gives universal juridical truths, or laws that satisfy Bentham's requirement of executing themselves, and *cannot* be disobeyed. The laws of nature are only the records of natural facts, but it does not conduce to clearness or accuracy of thinking to call every uniformity in nature a law, because the real uniformities observed in nature are distinguished, or distinguishable, in thought, according to what we find to be the cause, or constant conditions, of their occurrence. Such distinctions, no doubt, are mental, and have more to do with the subject than the object of knowledge; they may even be treated as empty and metaphysical, yet they have their importance in thought. The material cause of any natural uniformity is the cause or set of conditions, whatever they may have been, of the facts in which the uniformity is observed, but it is frequently possible for a rational explanation to connect this or that particular relation of uniformity with other sets of constant relations, and when this is so, it may be convenient to call it a law; but a simple statement of facts, standing by themselves and throwing no light upon any other class of facts, fails in the chief purpose of a law, which is the subsumption of fresh cases as they arise, it is at best a private bill, or the bylaw of some natural vestry.

That these considerations are not altogether foreign to the matter of "laws properly so called" appears both from Bacon's weighty aphorism, "*Ratio prolifica consuetudo sterilis est, nec generat casus,*" and from the magnificent maxim which meets us in every highly-developed system of jurisprudence: "What is not reason, is not law;" from which it would appear that the only laws which man must be conceived incapable of breaking, in order to vindicate his right to be considered as a possible object of scientific knowledge, are those laws which are intrinsically reasonable, or those, the precepts of which follow, by the logic of facts, from the most elementary axioms and postulates of social life

As man is generally defined as a rational animal, this conclusion seems to bring us hopefully near to the necessary certitude of identical propositions, but we have still to distinguish between the law and the fact. There are a few very simple general laws to which we know of no exceptions; all matter gravitates, and all human societies obey *some* law, but when we come to classes of bodies of at all a composite character, the law which is found to hold good of the class, and of every individual belonging to the class in so far as it is a normal specimen of its kind or species, does not of itself furnish us with any security that any or every specimen shall be normal. Rational law cannot pretend to do more than state the rules of conduct normally followed by the normal or rational man.

The normal citizen obeys the laws of his country, because these laws on the whole represent the permanent will of himself and his contemporaries concerning the conditions of relationship amongst themselves; in ninety-nine cases out of a hundred it is the spontaneous wish of every civilised man that property should change hands by consent and not by compulsion without equivalent, *i.e.*, that trade should be allowed and theft forbidden, that no one should die except from disease, accident, or judicial sentence, that the customary constitution of the family should be sustained, and so forth; and in matters of more detail, the average citizen willingly commits himself to the guidance of specialists, whose trade it is to apply the general principles of law spontaneously agreed upon to the innumerable cases, hardly any exactly alike, which arise from time to time. It might seem, no doubt, absurd to say that any special law of inheritance follows by physical necessity from the nature of man as such; but given one or two leading principles, such as the equal inheritance of all children, as at Rome, inheritance of the oldest male in the direct line, as in feudal law, or primogeniture without distinction of sex, as in the Basque country, a number of other regulations follow naturally from the application of the rule under the actual conditions of relationship and the chances of life. A child can understand the first principle, as a child can understand the axioms of the first book of Euclid, but it takes a lawyer or a mathematician to develop all the logical consequences which follow in our world from such premises.

Systems of positive law, as has been said, enumerate the necessities imposed on men by each other's wills, and a philosophy of law, in the narrower sense, deals with the question—Have these necessities any common quality, and how is it to be recognised?—as ethical philosophy deals with the common quality (if any) of moral precepts, and the philosophy of religion with the common element (if any) in the various manifestations of pious feeling.

Hitherto we have only found two unmistakable signs of a true law, generality, and what, if the barbarism may be excused, we should call *obeyableness*. But this latter quality throws as little light as the alternative note of authoritativeness on the nature or substance of natural human law—the natural characteristics of the normal working of social relations. A law must be obeyed as well as imposed, but what are the conditions of obedience? The habitual will of every one—including myself—gives laws to the community; and the habitual will of the rest of the community, gives laws to me; the reason that I and they nevertheless obey the same laws is that we have all, most commonly, motives for doing (or forbearing) what we have motives, most commonly, for wishing others to do or forbear; and law only becomes burdensome in the exceptional cases when the individual will wishes to break out of bounds and emancipate itself from the normal succession of cause and effect, by taking to itself some unconditioned good. The true lawgiver is the sum of effective motives, but the character of the accepted law depends on the sum of present susceptibilities to motive. Looking upon every will as at once active and passive, ruling and obeying, we want to know what are the classes of actions that it will agree, in both capacities, in calling lawful and necessary for men?

The morality of laws is often alleged as the condition of their true and permanent force, but this view cannot be accepted without question while a rival school holds that the precepts of morality themselves are only binding as expressions of an omnipotent lawgiver's will. The quality we know as justice may be by nature equally characteristic of the objective rules of conduct called law and the subjective rules of conduct called morality; and the explanation of this fact, if a satisfactory one could be found, would show us the common element essential to all conscious constancies of relation in the intellectual life of man. But if the development of real relations necessarily precedes the discovery of a correct theory or formula for the relation, law must have exhibited a spontaneous tendency towards justice, before justice could have been accepted as the natural standard of the ideal in law.

Substances of the same kind, acting under similar circumstances according to the same laws, do not habitually produce entirely heterogeneous results, and we may therefore expect to find a degree of family likeness amongst the simple acts and forbearances habitually prescribed by law or opinion as just. But definitions of the point of resemblance are themselves so many and various that it may well seem hopeless to give a satisfactory account of it. The easiest theory, that those things are just and lawful which are actually enjoined by law, even if it were otherwise adequate, would still be open to the objection that it only shifts the point of uncertainty, for we should still ask, what kinds of acts are generally enjoined by law? To define the just by the useful is to substitute two uncertainties for one, unless it is explained to whom the just act is useful, and even then the further question, what is use? would be found as difficult as the one for which it is substituted. Theories in which the conception of moral right is blended with and colours that of natural justice are more properly considered under the head of morality than that of law, and a perfectly self-supporting metaphysical theory of the foundations of natural justice has scarcely yet been invented.

The idea of justice, according to the ordinary English use of the terms, is more abstract than that of law, so that it is convenient to borrow the word *jus* for the somewhat intermediate conception, reached in the same way as other abstract ideas, of the common quality possessed by some actions of "having to be done," without desire, in obedience to external constraint, voluntarily submitted to. Having seen how this idea in its most general acceptation might and probably did arise, we have to inquire into the steps by which, historically, the notion of *justa*, things just, rather than lawful, or things according to law as it ought to be, whether it was so or not, detached itself from the simpler, more positive experience of ages in which fact was law, not merely, as we endeavour to show is still the case, by a hidden philosophical necessity, but plainly and notoriously. In other words, we want to know what are the general characteristics of the relations of men in their conduct to each other, which are made necessary (or real) by their nature as men:—not, What is justice? but, What kind of actions are just?

The proof of law is the fact of its observance, and the philosophy of "precedents" is simply the assumption that whatever has been habitually done heretofore was done for good reason, and will therefore continue to be done until cause positive be shown for its omission, when, such cause not having existed in the preceding case, the precedent ceases to be binding. Early laws are rather declaratory of existing usage than imperative as to future practice, and there is much to be said in behalf of the probable reasonableness of this kind of customary law; for, in the absence of disturbing forces—of religious or aristocratic prejudice, of an overbearing particular interest, or a petrifaction of the judicial faculty—it may plausibly be concluded that only those customs will permanently prevail amongst a people which that people freely chooses to observe, that is, such as the common interest and inclination approves; and if the function of reason in practical life is to show how all possible satisfaction may be given to all real desires, evidently the most reasonable laws will be those which state the formula that includes all the recorded cases, or gives the soundest generalisation of real practice.

But in primitive states of society cases are rare, and the declaration of the law has to be postponed until it has been empirically made, in all cases that cannot be referred to an intelligible standard of natural absolute right or reason. We need not stop to inquire whether such a standard is ever applicable; but when points that are naturally indifferent require to be fixed by law before there is a real consensus of usage respecting them, even acute lawyers in historical times are reduced to strange perplexity in seeking for the law which does not yet exist. Custom itself is not felt as binding until the consensus which established it is beginning to give way, upon which it becomes law or obsolete. But when a real tendency towards customary usage is struggling into objective existence, a community that has already formed, from experience, the idea of *jus* in general, hastens to conclude that there must be latent somewhere, either in the clouds or in the wisdom of their ancestors, or in the eternal nature of things, a law applicable to the present exigency, if only they knew what it was.

In nearly all the countries of Europe the law of succession to the throne passed through such a phase; it was really uncertain—not habitually violated—during all the time that usage was as various as the supply of possible pretenders; and the acquisition of general proprietary rights, by inheritance or contract, has usually been regulated in the same gradual, tentative way by the consecration as legal of the power proved to be strongest in the greatest number of leading cases. The general principle, hardly perhaps precise enough to be called a law, according to which all such vexed questions tended finally to decide themselves, was the desirability in human affairs of leaving as little as possible to the disposal of arbitrary accident. The aim of all civilised legislation is to minimise (by distribution or otherwise) the action of chance, and to make it more and more difficult for the merely natural accidents of life to carry with them serious modifications of legal and social status. And side by side with this tendency, a kind of natural selection among quasi-prescriptive rights goes on, till the claims which can oftenest point to prescription in their favour come to be systematically recognised as legal, and the description of such claims serves to supply a rule to which others as they arise are referred.

It is a familiar historical fact that "case" usually precedes "statute" law, or, what comes to the same thing, that the office of judge is more ancient than that of legislator. "Law" is supposed to be there, and is, of course, in its nature certain, but doubt as to what *is* law cannot always be guarded against. The first step towards a settled state of society is to proclaim the sacredness of what is, and this is done by the legislator as *richtend*, not as *gesetzgebend*, as judging, not as ruling. The division corresponds roughly to the distinction met with almost everywhere between written and unwritten law, the latter of which is naturally preferred until cases become overwhelmingly numerous, just as written laws are allowed to remain undigested till the extreme limits of legal libraries and memories have been reached. Unwritten law has the advantage of a reasonable elasticity, for until lawyers and others begin to theorise about the beauty and fixity of the law, it is always as far from fixed as daily convenience may require. The last truth that men are willing to recognise in theory is the instability of their own tastes, habits, and even principles; but in practice, when their natural forgetfulness is not interfered with by statute or

CUSTOMARY AND POSITIVE LAW.

record, they have no scruple about allowing that what was law once may cease to be so, and that be law now which of old was not—a maxim of course to be admitted and applied with judicial caution. But the power given to judges of deciding in the same sentence what rules are actually in force, as well as to which of these rules a particular case must be referred, is so discretionary as to be only tolerable while the judge acts really as mouthpiece to the common mind, and when the mind of society comes to be divided, by class prejudices or class interests, judge-made law cannot be expected to give universal, or even general satisfaction.

The primitive judge was a personage of great importance, because the task of formulating the just and acceptable generalisations concerning the custom to be followed by the community required a combination of rare intellectual and moral force. Law is virtually made by the causes that lead to its being obeyed as soon as it has been promulgated, but it is not known, and therefore not obeyed *as law* until it is promulgated, and accordingly the authorised legislative power, whatever it be, which declares the law, is, as we have seen, credited with the supposed higher function of making or laying it down. In primitive communities, judgments and laws possess the like semi-sacred authority, and the question of the justice or wisdom of customary law really does not arise as long as it is really customary, *i.e.*, as long as its binding force is undisputed. It might even be said, as one of the many paradoxes with which the subject abounds, that the idea of justice, as a quality that ought to be possessed by judgments, is not formed until judgments become uncertain or of disputable justice, and cease to be necessarily satisfactory and binding. It is scarcely possible to think of a just judgment except by comparison or contrast with judgments that are not just, and as such criticism as this presupposes some other standard of justice than what lies in the breast of the sovereign judge, whenever it becomes articulate, we may expect to find general rules or laws ready thenceforward to supersede the discretionary resolution of cases. Somewhat as the primitive ruler is able to give wise judgments before he or his people feel the need of laws, the people intuitively estimate the wisdom of his sentences before they have reached the point of distinguishing any kind of general rule as necessary, and *a fortiori* before they can distinguish general rules into those that are essentially obeyable and those which are not so. In point of fact, the just judgment was the one which corresponded to the existing social opinion, and gave effect to the latent will of the community concerning the righting of wrongs as they arose. Criminal law, which develops before civil law, generalises these judgments upon anticipated offences, and the formula for avoiding offence, given at the same time, contains the rudiments of positive law. But we are nearer having a direct intuition of the just, or what constitutes an acceptable judgment in particular cases, than of the naturally lawful, or what constitutes an obeyable rule for all known or imaginable cases. The just may turn out to be, in judgments and laws alike, nothing more than the naturally selected practical Best, but its identity is more easily recognised in the concrete form, and for the same reasons, its nature is more easily detected and its qualities described. It is easier to compare things than conceptions, and acts or forbearances than the relations of acts, and our only hope of solving such a problem as What constitutes the practical Best in human relations? must lie in reducing it to its simplest terms.

The most recent independent attempt to approach the subject from a positive standing-point is that of M. Littré, which should perhaps be welcomed as a step in the right direction. According to him, justice is to give to every one that which belongs to him, what that is having to be ascertained by the help of the axiom $A = A$. The application of this principle, or rather the practical discovery that moral equivalents exist, is no doubt a real step in the evolution of a sense of justice, the Pythagorean doctrine on the subject being, perhaps, its earliest expression. It only misses the root of the difficulty because it presupposes the man who is to be dealt justly with to be already possessed of something which—or an equivalent whereof—justice is to secure him in the use of for the future; but it does no more than the familiar *suum cuique tribuere* to account for the justice of the original possession.

On this point Kant is more nearly satisfactory, and if we take leave to omit a good deal of scholastic *a-priorität*, his view states, if it does not explain, the facts of the case fairly and clearly. In this system that which belongs to a person is that which he normally has, *i.e.*, what the general rules of conduct followed in the society of which he is a member, allow such members to acquire or to keep. The rules themselves are only generalised statements of the common practice, so that in proclaiming the general sacredness of what is, law really only affirms its own existence: it declares what is to be in the main conformable to law.

At this rate it would seem that we cannot, without arguing in a circle, regard justice as an intrinsic quality of acts: yet our feeling rebels against the inference that if we were all habitually to act unjustly, acts which we now call just would change their character and become worse than blunders, crimes, or violation of the natural law. We distinguish instinctively between various kinds of real tendencies and relations, and call some of the things which are "just," and others evil and indifferent; what we feel most set upon doing is what we think best to have done, and we have no ideal standard underived from reality; yet we cannot feel that the tastes and judgments of men are generically superior, in the matter of reasonableness and persistence, to their actions, since our thoughts and feelings seem to be for the most part developments of sensibility consequent on prior developments of energy. Our idea of justice is not coextensive with either the real or the good; it is a name for our estimate of acts as they affect men among themselves; and this estimate, we find upon analysis, depends upon the measure of permanent reality or goodness in the tendencies exemplified. The sentiment in our minds which makes the just a name to conjure with, is quite distinct from the objective qualities of the acts which have come to inspire the feeling, and we must not expect to find any metaphysical counterpart to it in them. We do not consider certain lines of conduct just *because* they represent the practical Best; certain aspects of the practical Best are distinguished as just, because they *are* distinct, to the mind and feeling, from other aspects; and it is not necessary to import any sentiment at all into the question of what we naturally and reasonably judge to be the practical Best—for men in their mutual relations.

It is not exactly true that (as Bentham said) society is held together "only by the sacrifices that men can be induced to make of the gratifications they demand:" at worst it would be held together by the purpose, whatever that was, for which the sacrifices were made. But it is probable that, at a comparatively early date, men, who usually act first from impulse and then try to attach a meaning to their action, began to look for a rationalistic explanation of the social compact into which they had been led by an unconscious, disinterested gregariousness. As desires multiplied with the advance of society, it became easy to find such an explanation in the help which men could give each other in gratifying their desires; but when the additional power which resulted from co-operation began to seek fresh objects for itself, society had, so to speak, outgrown its members. Instead of a simple *consensus* of inclination, the same in every part, a complex whole, with which individuals could scarcely sympathise, and which they soon gave up the attempt to understand, was built up by a number of heterogeneous impulses, standing in no obvious natural relations to each other, and always liable to come disastrously into collision until the deliberate reason of the community succeeds in overtaking and controlling the wills of its members.

Pending such a development of practical philosophy as would make laws unnecessary, it is their function to determine the point at which the action of various natural impulses must be restricted or arrested so as to allow proportionate scope to opposing or incompatible impulses. In this way it is that early law comes to be chiefly penal or repressive, and in reference to penal justice, M. Littré is no doubt right in thinking that the discovery of the equivalence of equals was important. As he says,[1] it was an intellectual rather than a moral advance to contemplate the two forms of delayed defence, retribution and compensation, as alternative possibilities; but the idea of compensation, when it had once been reached, admitted of various moral developments, while retribution was in its nature as barren as revenge, of which indeed it is only a generalisation. Those classes of acts are naturally regarded as criminal which society in general wishes not to have committed, but for the community in general to sympathise so far with the anger of an injured person as to interfere to punish the offenders when the injury is irreparable, shows (like the practice of war) that the destructive passions are the first to become altruistic.

It is a description rather than a definition of primitive judicial sentences to say that they consisted in giving every man the equivalent of his deserts, and the description does not explain how, side by side with the earliest conception of *jus* (as the restraints imposed on human action by human authority), there grew up the further classification of restraints, not as actual and possible, desirable or mischievous, but as just and unjust. If law is only the general rehearsal and enforcement of usage, what is there in the bare fact of actual use to make it the standard of anything so sacred as justice? In the face of the common and flagrant separation between the right and the

[1] La Science au point de vue philosophique.

fact in human societies, how can it be maintained that there is no higher or other rule of right than a general practice much open to exceptions?

According to Grotius (who, it is to be feared, is even more metaphysical than Montesquieu), voluntary obligation, or natural law, is the mother of civil law, and the child of nature; and if we are referred to nature, as the last court of appeal, how is nature to pass sentence upon herself? Consciously or otherwise, we do in fact judge everything in terms of itself, and the significance of the judgment is simply owing to the lack of absolute uniformity, the more or less of typical completeness which characterises real existences of every kind. If men were perfect, law and justice would not so much coincide as disappear together across the threshold of consciousness; the name might be kept to denote the automatic harmony of social actions, but there would be no corresponding impression in the mind. Opposition or strife is the condition of phenomenal as harmony is the condition of real existence. We know things by what they are not rather than by what they are, and by what they are chiefly in contrast to the things that they are not. Nevertheless, things must be, somehow or other, if they are to make themselves the object of thought; and when they are, our only knowledge of what they are, or what they normally tend to be, is derived from themselves.

In pronouncing anything to be just or unjust, society or an individual simply assumes the office of the primitive judge, and classifies a case not provided for (or provided for inadequately) by positive law, in accordance with principles embodying the general practice of the time or place. An appeal to the inconceivableness of the contrary opinion is always an unsatisfactory form of argument, but considering the difficulty of an historical treatment of processes that are half completed before the dawn of history, it may perhaps be allowable to re-enforce this view by the suggestion that it would be a very singular kind of society indeed in which the normal practice of every individual were something entirely different from what was currently believed to be good and desirable. Of course there are pessimists who will say that England in the nineteenth century satisfies the definition of such a society on all points; but, on the one hand, the merely formal beliefs which do not influence the conduct only inspire lip-judgments, not real opinions concerning things just and unjust; and on the other hand, the lively belief of the pessimist himself much requires to be accounted for, since, in saying that the world is bad, we seem to take for granted that there are, or have been, or might have been, worlds that were good; only as we have never visited any other world than this, it is difficult to see whence, except from this one (granted by an exceedingly eclectic process), we can have derived the idea of goodness as a quality of worlds.

In order that law, or natural justice, should be able to consist substantially in maintaining the *status quo*, the forces by which society organised itself must not have been in the first instance mutually destructive or antagonistic, otherwise society would be consecrating its own lingering suicide; but things do not come into existence by committing suicide, and human societies do exist, and what they aim at consecrating under the conception of law and justice are exactly those tendencies and accomplished facts which make the life, such as it is, of the society. Everything which contributes to make the society what it is, and what it is content to be, is just in the eyes of that society; and nothing can be permanently regarded as just which does not on the whole contribute to the lasting good of the community as that is understood by its members.

The natural right which is most generally recognised at the present day is that of every one to do as he pleases, so long as no one else is injured by his pleasure, and it is evident, from what has been said, without attaching any metaphysical sanctity to the independence of individuals, that the interest, or rather the existence of society, is more intimately concerned in the maintenance of this than of any other right or faculty. The majority of human impulses are not anti-social, or society would never constitute itself at all, and for its complete organisation so many impulses have to co-operate that arbitrary restrictions upon any considerable number of them would defeat the purpose (which can only be the interest of the organisation) for which they were imposed. It is found in practice that as men cannot behave systematically better than they naturally will to do, they are best left to the free play of their best, or naturally strongest, impulses. Still it is only by degrees that this generalisation comes to be accepted in all its breadth, and it may perhaps be objected that if there is a certain normal type of humanity toward which individual men tend more or less to approximate, and which it would be their perfection to realise, law, speaking in the name of the general good, might enjoin whatever sacrifices of private inclination appeared to the legislative mind conducive to that end, and insist upon the community behaving better than its own nature prompts. Such a confusion of the spheres of law and morality is not uncommonly met with at a certain stage of civilisation, and the contrary principle does not find general acceptance until a tolerably wide experience of various *régimes*, from the inquisitorial to the anarchic, has shown the practical convenience and expediency of the liberal maxim, and proved *a posteriori* the impossibility of securing profitable obedience to laws which the subject population is either generally averse to obeying, or altogether incapable of obeying with the indispensable minimum of intelligence.

If law is the formula of natural tendency, we can understand that the most elementary natural right of individual men should be to exist as they naturally do; but the just, or the practical best, as regards the relations of men among themselves, is not to be confounded with the ideal best, or good; it is simply the best result possible from the actual balance of real, more or less incompatible tendencies. The chief good of every existing thing is to exist as fully or perfectly after its kind as it can. If we put ourselves in the place of any existing unit, those things are good, for the unit, which promote its natural tendency to exist as much and as perfectly as it can; the unit is good in relation to other units, in so far as it furthers their several tendencies towards perfect existence, and it is bad, for them, in so far as it impedes the same. In ruling human societies, the practical best is the course which entails least permanent sacrifice of natural human power and will. The judgments which common sense spontaneously upholds as just are those which secure individuals in the possession and exercise of their own natural powers of doing and enjoying, subject to a due regard for the similar liberty of their neighbours. Just laws, or statements of real human relations at their best, are those which secure every class in the possession of its natural right to be its best self, that is to say, a self as much alive as possible, and related by as many good offices as possible to as many as possible of its coevals. Natural right or justice does not secure to individuals or classes the indulgence of all their wishes, either at their own or at the public expense, but it demands for them full exercise and development for all their permanent tastes and all their serviceable faculties.

Assuming the natural good or interest of the social organism to consist in the normal and harmonious development of the greatest possible number of natural faculties in the fullest possible perfection amongst its members, it is evident that the last relics of a belief in the natural "rights of man," apart from use or law, must be given up, as completely as Austin himself could desire. Right and justice are not arbitrary creations, they have a natural and necessary being in every human society, but they do not exist absolutely in vacuous eternity, out of all relation to the acts and sufferances of sensible beings. It is of course possible, and sometimes useful, to classify rights in order of generality, and as the correlative of *jus*, or obligation in its widest sense, we may understand by the natural rights of individuals, their claim to all the advantages which the general good requires them to enjoy. But the individual's property in such advantages is not absolute (though it might possibly be argued that a jural right is the only true and inalienable property), and it should be remembered, in asserting any claim to them, that it is the public, not private, interest that weighs in favour of its recognition.

Justice is fitly represented with a balance, for the just is always half on one side and half on the other. One man's right is another man's obligation, and men's obligations to each other are reciprocal. Justice consists in the perfect proportioning of these obligations, and gives effect to the natural claims men make upon each other, in order of their inward strength and outward usefulness. The right of the strongest claim to be attended to first does not lie in the bare fact of its strength, or power to compel attention, but in its strength as compared with other claims, that would be as good if they were as strong, that *are* as good if they are supported and re-enforced by external sympathetic tendencies which make the balance of power lie on their side. Justice consecrates the permanently dominant tendencies of men, and the special, almost religious feeling with which the decisions of justice are received, is a spontaneous evidence that the permanent realities of tendency in the relations of men have moral qualities over and above the bare fact of common reality. When our natural feeling, and our thought and feeling about the feeling, point one way, the tendency is normal as well as natural, that is to say, it harmonises with all the fixed conditions under which the kind exists, as well as with a portion of its instincts. Our respect for the just comes, not from its being what the majority do, but from its being what the majority wish to have done. The treacherous element of self-will is eliminated, and the practical best is estimated dispassionately by the common reason after weighing and balancing the common impulses.

To wish for a thing, or to find it useful, does not give a natural right to its possession or enjoyment; possession itself may be nine parts of the law, but it is not even one part of justice; only, as it happens, for the actual possession of anything to have become firmly established, such possession must have been originally fairly compatible with or conducive to the general interest, which is then concerned in protecting its security. It is a part of that imperfection of human affairs, to which, as already observed, we owe the existence of law and the conception of justice, that even the most elementary natural rights can lapse into disuse. There are whole classes, sometimes amounting to the majority of a community, who do not possess or exercise faculties which it would be eminently conducive to the general good for them both to possess and exercise—to which, therefore, they have the most indefeasible right; but this right, in the successful assertion of which the common good is deeply interested, is not vested in them as individuals, as classes, nor even as the majority, and the common good requires that the members of any oppressed section of the community should have the magnanimity to demand the emancipation to which they are entitled as right, not as *their* right. Neither the capitalist nor the *sans-culotte* have abstract rights against society; there *is* a social right, if we knew what it was—a just practical Best—and both have a right to what it is best for the commonwealth that they should have—and to nothing more, less, or different; but they themselves, unfortunately, are likely to be the last people to help us in ascertaining what that true "natural right" is.

The legalisation of local or class usages is an intermediate step between the practice of societies where all customs are generally binding, and those in which the law is chiefly occupied in protecting the free initiative of individuals. The saying acted on from ancient times, "*Cuilibet in sua arte credendum est,*" tacitly admits that there is (for instance) no typically just "law merchant" existing antecedently to the establishment of usages amongst merchants; and law and justice would have no further concern than to sanction and enforce such usages, were it not that political wisdom is not a part of any one's special "art," so that no class is "to be believed" on the question what is just or otherwise from its members in their unprofessional relations to each other or to a different class. The precepts of class morality afford a fairly sufficient rule of conduct while classes are as homogeneous as primitive society, and individuals are satisfied with the simple routine existence of their order; and when this ceases to be the case, the precepts of personal morality in social matters are still regulated by those of class or customary morality. Most of the dangerous vagueness attendant on ideas of "natural right" comes from a confusion between the dictates of public and private morality, or rather from the optimistic assumption that the two will always spontaneously coincide. People assume themselves to have a natural right against society to do, at least, whatever they do not themselves feel to be morally wrong, and certainly no duly enlightened conscience would affirm an act of extreme social inexpediency to be morally right; but then few consciences are so enlightened as to be capable of estimating the social tendency of private acts, and therefore, though it may be practically impossible to improve upon the principle of respect for the free initiative of individuals, it cannot be maintained that all the results reached in accordance with that principle are absolutely just or right.

In considering what classes of actions are regarded as naturally lawful or just, we have rather lost sight of the question, how law comes to possess a binding and constraining power, though the answer has already been partly taken for granted. It is necessary for the maintenance of society that men should make certain sacrifices of their own inclinations in their dealings with each other. The law ordains that these sacrifices shall be made, but men do not feel obliged to make the sacrifices because the law commands, the law commands because men feel obliged to make them. And there is nothing very wonderful or mysterious in this feeling of necessity; it is no news that human life is determined by other conditions than human desire, and consciousness of these conditions *is* consciousness of constraint, whether the constraint be direct or alternative. It might be surprising that men should acquiesce in these conditions if they had the choice of an "unchartered freedom" in their reach, but, if freedom must be unchartered, that is a fresh, and to man as he is, an unacceptable condition.

From the earliest to the latest speculation on the subject, the question concerning law and justice has been whether they are based upon nature or are of human— meaning personal and arbitrary—institution. We say human institutions are based upon human nature, are its voluntary and necessary expression and manifestation, or, in other words, that law is the organised liberty of all the members of a society, and obedience to law merely the *Wille zum Leben*[1] of the social organism. The obedience becomes conscious in man as all his other actions do: "rational action arises out of instinctive action when this grows too complex to be perfectly automatic."[2] The multitude of actual observances leads men to classify their conduct, or reduce it to rule; the multitude of rules leads to the substitution of the general conception of rules necessarily obeyed, for the thought of innumerable special conditions of necessary action, and it is not till this point has been reached, after long and hereditary experience, that the existence of a positive law, enjoining or forbid-

[1] Perhaps "vital self-will" is the best equivalent for this untranslatable phrase of Schopenhauer's.
[2] Herbert Spencer's Principles of Psychology.

ding actions of a class, can be said to serve as a motive for their performance or omission.

Most writers on the philosophy of law, having begun the treatment of their subject at a time when positive legislation was already complicated enough for obedience to it to be an act of faith rather than reason, naturally began by trying to account for the faith; and though their method was scarcely sufficiently historical for their attempts in this direction to be perfectly successful, the list of alternative explanations logically possible or conceivable was almost exhaustively discussed. In Greek philosophy generally, the nature of justice in itself was the object of inquiry; but the Romans were brought, by the practical experience of which the *jus gentium* was the result, to the notion of a more comparative treatment, and seeking the common element in real systems of law, naturally postponed their researches into the origin of law in general; for classification seems of itself a step towards explanation: when several things of a class exist, one seems partly to account for the other, so far as the mere existence is concerned, and what seems chiefly to need explanation, is the being of the class as an ideal entity, or the common properties by which it is constituted. To the later Latin jurists, and to most modern publicists, what seemed to want explaining was not the existence of this or that law, or of law in general, but the agreement of all, or most law; why laws tended to be just, and for what reason they were generally obeyed. Merely logical explanation, however, though the only sort satisfactory to some minds, adds nothing to real knowledge, and can at most connect one phenomenon with a wider phenomenon of the same kind. Thus the civil law is referred to, or included under a natural law, as by the Romans; this natural law is in its turn explained, as by the schoolmen, from a natural reason, which comes everywhere to the same conclusions, or by a natural morality, as in most writers of the sixteenth and seventeenth centuries, expressive either of the divine nature or the divine will. The genealogy itself was inspired partly by the common wish to arrive at something more ultimate than a fact, and partly by the more reasonable hope of finding, as it were, a "source" for the law, which is felt, and truly, to be not altogether self-imposed. But we do not find that there are any real historical processes corresponding to the steps in this genealogy, for the relief of law by equity does not represent any permanent distinction in principle, as if there were two kinds of justice for suitors to take their choice between, one a degree more general, abstract, and stable than the other.

Voigt,[1] who admits that equity can be thought of as agreeing with law as well as at variance with it, virtually reduces the idea of the just or the "fair" to a commentary on the variable relation between the law and morality of each period. Equity, when established law is supposed to be just, may serve to determine the application of the law to cases; otherwise it is simply an artifice for keeping the administration of law on some points of general interest more nearly abreast with the latest popular notions of justice than the text of the statutes administered; and not a convenient artifice, because as soon as courts of equity are established, their practice tends to stiffen into a system, and has in its turn to be relieved by courts of appeal deciding merely on the merits of the case; while it is plainly not for the interests of either law or justice to perpetuate a state of uncertainty amongst litigants, as to whether their causes will be tried according to rules of law, equity, or common sense.

Another recent German writer[2] ends his investigation of the philosophical element in Roman jurisprudence by declaring that the binding force of the *jus gentium* rests

[1] Die Lehre vom jus naturale, æquum et bonum und jus gentium der Römer.
[2] Hildenbrand, Geschichte und System der Rechts- und Staatsphilosophie.

on the *consensus* of the human species, that of *jus civile* on the *consensus* of the state, and that of *jus naturale* in the subjection of man to the laws of nature—considered in relation to God; in lieu of which last clause, by which the symmetry of the statement is somewhat impaired, we should propose to read that the force of the laws of nature rests on the wide natural *consensus* of existing beings to exist as they do.

The source, from this point of view, of the external constraint which comes into the consciousness of the narrowing subject class as law, is always the fixity of relations amongst things natural and real, and the readiness of the will to acquiesce in restrictions which it perceives to be natural and unavoidable, certainly does not require more explanation than the reality of the restrictions themselves. As the judicious Hooker observes, " Let Reason teach impossibility in anything, and the Will of man doth let it go." And though such letting go may be altogether against the inclination of the will, which would gladly have had the thing possible, there is at least an intellectual relief in perceiving the order and relations of the impossibility. Coleridge, in speaking of the satisfaction found in accounting for a pain, says, "There is always a consolatory feeling that accompanies the sense of a proportion between antecedents and consequents. It is eternity revealing itself in the form of time." And this is only a transcendental expression of the gospel of necessarianism. To see two events as cause and effect is to see them in an inseparable relation, as, in a sense, one to the mind, after which it becomes impossible to separate them in serious practical speculation; to know that things, being what they are, could not in any single particular have been other, or therefore better, is to see in this the best of all possible worlds, because any fictitious possibility which the play of thought or fancy may suggest is unreal—or it would be realised—is not *really* possible.

It is curious to observe how all theories of the origin

CUSTOMARY AND POSITIVE LAW. 65

of law, whether metaphysical or political, whether, that is, they refer to nature or to will as the ultimate source of its authority, gradually gravitate towards the recognition of a power felt to be supreme of fact and of right, as the only logical base of legal obedience. The power must be supreme of fact, or there is no true compulsion; it must be allowed supreme of right, or the will itself is not compelled, and when both conditions are satisfied in the voluntary obedience to an irresistible force, or the complete identification of the weaker with the stronger tendency (we cannot here say will without anthropomorphism), the reign of law is established.

When the individual is first becoming conscious of his own personality as distinguished from that of others, he seems naturally to personify all the necessities he encounters, as a preliminary towards complying with them. But this uncritical docility does not easily survive the multiplication of laws resting on the same authority; these supply a standard for themselves to be tried by, and unless they are all such as the subject will can and does spontaneously accept, the law and the lawgiver lose their authority together. Within the range of modern history we can trace three main phases of feeling about or towards the nature and conduct of this Supreme power, with three corresponding forms of doctrine concerning the ground and extent of man's subjection to it. Scholastic philosophy, taking for granted the foundation of a sincere theological faith, confines itself to an *ex parte* statement of the positive elements in the divine law. The expositor recognises a real distinction between things *mala in se* and things *mala quia prohibita*, but it does not occur to him to criticise the existence of things in themselves when he is praising the excellence of the divine appointments which cause such natural evil to be condemned by the common law of nature. The precepts of revelation are not conceived as possessing the same elementary kind of philosophical necessity. Obedience to them is only necessary to man because

E

God has willed the command, and it is an act of faith to believe that whatever God commands is both naturally and supernaturally good. From the twelfth to the sixteenth century philosophy was spontaneously on the side of authority; the laws of God and man were better than anarchy, and the time had not yet come for trying all ordinances, whencesoever derived, by some common ideal standard other than their objective authority. Revelation made a duty of loyalty to political superiors, so that positive law might be conceived as in effect declaratory of the divine law, while the transgressions of political potentates failed to compromise the divine authority, since they might always be condemned by a still higher organ of the divine will—the authorised spiritual power. Suarez, one of the latest and most circumstantial exponents of this philosophy of law, explicitly asserts a "natural right" of sovereignty in the people over whom the prince rules by divine sufferance and human consent, and with this concession we come to the end of the period during which goodness is praised as conformable to the divine will, while the divine will is never summoned to prove its conformity to its own creation—natural goodness.

In the theological period, it may be observed that law is conceived more dynamically, and as it were constructively, than is usual, as enjoining what men are to do, rather than as stating the conditions subject to which they may do as they feel inclined, and it is in this way parallel to the precepts of customary morality, which are of absolute force for a time, but have not the logical necessity belonging to relations deduced from other relations. It was reserved for the civilians to stultify the premises which they borrowed partly from theology, by inquiries in which Puffendorf especially is much entangled, whether God has "a right" to command the obedience of His creatures. The arid abstractions of scholasticism are at least precise and internally coherent, and Suarez keeps clear of the absurdity of proffering a reason for the ultimate fact, which explains itself to every *bona fide* believer in a Deity, since religious belief is simply being bound by the will, so far as known or conjectured, of the deity believed in. In his own dialect, "lex participata supponit legem per essentiam sed lex per essentiam eterna est:" and boldly confronting the difficulty of a free will in a fixed nature, he concludes that God Himself acts by the rules of His own right reason, while the laws He has appointed for man are, as a fact, just and according to reason, as well as efficacious to oblige, the two things required in the idea of law.

A sincere belief that the divine ordinance is the sole source of lawful obligation naturally affects the resolution of the question much debated by casuists, Whether by human laws the conscience be obliged or no; "for if conscience be not," says Jeremy Taylor, "then nothing is concerned but prudence, and care that a man be safe from the rods and axes; but then" (he was not alone in thinking) "the world would quickly find that fear would be but a weak defence to her laws; which force or wit or custom or riches would so much enervate or so often evacuate." The will of God as conceived by any one generation binds those of that generation who recognise nothing in His will that their will does not fully identify itself with. But men make gods after their own image, and the image frequently survives the maker, whose descendants may, for a space, be bound by belief in the existence of sanctions of such cogency as to compel an obedience that has become reluctant; only as the force of sanctions is relative and dependent on the disposition of the subject will, should that become increasingly reluctant to obey, the law, if it is so far from necessary that it *can* be habitually broken, is *ipso facto* abrogated, shown not to state necessary relations following from the nature of things real.

The last question for the advocates of the political theory of law, or its origin by institution, is thus seen to be: Can the divine will be resisted and the divine law be disobeyed? And the answer to this belongs to theology, not to moral or political philosophy, though it cannot fairly be evaded by theists, whose systems depend upon the answer that can be given to it. We need only observe that Calvinism, the only theology since that of mediæval Catholicism with any pretensions to scientific completeness and insight, honestly allows that an omnipotent ruler, creating, ordering, and sustaining everything that exists, neither is nor can be conceived as having His purposes frustrated by the creatures of His own will, and that therefore the law of God ordains the condemnation of sinners in a sense which makes an expression of ordinary moral disapprobation for sin inappropriate. Modern theology virtually has to make its choice between this opinion —that what God does is right in some supernatural sense, even when it seems and is humanly speaking bad (as in the election of sinners to damnation)—and that of rationalistic optimism, according to which everything however really or apparently bad will somehow come to good in the long run. But neither of these hypotheses exhibit such a necessary relation between the will of God and man as to enable us to deduce the uniformities of human conduct from the nature and being of the two. A legislator who makes his subjects as well as his laws has failed in one or other of his functions if the laws are habitually broken, whether the reason of the breach be that the will of the subject rejects them as bad, or that the nature of the subject *is* bad, *i.e.*, imperfect or abnormal and irregular in its manifestations. And since the laws which we have best grounds for calling divine are seen empirically to be but imperfectly binding on man, we conclude the relation between man and God—if there be a God—not to be the relation of omnipotent sovereign and lawful subject; and accordingly a secular theory of law must seek elsewhere for the seat of supreme power and the source of real obligation.

The second stage of feeling and speculation had, as

already implied, less internal consistency than the theological theory in its purity. Criticism did not go so far as to question the morality of the divine law, but the schism which agitated Christendom seemed to leave every portion of so-called divine law open to discussion, in which the claim to authority had to be justified by an appeal to the merits of the law; and, in fact, the civilian founders of the Utilitarian philosophy virtually took their own estimate of natural right as the expression of that law of nature which they could, on the one hand, invoke as an authority with secularists, and, on the other, praise to the religious as a precious gift of all-wise Providence. Bentham and Austin have little to add to Puffendorf's assertion that God prescribes to men the duties calculated to give them the happiness they so earnestly desire; and Bishop Cumberland (who describes moral obligation as an act of the legislator showing the particular conduct enjoined to be necessary for the person who is to follow it) concludes that, given the knowledge of a necessary dependence between the pursuit of the common good and the happiness of each individual, each individual is certainly obliged to seek that good, which proves the law of nature to be duly and truly "promulgated." Writers, on the other hand, who attribute a metaphysical sanctity to the chief moral conceptions actually entertained by mankind, either derive those conceptions from the Essence of the Deity conceived as absolutely good, which Cumberland not unfairly objects to, as virtually defining a thing by itself; or else confine themselves to arguing that the sanctity in question cannot be explained by an arbitrary act of will. "When things exist," says Cudworth, "they are what they are, not by will or arbitrary command, but by the necessity of their own nature;" so that, given things with ultimate moral qualities, the moral qualities of their mutual relations would follow by a logical necessity. Leibnitz is at the pains to protest against Puffendorf for making duty consist in obedience to law, and law consist in the will of a superior that such and such acts shall be done, when the very schoolmen declare "voluntas non est regula," and no one is content to rest his claim to authority on a law of his own making commanding obedience. To which Barbeyrac retorts that "the nature of things" cannot impose an *obligation* on us, which, with lawyers of his school, includes the idea of "right" in the person imposing it, a right, according to them, which no one but a recognised superior possesses: but this, as we observed at starting, is an ambiguous qualification, and, the one word "recognised" virtually concedes Cudworth's position, that "it is not the mere will and pleasure of him that commandeth that obligeth to do positive things commanded, but the intellectual nature of him that is commanded." Real as is the difference involved in the two shades of opinion, it has had no influence on the theory of law itself, for the only practical question between the disputants was whether the precepts of a naturally binding law should be strengthened by the discovery of a pre-established harmony between them and the divine will, or whether the perfection of the divine nature should be demonstrated by the excellence of the precepts appointed for the regulation of the natural world.

The third period of criticism is that into which we have drifted since conceptions of natural perfection and ideal order have begun to form themselves, in comparison with which the "laws of nature," at their best, are harsh and ruthless; and while we conceive these ideals themselves to be altogether of natural growth, now that they are formed, they serve to condemn, not the laws of their own formation, but the facts which retarded it, and still retard their realisation. These conceptions do not owe their virtue to any belief in the sacredness of their source; we know their power consists only in the strength of conviction with which they are cherished, but no one questions their "right" to adhesion should they happen to receive it, the only question is whether the inevitable tendency of natural fact will procure it them. The consciousness of obligation is in the subject, but the reality of obligation, or compulsion so exercised as to control and alter the direction of the subject will, must exist in nature if the obligation is to be felt permanently as binding. The great law of nature which no man can break or annul, is the existence of all natural objects after their kind; and this law has no other standard of right than the facts it proclaims, for, though the general good consists in the orderly existence of kinds in their perfection, it is only because real existence is orderly that we regard what is abnormal as imperfect of its kind and so contrary to the general good, of which the observance of law is the chief condition. No one but a madman would ask if fire has "a right" to burn us; it cannot help doing so, and the "right" of human societies to make laws regulating the intercourse of their members, and the right of moral causes to produce effects after their kind, are of the same natural hyper-rational sufficiency.

The few frail or diseased wills that cannot accept and identify themselves with the supreme tendency of the universe to exist as it does—or as it best can—cease before their time out of the land of the living sharers in the tendency; but the immense majority of men submit peaceably to the laws imposed on them by the force which they feel to be irresistible—the tendency of contemporary being; and this for reasons substantially identical with those acknowledged by the most intelligent advocates of the theory which ascribes the force of law to its imposition by a superior will. Sincere theists who believe all things to follow the laws divinely appointed for their guidance, obey the laws they feel to be binding on themselves as a religious duty, because their will is one with the will of the God they believe in. Consistent naturalists see in the fixed relations of the natural world the norm of natural human life, and in the fact that nature is thus and thus become conscious of an efficient—though not of a final—cause for living according to nature.

III.

MORALITY.

"Constat itaque ex his omnibus, nihil nos conari, velle, appetere, neque cupere, quia id bonum esse judicamus, sed contra nos propterea aliquid bonum esse judicare, quia id conamur, volumus, appetimus, atque cupimus."—SPINOZA.

"Die Abhängigkeit eines nicht schlechterdings guten Willens, vom Princip der Autonomie (die moralische Nöthigung) ist Verbindlichkeit. Die objective Nothwendigkeit einer Handlung aus Verbindlichkeit heisst Pflicht."— KANT.

"Subject to himself—which were not subjection, but freedom."—HOBBES.

"Motives are symptoms of weakness and supplements for the deficient energy of the living principle, the law within us."—COLERIDGE.

Feeling of obligation merely consciousness of causation—Habit not a cause—
Difficulty of separating the practical and speculative side of moral problems—Duty always conceived in relation to a person bound by the duty and conscious of the bond — Divergent theories of obligation, theistic, sentimental, and utilitarian—Right being relative to the conscience, what is the good commonly thought right or moral?—Three kinds of good: natural good, the perfection of a thing after its kind, ascertained not *a priori* but by eclectic experience; sensible good or pleasure, included in, but not coextensive with natural good; moral good the pursuit of natural good through natural obstacles which make the pursuit self-conscious—Such obstacles threefold: 1. The imperfection of the world, including human society, which may make the natural exercise of normal faculties difficult or painful. 2. Imperfection of the organism after its kind; conflicting appetites, the indulgence of some of which is incompatible with complete natural perfection. 3. The instability of the specific type, the goal of natural perfection receding with the evolution of fresh faculties—Utilitarianism wrong because the pursuit of natural and that of sensible good do not always coincide, and because it fails to include evolution, or development of the moral ideal—A morality of some kind, or formula of obligation imposed by the nature of the agent in its fixed relations with the surrounding medium, exists necessarily, supposing men to have a specific nature, with certain tendencies that are liable to be impeded, but do not therefore cease to be real, only become present to consciousness, if so it chances, as a constraint upon the equally natural (but not morally necessary) inclination towards a sensible good—The tendencies commonly called moral, those which conduce to the natural good of the kind—A kind could not subsist with essentially self-destructive tendencies—Practically, morality begins with the discovery that it is not always possible to do as we like, that some sacrifices are unavoidable: the sacrifices which it is called moral to make are those which men are conscious of a real natural tendency to make or to desire to make, those, namely, which conduce most, not to the sensible good of the individual which, by the hypothesis was unavoidably sacrificed, but to its natural good or perfection—The sacrifice of the natural good (*e.g.*, life) of the organism only liable to become moral because the individual man is member of a social body, so that his natural perfection includes the discharge of social functions, after their kind, *i.e.*, in the manner most conducive to the natural good or perfection of the social body.

III.

MORALITY.

IN the foregoing section we endeavoured to assimilate human laws "properly so called" to the scientific laws of nature, by suggesting that consciousness and causation are not incompatible, and that the sense of constraint which undoubtedly belongs to human law is most intelligible and explicable if conceived as the mere addition of consciousness to a real causal, or fixed order of relations, as, in fact, the *consciousness of causation;* not the mere perception that a fixed order exists, but a direct consciousness of the steps in such an order as succeeding each other, without, perhaps against, the desire of the conscious subject.

A real tendency or impulse in the subject towards the effecting of any particular result, becomes present to consciousness as a desire for that result. Such a desire may be felt as an additional force or motive for following the impulse or tendency of which it is the consciousness, but conscious volition is not consciousness of constraint, and to produce this, we must conceive a second force, independent of the first and brought into relation with it.

Men become conscious of law as a check on desire; yet their desires are in the main normal (or the abortive race would perish), and they on the whole desire to be governed by the laws which they feel to be at times a restraint, at times a protection, and for the rest a just and reasonable custom. The feeling of voluntary action under constraint, or in other words of free human action subject to law, is given when the subject is conscious of a present, spontaneous impulse to act in a given way, which impulse is impeded or diverted by the existence of other present, persistent forces, towards which the subject stands already in a necessary relation of coexistence; the permanent outer influence overrules the ephemeral inner desire, and we gradually come to class together as lawful those desires which habitually conform to the objective pressure.

In distinguishing the laws of human conduct as political, moral, or religious, according to their presumed source, and the sphere of their apparent jurisdiction, we only follow a classification too general to be quite baseless or unsound. When external constraint is absent, there must still be law wherever there is intelligible life, and we suppose that even if men did not naturally associate with each other, every human organism would still possess certain fixed properties or dispositions, by which its conduct under various conditions would be regulated, and which, consequently, would be, at least to some extent, a possible object of knowledge. Even when the power of custom is strongest, and men have so few unshared impulses that an impulse to do something of itself indifferent, may be disapproved of as abnormal, merely because it is not shared, there is still always a part, and as civilisation advances, and custom makes way for law, an increasing part of the daily existence of each several member of the community left at his own disposal, subject to no other restrictions than such as his own nature and the general constitution of the universe may impose. Unlike law, and like custom, which is a fusion of both, morality has as many positive as negative rules; for though a man's neighbours are not always concerned—as they in time discover—in prescribing to him exactly in what way he is to act, he himself finds it natural and necessary to act always in *some* way, and all ways are hedged in by fixed conditions; and to go on acting consciously and regularly in any way whatever, without the immediate instigation of personal desire, is to act from habit, calculation, or duty.

The effect of habit is generally seen in the repetition of acts not themselves productive either of pleasure or pain, nor yet regarded as means to a more remote, probably pleasurable, end. Custom is only the habit of a number, and both owe their strength, partly to the original cause, whatever it was, which led to the formation of the habit or custom, partly to the peculiarity of human or animal nature (much conducive to the fixity of types and species), that other things being equal, any action is more easily performed a second time than the first, or that, of actions of equal natural difficulty, the one that has already been performed once, will be easier than the one which has not. But the difficulty of breaking a habit, and even of altering a custom, is rather physical or material than moral; the existence of a habit is not felt to be a motive to the will for perseverance in it; it is not recognised to be a duty to keep the specific type unaltered; in fact, to be conscious that habit is the disposing cause of an action is distinctly *not* to feel the action as obligatory, and if morality consists in the consciousness of a subjective necessity, as law in the consciousness of a necessity imposed from without, it is obvious that the idea of right, or of things that in common parlance " ought" to be done, cannot be derived from usage. Habit is only a real motive through its effect on the organism, and Aristotle's *dictum* that no law of nature can be altered by habit is explained when we remember that a true law implies more than one set of constant relations, and that the conditions of the relations, on one side at least, cannot be directly affected by a mere act of will; and since, as the same authority observes, all habits are formed by acts of like nature, the habit does not explain the action: a habit universal enough to modify the specific type must have been natural to begin with.

The chief difficulty of this part of the subject is inseparable from its nature. We cannot separate the intellectual and the practical aspects of the problem. Our daily conduct must be influenced by our moral theories; and our theories are based on history and reason without reference to expediency. But, in morals alone, the credibility of a view is associated with its practical merits, and the best judges do not feel as if a theory were true unless the statement of it inspires something more than assent. We take for granted that the true ethical system upholds all moral obligations, and therefore it seems that every moral philosopher is *ipso facto* a preacher or teacher of morals, and his philosophy is faulty if it can be believed without being acted upon. An intellectual truth ought to be convincing to every sane mind, but many persons of sane mind are morally perverse, and the apprehension of an abstract truth does not necessarily affect the will. To know whence the majority of mankind derive such moral virtue as they have, is not necessarily to feel moved towards the acquisition, in one's own person, of more virtue than before. And yet, if the argument is given in its logical simplicity and aloofness from personal feeling, it seems incomplete, because the feeling of the majority is the minor premise which we have no right to ignore.

On the other hand, the argument has no right to assume that any given reader is one of the majority, whose feeling supplies the base of our general conclusions. The science of morals is on a par with the science of medicine. It treats indifferently of the conditions of health and disease, and has no power to alter concrete matters of fact, or save the heir of diseased appetites from the natural consequences of their indulgence or repression. It proclaims the sanctions of the law of nature, and leaves men to obey or defy the law as they please. But the law is there, and those who are not inclined to defy it, have a right to treat the substance of the law and its natural mode of administration, as part of the same subject, and to take its working for granted in the exposition of its principles.

Voluntary spontaneous action, while unchecked, does not give the idea of necessity or constraint, and whatever theory be adopted concerning the nature or source of the common notions of duty, morality, or moral obligation, it will scarcely be denied either that such notions really exist and are of force, or that their force in particular cases is felt as binding. Moral actions are actions done because the doer of them believes it right that they should be done, and right is seldom more clearly defined than as that which some one "ought" to do. When men at a certain stage in the development of moral ideas, say we or I "ought" to do so and so, and are asked "Why?" they sometimes give as the reason that quality in the act by which they have recognised it as incumbent. They knew that it was what had to be done by the token that it was good, fit, admirable, useful, or the like; but the further question, why what is good, fit, admirable, or useful has to be done, is apt to elicit the most conclusive, and, saving the prejudice of logicians, the most logical of answers: "Because it has." But if we examine further into the nature of that which has, or ought to be done, we find nothing anterior to the speaker's conviction that *he* must and will do it if he can.

If we consider the current ideas of duty, we shall find that they all include the conception of relation to the person on whom the duty is incumbent. The verb expressive of right doing is irregular, and though the categorical imperative is not a "shalt" but a "must," it is only in the first person singular that we read always "ought," which is practically a "must" acquiesced in by the will. "I ought" has a meaning for everybody, and "we" or "you ought" only extends the obligation to other men in the name of a common humanity. But we have no conception of duty, our own or other people's, apart from the inward conviction or subjective sense of moral obligation. We may say, it is the duty of this or that man or woman to act thus and thus, but the judgment always rests on the preliminary assumption that the person in question has the same sense of right and wrong as ourselves. The further assumption of the existence of some uniform, objective rule of right conduct exterior to the consciences of mankind does not interfere with our belief that people in general ought to do what they themselves think and feel to be right; and we involuntarily form a quite different judgment of persons who, we think, have mistaken their duty, and of persons who knowingly fail in the performance of the duties they recognise. In the attempt to determine our neighbour's duties, we are always divided between a conviction that the right is one and unalterable, and an impression, based on personal experience and the natural meaning of words, that it cannot be morally right for any one to do what he believes to be wrong.

The inference is obvious: the class of actions enjoined by the moral law may be determined conjointly by the nature of the individual man, and that of the real world in which he is circumstanced thus or thus; but if consent is necessary to all law, the sanction of morality, the source of the inward feeling of obligation which we have to explain, must be sought "within the breast." The existence of morality as a something binding the will is purely and necessarily subjective; we have the *data* for passing moral judgments on ourselves, but on no one else; though, in practice, it may reasonably be assumed that beings of the same kind will experience the same natural necessities, and will follow in their conduct the same laws, moral as well as physical. But the real and satisfactory explanation of the phenomenon would certainly be a full and intelligible account of the growth and limitations of this subjective sense of obligation, as attached under certain circumstances to certain kinds of action.

Positive law regulates the overt acts of man in society; the moral law regulates the disposition of the will in accordance with which men act. Positive law, it is admitted, should be moral, and certain moral duties may be fitly enforced by legal sanctions. But the fact that the two systems of regulation coincide for a part of their extent, does not make them mutually dependent, the external power or source of obligation is not the same, and the inward consent of the will which gives effect to the outer pressure has, in each case, a different set of antecedents and a different history of growth.

In speaking of positive or customary morality as an early phase of social law, we did not find that the generality of a practice explained its existence, though it might help for a time to perpetuate it. An observance that is only kept up because it has been customary is sure, sooner or later, to pass into disuse, for individuals do not feel bound in conscience by the habits of their neighbours any more than by their own. There must be a cause or motive in present operation to affect the will with the sense of necessity or constraint which is as essential a part of morality as of law. The present opinion of the majority of mankind does not give such a cause or motive, because mankind is made up of individuals, and it is the opinion of individual men that we want to have explained. Morality is a matter of personal opinion or sentiment, and conformity to the opinions or sentiments of the majority is not felt to. be in itself a moral duty. There is nothing intrinsically immoral in the position of *Athanasius contra mundum*, and the general similarity between the moral judgments which we all naturally pass, the substantial *consensus* of human opinion as to what is right and wrong, what ought, and ought not to be done, is sufficiently accounted for by the judgments and opinions being formed under the same general conditions by beings of the same kind or nature. But the existence and the tenor of the opinions on those points separately reached by individuals is as far from explanation as ever.

The opinions that men have entertained about their own moral ideas differ more than the ideas themselves, and the only objection to an eclectic theory, taken entirely from known and accredited works on ethics, is that in each one, amongst nine points of agreement with the rest, there is

F

always one point of difference, so that, whether the one or the many are right in any particular case, it is evident that the many are never right in all. When possible points of divergence are practically innumerable, and yet so far from essential, controversy is apt to be lengthy in proportion to the number of common premises, which, unaccountably, fail to lead disputants to the same results. Every system has a different reason to give for dissenting from each of its rivals, and each reason involves some assumption to which rival systems would agree in demurring, though, again, all for different reasons. The objections that can be urged against a merely naturalistic theory of the origin of morality take a different form according to the objectors' own opinions, and the answer that would meet one statement of a real difficulty may fall, or seem to fall, wide of, perhaps, the same difficulty stated in a different way.

What has been already said of the theories which ascribe the force of positive law in the last resort to the will or act of a divine legislator, applies equally to the cognate explanation of the existence and cogency of the moral law. The many advocates of a pure and lofty morality, who believe its precepts to be of divine institution, are conscious of no other ground than this belief for the morality they practise, and are, therefore, sincerely persuaded that without religious theism the existence of morality would be left to the accidents of natural temperament and hereditary disposition, and could not be expected, as a rule, to survive exposure to the natural obstacles and hindrances to virtuous life with which the world abounds. They argue, like Voltaire, that if God did not exist, it would be necessary to invent him, as the cheapest way of strengthening the hands of the police ; and there are some timid sceptics who so far agree with them as to half believe in the desirability of both respecting and preserving the illusions of the majority, while the fulness of irreligious truth is reserved for the few whose passions have been chilled by a life of study, or who have learnt by experience the reasonableness and prudence of self-control.

If, however, we suppose human ideas, feelings, and beliefs to have been evolved by a continuation of the natural process which fixed the nature of the things thought, felt, or known about, and to correspond in essentials to their material counterparts, we shall find it difficult to account for the rise of a general illusion or baseless belief, and almost impossible to understand how such an illusion should be an essential condition of the prosperity and subsistence of the species entertaining it. Theologians and naturalists may join issue if they please on the preliminary question whether a Deity exists, but nothing save confusion can result from their going off into speculations, not whether there is a God or no, but whether it would be a good thing if there were, and further, supposing that to be conceded, whether it would be a good thing to believe there were, even if there really were not.

The objection which the various theories of morality that may be classed as sentimental would lay most stress upon, as against a theory of mere realism, is psychological. Morality includes a sentiment about certain acts, as well as a real tendency, desire, or intention to do them; and if moral acts are done by a simple natural necessity, it is asked, and with reason, why we do not consider all acts performed in accordance with natural laws as moral. The objection admits of being retorted, for granting that the moral sentiments of men were all alike, and sufficiently strong to determine their conduct, there is nothing in the habitual prevalence of certain sentiments to give the feeling of obligation, to make men think it their duty to have the same sentiments as their neighbours, or to have always the same sentiments themselves. And as simple feeling in our own persons does not give the idea of morality, *a fortiori*, it is not to be expected that reflected emotion or feeling for others should do so; and accordingly no further light is cast on the question by the half-and-half form of utilitarianism, which supposes men to feel bound to do as they like, but premises that many of their likings are sympathetic, that is to say, mainly determined by the selfish desires of one another.

The so-called selfish systems fail in that they obliterate the distinction, which it is desired to explain, between different classes of actions, by tracing them all to the same motive, as if additional strength were all that was wanted to make a tendency sanction its own persistence. All voluntary actions are in a sense selfish, done, that is, because we would on the whole rather do them than not, and if they were all equally selfish, and self-interest were the root of virtue, they would all be equally virtuous. Utilitarianism only escapes the reproach of sanctioning egotism to an extent which utilitarians themselves allow to be immoral, by assuming that the conduct which conduces to the greatest happiness of the greatest number, so generally conduces to the greatest happiness of each individual as agent, as to have become indissolubly associated with ideas or sentiments of approbation, which in the course of time have transformed themselves into moral judgments. This optimistic explanation of virtue by a pre-established harmony between its dictates and those of general and particular utility, which is accounted for, in the decadence of theology, by the beneficence of the Creator, might perhaps be satisfactory if the coincidence were absolute; but reasoners of Paley's school only address themselves to common sense, and it is impossible to explain to common sense what a good utilitarian God can want with punishments, temporal or eternal, to make his creatures do as they like best; while it is evident that there is nothing in a theory which rests morality on association to account for the belief that the association on which it rests *ought* to be kept up unbroken.

The fact that men have moral sentiments, and perform acts dictated by a sense of moral obligation or duty, has thus been variously accounted for, by the fact that they naturally have feelings, interested or disinterested, about acts; and by the assumption that there is an external rule or standard of right, which is the source of a unique sentiment enjoining conformity to itself. This rule again may be conceived as abstract, and lying in the nature of things, in which case the private conscience of the individual must be held to declare the law which it obeys; or concrete, that is, the expression of a personal will, more or less directly revealed to its subjects, in which case the conscience is not held bound to pronounce upon the law, only to declare the application of the law to the cases that may arise.

All these formulæ no doubt contain a measure of truth, but they do not seem to carry us to the root of the matter. Our moral conceptions are too complex to be referred to a single ultimate instinct or propensity with a corresponding definite development of the organism. A number of feelings go to make up the state of consciousness which we call sense of duty, and many of these feelings are themselves compounds of physical temperament and moral experience, personal as well as inherited. We are born with a certain number of moral feelings, inherited through our immediate ancestors from the long series of men and women who have lived under conditions favourable to their growth and transmission; each one of these feelings has a history of its own, and the children of the present day are born with a rudimentary disposition to say " I ought " in particular cases, as they are born, variously, with a disposition to draw or sing, kiss or quarrel, as well as with a disposition to walk and eat. The disposition or aptitude is of the most rudimentary kind, but it is not really more difficult to understand how experience, continued through ages, of the constant relation between causes and effects should have tuned the minds of men to the perception of the relations, than it is to understand how the sensibility of the human ear to musical intervals has developed into a capacity for composing and retaining long and highly elaborate melodies. Just as some people are born without a musical ear, so others are insensible to the force of moral considerations; but the average man can tell one tune from another, and is more or less shocked by a discord, and in like manner the average man feels the pressure upon his own individual will of all the unknown natural sequence of motive in the past which caused his ancestors to do on the whole more often the right thing than the wrong. "Ought" is what I feel obliged to do, because for ages and ages the stream of human tendency has set in favour of such doing, and my present inclinations have been moulded by the stream; if completely, I do easily and willingly what I ought, if not, I may leave it undone and repent, or do it grudgingly and with pain, or I may set myself against the stream and deny the obligation; but in the ordinary use of words, I am a "good" or "bad" man in proportion to the completeness and spontaneity of my obedience.

But it is not merely true that we have for the most part, by inheritance and choice, a formed habit of not stealing or murdering, of working, if needs must, for our living, and of cherishing parents and children. These habits might be formed, as the Tartars ride and the Fijians swim, by inherited aptitude and acquired proficiency without giving room for a science of morals. The peculiarity of the sense of moral obligation is that the obligation felt is towards a precise action or abstention, while the source of the obligation is unknown or unfelt, and its nature altogether abstract; the reasons for doing or leaving undone lie not in the deed itself, but in some quality of the deed which makes it "right," and in some quality of ourselves which makes us mean by "right" what ought to be done.

Still the question remains, What do we mean by "right?" and what classes of action are enjoined by the moral law? The just in positive law is the practical best for the community—*i.e.*, whatever course conduces most to the perfect and satisfactory development of its members, in which ideal the greatest happiness of the greatest number is included. The right in morals is also the practical best for the individual subject to do, such bestness being estimated by a special feeling in the subject towards the nature of the act, quite apart from its consequences; and what we have to do is to discover what descriptions of act inspire this feeling.

If we say that it is right to do good, we do not at first seem to have made much progress, for the question, What is good? has been as much debated and solved, or not solved, in as many different ways as the question "What is right?" But either the idea of good was originally less complex than that of right, or more progress has been made towards a sound analysis of it, for it is a more satisfactory substitute for an answer about the nature of good, than those generally offered by moralists about the nature of right, to say that there are three kinds of good—viz., natural, sensible, and moral good.

By natural good we mean, as will probably be allowed, the perfection of anything after its kind, understanding by such perfection only a statement or inference from experience, that there are certain types to which beings of different species do actually tend to approximate, and this so generally that, though the perfect type may never be realised in one individual specimen of the class, still, every particular partial divergence from it appears as an exception to the general rule. There is in this no reference to any metaphysical ideal, or mystical archetype, though the Platonic ideas, and the Aristotelian mean may be regarded as forms of the same conception. The natural excellence of the latter especially could by no means have been ascertained deductively; to give any significance to praises of the mean, we must suppose real extremities of excess and defect to exist and to be felt as naturally faulty; and the only reason against making moderation the standard of merit is that excess and defect are not estimated by their relation to that degree of the quality in question which lies half-way between them—because it is half-way—but because it represents the normal development, in the direction given, of beings of a particular kind, which it is the aim of science to characterise more completely than by averages.

Imperfection, then, is only departure from the class type; a crystal may be faulty, a diamond clouded, a plant stunted in its growth, an animal weakly or misshapen, a man vicious or diseased; but in all these cases the standard by which we decide the existence and the degree of imperfection in a given specimen of the kind is only the kind itself, or what we have learnt to regard as the normal development of objects belonging to it. This is practically the point from which intuitive theories of morality start. They suppose the normal man to be virtuous, that vice is a disease of the mind or will, and they only fail to explain the source and nature of the peculiar disfavour and uneasiness to which sufferers from that particular form of disease are alone exposed,—why divergence from the class type should be felt to be "wrong" by those who diverge, as well as by an impartial spectator. The stoical morality also, admirable and fascinating in many ways as it is, fails altogether to account for the impression under which men labour, that they *ought* to be good of their kind, or live according to its nature. In fact—though such distinctions have a fatiguing air of subtlety—we must submit to see in men's natural feelings about the moral quality of acts a phase of their natural feeling about the acts themselves. The so-called instinctive condemnation of injustice, cruelty, or falsehood, is simply a generalisation from the feeling excited in practice by unjust, cruel or faithless conduct, and the natural objection men have to being wronged, hurt, or deceived, is not more mysterious than their general preference for food over poison.

The practical best for things in general is, of course, the

maximum possible attainment of natural good throughout the system, but the feeling with which we regard "good" as the supreme end of desire comes from the fact that we give the generic name of good to all those ends of desire which can be permanently sought and attained without undesirable consequences. Things are divided by nature as good, bad, or indifferent, and those ends of desire are called good *par excellence* which are naturally good all through and in every relation; the verbal distinction answers to a real distinction between classes of effects and the feelings which answer to these classes. The good qualified as "moral" or "sensible" is also an object of desire; but conditionally, not absolutely, generally, not always. Everything that is fitted to be an object of human desire is good in so far as so fitted: and the objective conditions of life gives rise to many degrees and varieties of goodness.

The only things which are found good always and under all circumstances are those which conduce to natural perfection, and not merely to the natural perfection of one individual or class, but to the perfection of classes or individuals in so far as their perfection harmonises with the perfect development of other kinds. The natural good or perfection of man himself consists in the possession of abundant faculties, active and passive, fully developed, and in regular and equal exercise. The condition of natural personal perfection may be summed up in one word "ability"—ability to do, feel, and perceive as much and as well as possible. But for perfect accomplishment, or the highest realisation of the possibilities of perfection, the ability must find due scope for appropriate exercise, and it depends upon other circumstances than the will and power of the individual to determine whether he shall be able to attain the highest degree, or live in the fullest state of natural perfection physically within his reach.

We cannot pass at once from natural to moral good, but

the connection between natural good and sensible good or pleasure is comparatively simple. Sensible good is included in natural good, but is not co-extensive with it, and the confusion of the two, or still worse, the exaltation of the former as the higher, more comprehensive term, can only be the work of a shallow inaccurate psychology. We see this at once in the case of physical perfection; strong and far-sighted eyes are physically better than weak ones, yet a short-sighted, squinting artist may derive more pleasure from his imperfect powers of vision than a human hawk with no sense of beauty. Acute hearing is a perfection, though Beethoven was deaf; muscular strength is a perfection, though a champion pedestrian may get less pleasure from his 1000 miles than a feeble cockney like Charles Lamb out of strolls measurable by the yard. Similarly the power of ruling men, the power of inspiring love, the power of inventing and creating, the power of seeing what is true and of being deeply moved by the vision, these are all natural perfections, not necessarily associated in practice with the keenest possible delight in the exercise of the acknowledged power. A small domestic tyrant may have more carnal satisfaction in the consciousness of his vexatious sway than the saviour of a nation in the discharge of his beneficent mission.

Pleasure comes from the equilibrium between power and desire, or correspondence between the inward impulse to do, and the result of the thing done. But though it is a perfection to maintain such an equilibrium, when the power of achievement is ideally high, or exercised under ideally favourable circumstances, it is not exactly a perfection to be content with powers or results that fall below the average, or below a distinctly conceived ideal. Such content sets the final seal of inferiority; for discontent with the worse may always be—though it often is not—a prelude to improvement or change for the better.

Still, pleasure, though not an infallible sign of perfection, is undoubtedly a real element in natural good. It would be futile to attempt to analyse the ultimate, irreducible experience to which we give the name; we all know what we mean by pleasure, though we find pleasure in the most various and opposite pursuits and sensations. The pleasure of the saint and of the sensualist, of the student and of the athlete, are alike in the one indescribable quality which makes the *bien être* for each enjoying self. Most rich languages, however, distinguish between "wellbeing" and "being good;" the one phrase serves to describe subjective contentment, the other objective perfection, and we have no more right to expect or assume the existence of a pre-established harmony between the two, than we have to assume a pre-established harmony between the demands of the palate and the digestion. Generally speaking, food is pleasant and the exercise of faculty enjoyable, but a man may get his taste from one ancestor, and his stomach from another, and the demands of the two may be incompatible; or, again, the promptings of taste may be his own, a new product of the latter ages, while his powers of assimilation are still at the ancient level. It is not a paradox, but a commonplace, that the good and the agreeable are disparate. All naturalists will agree that pleasure is a natural good, and even that it has a wider range than other concrete goods, but it has never yet been found possible to develop a theory that combines in a consistent system the recognition of pleasure, not only as good, but as the true *summum bonum*, with the recognition of the unexplained, undeniable excellence of other spiritual ends.

The objective conditions of pleasure are still very imperfectly understood; but so far as we are aware, it seems always to be attendant upon the free and normal exercise of some natural faculty, and pain, upon the disturbance or arrest of such exercise. It is not, of course, true that every natural act is distinctly pleasurable, nor that every pleasure attends an act conducive to the natural good of the organism as a whole; but in general, allowing for the complexity of organisation, which may make the simultaneous exercise of disparate faculties difficult or impossible, it is true that pleasure attends upon, or, perhaps, is actually the sensation of, a normal activity of the natural powers; pain, of abnormal or impeded activity. Why some normal actions are attended with pleasure, while others are performed unconsciously, with automatic regularity, and what is the difference between the two classes, are points that physiologists will doubtless in time determine. Meanwhile, it may be conjectured with some plausibility that pleasure accompanies the exercise of natural powers, or special organs, at a certain period in their evolutionary history. Animals that only breathe and digest may be supposed to find something dimly pleasurable, or analogous to pleasure, in the consciousness of those processes, which in more highly organised animals are not conscious at all so long as they go on with normal regularity. We know that ordinary human pleasures of a semi-artificial kind are apt to lose their zest after constant indulgence and repetition, and analogy would favour the supposition that powers which are in constant necessary exercise would at length come to be exercised with indifference, if not with absolute insensibility. There is nothing in this supposition at variance with the most general conclusion given by Professor Bain,[1] that "states of pleasure are connected with an increase, and states of pain with an abatement, of some or all of the vital functions;" for "increase" and "abatement" are terms of comparison, and the vital functions which we suppose to become indifferent and unconscious are only those of which the variations are imperceptible; since every act of consciousness implies some organic modification or change in its subject, the absence of change, either in the intensity or in the mode of exercising vital functions in constant operation, almost implies the absence of sensibility, pleasurable or the reverse. Pleasure, on this hypothesis, would be attendant on the

[1] The Senses and the Intellect, p. 286.

exercise either of comparatively newly-acquired faculties, or of faculties that only come into play occasionally, or intermittently.

Supposing this to be correct, sensible good, though always the same in reference to the conscious subject, *i.e.*, always some kind of pleasure, varies in its objective conditions or constitution with any variation of the specific type which is the standard of natural good. If we accept the doctrine of evolution in its general bearings, we may suppose, as it were, a belt of pleasurable consciousness of power, bounded at one extremity by the high-water mark of actual development, and not necessarily increasing in width as that gradually rises to a fresh level in the scale of creation. We can no more suppose sensible pleasures to be habitually associated with acts destructive to the sentient organism, than we could suppose societies naturally to institute laws destructive of all society; for we know that the pleasurableness of an act is a strong motive for its performance, that would in practice certainly overrule any abstract desire for the continuance of the species in its purity.

Utilitarianism rests morality upon the coincidence, which is certainly general, between natural and sensible good, and the conditions of their common realisation. It makes moral good practically a compound of the pleasure naturally desired, and the perfection naturally admired or preferred; and it only breaks down when we try to apply its test to the cases which are unfortunately also of very general occurrence, in which pleasure and virtue lie along divergent paths. Virtue, by which we understand the deliberate pursuit of perfection, is only valuable on utilitarian principles for the pleasure which it gives, so that, on these principles, if it ceases to give pleasure, or gives less pleasure than something which is not virtue, it ceases to be valuable or good. But, of two things one; either this never occurs, in which case it is inexplicable that we should have two names for the natural appetites of man alone, out of all the animals that spontaneously seek the gratification of their natural wants: or else, when it occurs it is right, or at least not wrong, to prefer the sensible pleasure to the natural good. In other words, the theory has to choose between a somewhat extravagant optimism, and what, without any appeal to vulgar prejudice, must be called a comparative laxity of moral precepts. Children are told that to be good is the way to be happy, and it would be strange that they should always decline to accept the comfortable doctrine if the sequence were really so simple and direct. But, if happiness were attainable, and the highest wisdom and virtue consisted in attaining as much happiness as possible, the notion of morality would either disappear with the feeling of constraint that is a part of it, and only arises when the natural pursuit of pleasure is interrupted; or it would be reduced, as it practically is by Bentham, to the art of being happy under difficulties. Mark Tapley may be as sound a philosopher as the Emperor Marcus Aurelius; but we do not believe that he, or any other follower of Bentham, ever felt obliged in conscience to be happier than a spontaneous inclination—which is not duty—made him.

In one sense, the existence of these two forms of consciousness (obligation and pleasure) is explained when the history of their growth and origin has been traced; but why, when they are developed, each is what it is and not something quite different—or, indeed, nothing at all—is a question with which positive thinkers may decline to embarrass themselves. It is unphilosophical to ask for the logical reason of matters of fact, as well as unscientific to ignore the reinforcement of certitude belonging to matters of fact so universal as to have become a premise for the reason. The mental state which we call enjoyment is not the result of physically simple causes; we have not a special organ for feeling happy, but we have a special mental feeling which attends upon analogous states of special organs. Similarly, we have not a special organ for the apprehension of what is right, but we have a special mental feeling towards analogous lines of conduct; and we shall scarcely be able to get nearer to an explanation of the feeling than an analysis of those qualities of conduct which seem to be its *sine qua non*.

For practical purposes, the utilitarian and the Perfectionist theories of morality agree on all points except in their estimate of the comparative power of pleasure as a motive. If there is one psychological truth of axiomatic evidence, it is that people find it pleasant to do as they like, or rather, their liking and the pleasantness of the action are correlative—two aspects of a natural agreement between the agent and the act. Something has already been said of the character of those acts which are naturally pleasant, and, subject to correction, we assume them to be those in which the less hackneyed powers of the organism find their appropriate exercise. An act is found pleasurable in proportion to its essential naturalness, *i.e.*, to its fitness for exercising existing organs of action and impressibility in a healthy manner. But such exercise may lead to diminished as well as to heightened sensibility, for, although a faculty is strengthened by its exercise in taking in different, numerically distinct impressions, the same subjective feeling is apt to grow faint with repetition, and may in time cease to be distinguished in consciousness at all. A pleasurable act, when (in the lapse of ages) it has been repeated often enough for its periodical repetition to have become, as it were, an organic function, continues to be performed, if possible, with more inevitable regularity than if it were voluntary, but with less and less sense of pleasure, until, finally, its performance is a matter of indifference to sense, but has become a part of the natural life of the organism, and its unimpeded performance an element in the natural good of the species.

Will is conscious tendency, and as there are states of consciousness unattended by pleasure or pain, desire is distinguished as the will to follow a tendency which produces pleasure. Now it is possible that the hope or imagination of the greatest possible pleasure may be irresistible, when it exists, and it is further true that so many of our acts have the hope of pleasure or the fear of pain for their motive, that we readily assume these motives to be universal, to lie latent in consciousness, when we fail to be aware of them. Without this assumption, utilitarianism crumbles to the ground; for a formula is useless which leaves the intermediate bulk of indifferent actions unaccounted for, besides stumbling over the extremes of infelicific self-indulgence or self-devotion. It is inaccurate to speak of motives except in relation to consciousness, and not all acts of will are preceded by conscious self-determination. Men will and choose consciously, sometimes moved by a physical impulse, sometimes by a present physical inducement, sometimes by a mental representation of inducements, real or imaginary; but consciousness includes only a part, not the whole, of the organic life of man, and it cannot be too clearly understood that the higher forms of consciousness are not the cause but the product of lower processes of animal life.

It is conceivable that a universe might be so providentially arranged that every natural tendency should be normally felicific, and no natural tendency impeded in its course. But this is not the case in the world we live in. Many natural tendencies give little or no pleasure to the subject of them. Many of them if freely followed would become productive of pain either to the individual or to other conscious subjects; and this fact, conjoined with the influences of the natural human affections in developing a sympathetic concern in man for man, hampers the will as well as the conduct, and it is found not merely physically impossible to do all that we wish, but morally impossible to will to do all that we wish to will. The notion of a natural impulse, persisted in in defiance of external obstacles, and passing into consciousness in a form slightly modified by the opposition it has encountered, brings us some way towards a conception of moral necessity that shall not err on the side of optimism, and that recognises no duties of imperfect obligation, except as the correlative of imperfect knowledge or undeveloped sensibility.

All the vital force of a man's individual nature tends spontaneously to self-development, he feels impelled to be himself, as fine a specimen of humanity as he can, to realise, that is to say, all the capabilities of action and passion that are in him, so far as fortune, favourable or adverse, will allow. The appetite for happiness may be strong or weak, but as pleasure is found only in the gratification of secondary, special appetites, it is obvious that a man's chance of gratifying a general taste for gratification depends upon a thousand circumstances besides the mere strength of his wish, though that alone is a circumstance that may now and then have power to turn the scale. But if a man's strongest tendency is to be—rather than to please—himself, his nature will still struggle to assert itself through every check, though it will be compelled to many compromises.

To take real cases: a young man aims at self-culture, but he may only be able to secure leisure for intellectual pursuits at the expense of the not less necessary discipline of practical life; he may resolve to whet his intellect upon the grindstone of a bread-winning industry, or he may hope to train his imagination to supply the place of experience; but, in either case, he has to resolve, with more or less painful effort, to be his best self under difficulties— upon spiritual short-commons. The same necessity may be forced upon an individual by single accidents, the will of another, or the merest chance, a birth, a death, loss of fortune or loss of health, or the *contre-coup* of some change in the circumstances of others, involving the material interests of their connections. Many words, indeed, are hardly needed to establish the simple position that even when a man knows what life he is best fitted for, and wishes to lead it in the best manner possible, he may not be able to do so without sacrificing some of the pleasure or some of the efficiency which would be his but for adverse circumstances.

Now, it is possible to define virtue, or moral good, as the consciousness of a necessary (or actually existing) tendency, of which the conditions are fixed and stable, towards the natural good of the individual, as conditioned by the common life of the species, in all those cases when submission to the tendency is neither pleasurable nor automatic. All unimpeded tendencies we suppose to be one or the other, and we do not expect to find the discharge of the functions of natural life or the pursuit of natural pleasures attended by the peculiar sense of constraint which we call moral obligation. The actions that are so attended are of various kinds. The greater part of the waking life of men is taken up with conscious, more or less voluntary, actions, that is to say, co-ordinated volitions directed towards the attainment of ends thought or felt to be desirable. Those ends which constitute the natural good of man as a rational animal are not absolutely fixed, but at any given time they may be inferred in the same way as we determine what constitutes the perfection of a greyhound or a bulldog, by an intelligent eclecticism preferring out of all the rudimentary possibilities existing in nature, the combination that harmonises the greatest number of the strongest tendencies. A world so ordered that none of the real tendencies of which individuals were conscious ever came into collision or conflict with other tendencies of the same or other individuals, would be perfect after its kind. If the world had been so arranged that it was always easy to know and pleasant to do what is right, we should not perhaps regret, what we should no longer have or need, the conception of right.

Theologians have found comfort in the thought that the evil in the world might be, as it certainly is, a necessary condition for the moral education of mankind; we cannot know moral good without knowing natural and sensible evil; but it is by no means evident that the knowledge of moral good is a good in itself; it can only be so regarded in the metaphysical sense in which the Stoics made an end of conformity to nature. The knowledge of moral good is not a sensible good, it is not even a simple natural good, it only becomes so conditionally upon other things being as they are, that is to say, the world imperfect. We have the conception of right or moral perfection because the world is imperfect, and this conception is the condition of its perfectibility, if indeed it be perfectible; by which we mean that in the strength of this conception, man, the conscious register of the least material tendencies of nature, may continue to approach more nearly to the goal of a perfection that still recedes, but least dishearteningly from those who know the laws of mental perspective by which a goal ceases to attract those who have reached or passed it.

To be more precise; we conceive moral good as the pursuit of natural (not sensible) good under difficulties without which the pursuit would not be self-conscious. These difficulties may be of three kinds. The material obstacles which external nature (including human society) may and does oppose to the natural tendency of each single man towards the realisation of as much perfection after his kind as his particular organisation is capable of attaining; the less palpable, but more insuperable obstacles which certain tendencies of an organism that is not perfect after its kind, oppose to the full and normal action of other tendencies, the frustration of which constitutes imperfection in any specimen of the kind; and, lastly, a difficulty which Utilitarian morality seems incapable of meeting or including in a consistent system of precepts; that namely which is presented by the facts of evolution —the instability of the type to which it is perfection to conform.

Mr. Herbert Spencer observes that "survival of the fittest cannot bring the inclinations and aversions into harmony with unfelt conditions," and it is at least equally clear that the inclinations and aversions have no power by themselves to bring about their own extinction; the desire for one action that is at present pleasurable does not dispose to another action that, at a future time, might be pleasurable, nor to the same action in the event of its ceasing to be pleasurable. Evolution is not primarily a Utilitarian process, even though, as has been suggested, pleasure were only to be met with as an accompaniment to the exercise of faculties still engaged in the act of evolving themselves; for the process, while appearing as a condition of pleasure in general, sets a fatal term to the enjoyment of each real pleasure severally. The natural good of any species may vary indefinitely, with whatever modifications of the specific type actually take place, but as there always *is* a type, the standard of natural good is at least relatively fixed. Sensible pleasure, again, may be conceived as fixed in relation to the conscious subject, or individual member of the class, the type of which is supposed to vary, but such variation necessarily brings with it a partial disturbance of the agreement between natural and sensible good. The physical interests of man are the same as those of other animals, that is to say, self-preservation, and, perhaps, though less directly, the preservation of the species; but the interests peculiar to him as rational are relative, dependent that is upon the point of development reached by the active impulses at any given period in the history of the species, without reference to considerations of utility or pleasure. Men wish for this or that, not because they can get it, but because their antecedents have determined them to wish; and if morality consisted in the systematic pursuit of pleasure, or the indulgence of wish, it would be felt as a moral duty to resist the course of evolution whenever it promised to give birth to new wishes, unless, which is hardly ever the case, means of indulging the wish were provided first. But, as has been said before, whatever other duties men may acknowledge, they do not look upon it as a duty to preserve the species *in statu quo.*

There is no common measure of happiness to enable us to say that the more perfect being enjoys more of it than the less. An animal can only be happy with all the powers of its being, and if an animal has the chance of being happy after its kind, what inducement has it to become a different animal if it can only be happy at best? In point of fact, no man is either as happy or as virtuous as he would like, but the feeling towards those two kinds of defect is quite different; one is spontaneously named a misfortune, the other a fault. The one makes the universe so far the less cheerful, the other makes it the worse, in the technical sense which it is our business to analyse. For that badness which is the converse of the good we can still find no other paraphrase than imperfection, or departure from the type of specific excellence. Thus, though it is not in itself a crime to be unfortunate, it is a defect to fail in making use of average opportunities for securing success; and though it is not a crime to be made melancholy by misfortune, we reckon as a defect the morbid mood which finds no satisfaction in circumstances of average felicity.

Utilitarianism might pass muster in a theory of Social Statics, but it breaks down altogether if we seek its help to construct a theory of Social Dynamics. Happiness is relative to the desires of the organism as it is, and we want a clue by which to make or keep desires what they should be, through all the changes brought about in their nature or chance of indulgence. A change in the environment may alter the means by which a desired happiness has to be attained, or may make it unattainable by any means within the power of the organism as hitherto constituted. Such a change may either cause the old desire to atrophy for want of indulgence, or it may stimulate new energy to overcome the obstacles in the way of indulgence; and this new development of energy may be attended by a change of taste which may supersede the desire that provoked the change. In other words, whenever the circumstances of men change for the worse, without their own co-operation, the strength of existing desires resists the threatened privation, and unless the change affects the powers as well as the enjoyments of the unlucky generation, it defends itself by a real progress, the development of new ability to cope with circumstances.

The migration of a progressive race from a region of extreme to one of moderate fertility is an obvious example of this kind of influence, but by far the commonest kind of change brought about in the circumstances of men is that effected by the course of history, which leaves each new generation burdened with the debts and legacies of its predecessors. For nations, as for men, successive experiences modify the character, or the sum-total of impulses, abilities, and inclinations which determine the action at any given moment. The desires of the child are not those of the youth, but the desires of the man are after all an inheritance from the past that he calls his. The successors of an age of constructive faith possess by inheritance a taste for the pleasures of performance, as well as, very often, an acquired knowledge of the futility of special kinds of performance. It is in such straits that the counsels of Utilitarianism might fairly be called " unprincipled "—not by way of reproach, but as a simple statement of their intellectual looseness. To take the present time—which is variously called an age of scepticism, analytic, critical, indifferentist, and so forth—if we ask how the members of such a generation can attain the greatest possible happiness, some will say by being less critical of the advantages they enjoy, others by being less indifferent to the success of the work they might do, but there is nothing in the greatest happiness principle to enable men to decide whether they shall aim at attaining, say, the same amount of happiness, by limiting their wants or by enlarging their labours ; if content is the only thing to be aimed at, and clods are less discontented than critics, it should be a duty —not a pardonable weakness, but a positive duty—to cultivate cloddishness, and this no one seriously believes, though many half admit the premises for inferences of kindred absurdity.

The issue is not altogether between conservative pleasure and painful progress, but if progress is conceived as the winding road that leads up the heights of perfection, happiness may answer to the resting-place at every turn of the zig-zag; listless climbers hurried away from one seat by cosmic or historic force have no higher ambition than to reach the next turn and rest again in thankfulness, and it is nothing to these whether they rest at a higher or a lower level, so they do but rest. The theory of the perfectionist on the other hand is, that man has nothing better to do with himself than climb, and the proof alleged is that the higher he climbs up this allegorical hill, the more of a man he becomes; he breathes quicker, he sees further, he climbs faster, his ability is greater, even though he should now and then forget, for a stage, to rest, or spend the inevitable breathing space in impatient longings to be gone.

To each individual unit, no doubt, it is an urgent question, What is the greatest happiness possible to me? but science, even ethical science, is essentially unsympathetic, and speaking scientifically, the self-contained happiness of a human unit is of no more account than the blossoming of a flower or the breaking of a wave; it was and is not, it came and went, and the rest of the world felt no change. Human feeling is a kind of waste-pipe of the world's force, and all the motive power that spends itself in unproductive feeling counts for nothing in the history of progress, save in so far as the experience modifies the subject self. It is not of great moment whether each individual soul-chimney enjoys the flavour of the smoke it is engaged in consuming, but intense and varied feeling is a product and a symptom of rich and active life, or, in other words, of human perfection, and it is an imperfection in the objective universe if fine and normal feeling habitually suffers pain and privation.

It may, perhaps, be objected that we seem to put forward two standards of excellence, the perfection of the type as it is, and an ideal standard of perfection in the absolute abundance and variety of vital power; and this is true, but not necessarily inconsistent. The common quality of all ideals is to be as full as they can, and each special ideal only has its possibilities determined by conditions of time, place, and circumstance. The power of growing or developing is a natural excellence, because we look upon everything as naturally, so to speak physically, the better, *the more of a thing* it is: if a vegetable throws up a long leafy stalk at the expense of its root or blossom we do not praise it, but the more flowers or fruit it can succeed in bearing from the one stock, the better every gardener and grammarian must call it. And when organisms of a still higher kind include among their specific qualities a power of self-adaptation and self-development, the more of this power there is in each individual the better specimen of his kind he will be, always provided that the performance of the day is not sacrificed to the promise of the morrow.

The highest form of virtue or moral excellence, according to this view, would lie in the conscious tendency towards conformity to the type as it is going to be, but as, except in a few chosen specimens, it is not yet discernible to be. Experience, which gives no support to the view that men feel a moral obligation to preserve the ideal of their own generation unchanged, certainly warrants our assumption that it is from a sense of moral duty or constraint that some few men in most ages exhaust themselves in endeavouring to *raise* the ideal of their contemporaries. The natural action which has become easy, and not yet too familiar, is pleasurable; the natural action which is good, but has not yet become easy enough to be pleasurable, is virtuous. Virtue accordingly is not pleasure, nor a condition of present pleasure; it is the condition of good, which includes pleasure to distant generations—as pleasure may be the precursor of indifference. Without evolution, virtuous action would, with habit, merge into sensible pleasure, and vanish at last in unconscious natural good; and it is owing to the slow instability of an imperfect world that virtue remains, while what is virtuous changes, as some think all too slowly. Perhaps the most conclusive proof that morality consists in consciousness of constraint, not in any inherent property of moral acts, is that persons in whom the inability not to do a given moral act has become absolute, are absolutely incapable of recognising their own action as virtuous. There are some trifling acts commonly classed as virtuous which every one feels that there is no merit in performing, though their omission is still felt to be wrong because their performance, though easy, has not become absolutely automatic. There are ages when no more virtue is commonly practised than has become comparatively easy and natural, and at such times optimism flourishes, because morality is stationary. Morality advances when the sense of moral obligation is onerous and distressing, because the necessity then experienced by the moral teachers of the race is made by desires going forward after the unattained, not by motives already present to sense.

We are not yet prepared to describe in detail the kinds of action or forbearance to which men feel morally compelled; but moral conduct may be defined in general as conduct conducive to the natural good or perfection of the agent and those persons affected by his action, and the one morally right and dutiful way of adding to the happiness, which is a part of the natural good of sentient beings, is by ministering to their perfection, and removing objective obstacles in the way of their sane and profitable enjoyments. The moral sense is a naturally conditioned appetite for natural perfection, especially of certain kinds, the natural (superable) impediments to which virtually trace the outlines of special duties, social and self-regarding.

It will, however, not impossibly, be objected, on the one hand, that virtue is degraded by being ranked as a simple natural phenomenon, like hunger or sight; and, on the other, that virtue, if shorn of all her supernatural dignity and beauty, will lose her power to control the very beings whom we are supposing to be subject, by a natural necessity, to her sway. As the purpose of these pages is truth, not edification—when were men ever made virtuous by argument?—it is perhaps unnecessary to do more than allude to these probable objections; nevertheless, they will be met to some extent when we come to consider the particular provisions of the moral law as conceived from the natural, realistic standing-point. At present we are only concerned to show that a moral law of some kind, that is to say, a rule of conduct of strictly subjective necessity, is not only possible, but really laid down for every rational being by its own nature, the free development of which is conditioned by the equally natural, fixed order of the universe; that this law, as it owes its force to the consent of the subject, is only binding upon the individual conscience, which is subject and legislator in one; and that this law thus promulgated in every conscience will be the same for all men, in so far as they have a common nature, and an identical knowledge of the wider laws to which all existence, their own included, is in common subjection.

The force of this law is not derived from the incidents which bring its existence home to the consciousness of men; but after they have attained to a sense of the reality of the laws actually followed by themselves, they can trace the historical course of their own enthralment without incurring any risk of emancipation. There are some lines of conduct which we feel naturally bound to follow: these lines are such as have been naturally selected for approval, as most conducive to the perfection of all those concerned: if we try to imagine any other general rule of conduct for ourselves than the one so-selected, we are brought into collision with the spontaneous judgment of our fellows that this pseudo-rule is bad or indifferent; and there is no conceivable bad or indifferent rule which we ourselves could approve if proposed for his own guidance by somebody else. Our feeling is that other people "ought" to be good—good in themselves, and good to us—but we do not, except by a transparent fallacy of egotism, make the goodness of others consist in their willingness to indulge ourselves in pleasures that are not good. The self and the community agree because both seek a general rule for the right guidance of the other, and general rules refuse to admit of one-sided application. But the real reason of our subjection to a moral law is not the opinion of others that we ought to submit to special rules, but our own habits of feeling—habits formed, however, under the same objective conditions as the opinion with which they agree.

As has been said, no truth regarding human nature is more general, or more generally admitted, than the fact that men find it pleasant to do as they like; but there is another point upon which the experience of ages is no less unanimous, and herein it is that we conceive the first foundation of morality to be laid: the condition of being able to do as they like is practically unattainable by mortal men. Pleasure consists in the complete and appropriate satisfaction of each of our faculties or appetites. Happiness would consist in the full and simultaneous satisfaction of *all* the powers and desires of our nature, if such satisfaction were not a moral and material impossibility. Man is imperfect; he has unsatisfied instincts, or rather he has the instinct of dissatisfaction, which omnipotence itself would find it hard to satisfy. His best pleasures lie in the exercise of faculties which have to develop before he can use them, while he can conceive and desire the pleasure which their exercise will afford before their development is complete—which, indeed, it never is, any more than the bee's cell is a perfect hexagon, or the eye a faultless optical instrument. The foundation of morality, or the sense of constraint acting in favour of human tendencies towards perfection, is not, of course, to be found in man's imperfection, as such, but rather in the juxtaposition of his higher impulses with material and spiritual checks to the impulses. If man were morally perfect, the imperfections of the world and the flesh would be powerless to cause a moral struggle; if the world were materially perfect, the devil himself would have no temptations wherewithal to seduce the weakest sinner. If men always liked what was best they would do it without feelings of constraint; if what they liked always *was* best they would have no feelings of approval or aspiration apart from liking; but both the feeling of compulsion and the resolved submission to its force are facts of consciousness. Moral perfection is the deliberate pursuit of the elected Best, through every obstacle within and without; and the objective abundance of obstacles to which we owe the conception, by contrast, of a moral Best, also brings home to our experience the reality of a moral Bad. Man is the imperfect denizen of an imperfect world, and therefore, though morality may be as natural as hunger and as necessary as food, crime is as possible as starvation and malice as real as indigestion. But the existence of moral evil is only an historical fact, that of moral good is a logical necessity as eternal as pain and privation.

Children and adults with undeveloped faculties often have their minds occupied for a time with a single, not impracticable, desire, the gratification of which constitutes their idea of happiness; but the world is not so planned, or the laws of nature so adjusted, as to give every child the sugar-plum or the toy which excites its appetite as soon as it begins to cry for them; and this is the beginning, though as yet only the beginning, of the moral experience of the race. The toy and the sugar-plum are sometimes enjoyed, as well as often necessarily renounced, and with the natural man the wish is father to the thought that enjoyment is the natural rule, and deprivation the exception, an accident to be cried out at, or prayed against, or warded off with such small prudence as a limited experience may suggest. But natural necessity is inexorable in its alternatives. The desired enjoyment has either to be gone without or purchased for a price, and the evolution of moral principles takes place *pari passu* with the growth of general feelings as to the price worth paying for each indulgence as it offers. Ethical science sums up the empirical estimates of the comparative value of various natural goods, and shows them to be in accordance with a perfectly natural and intelligible standard—the supreme natural good of general perfection. All our permanent preferences are for things permanently and constitutionally good, good in themselves all through and in every relation, and to these we naturally think it "right" or practically best that passing partial goods should be systematically sacrificed. One after another the simpler, cruder, pleasures of the child or the savage are found to be hardly worth their natural price; they have to be worked or prayed for too hard, competed for too fiercely for the trifling reward to be worth the cost, and reason advises voluntary renunciation or quelling of desire in special cases long before the suit and service of perfection comes to be prescribed as the whole and sole duty of mankind.

But even then a fresh difficulty may arise; the taste for sugar-plums is outgrown, and men become curious in toys. The problem to do as one likes is complicated by uncertainty as to what on the whole one does like best. Physical necessity introduces us to moral necessity by bringing our appetites into collision with dispassionate forces as ultimate and irreducible, and far more powerful than themselves. The question then perforce arises with respect to any course of conduct, not merely whether we might have liked it if circumstances had left it altogether easy and attractive, but whether we can and do; whether we are content to like it; whether our judgment goes with our taste; or, whether its native pleasurableness is disturbed by half-a-dozen conflicting and irreconcilable wishes; for, if so, just because tastes are ultimate and above reason, it is vain to try to restore the lost appetite. Reason by itself is not a motive for action, only real facts and desires, and the compromise between reality and desire, which reason recognises to be necessary and imposes even on the reluctant will, is what we call moral duty, that which *ought* to be done. Till the need for the compromise is felt, and the formula for it accepted, the mind continues a prey to incompatible desires; no one pleasure draws it with the old irresistible force; one appetite has lost its edge with indulgence, another with disuse, and over and above the limitations which the capacities of our body and mind set to the pleasures they can enjoy, there is still the whole indifferent machinery of worldly circumstance, which now helps, now hinders our endeavour, but certainly makes it impossible for us always to have our will unless we can learn to let our will accommodate itself to the necessary limits of material possibility.

The discovery that easy, unbroken happiness for the mass of men is not amongst the results of existing natural laws is an indispensable step in the evolution of morality; but the search after happiness—which is only the pleasurable consciousness of natural good—is still natural even when it is found that the pursuit has to be carried on under difficulties. The difficulties only stimulate fresh faculties to assist in the search, and knowledge was, perhaps, first valued as an auxiliary to pleasure. But as every faculty that is exercised tends to assert its own activity as an end in itself, the impulse to know continues active even after knowledge has begun to disclose unpleasant truths. To seek knowledge is not the same thing as to seek pleasure, and to find the knowledge that pleasure cannot be found is not a pain, if it was really knowledge and not pleasure that was sought. We need not borrow the eloquent arguments which have gone to prove that life is an unmitigated evil; it is enough for our purpose that all agree in allowing it to be by no means an unmitigated good. It is not within our power to secure a constant succession of the natural innocent pleasures proper to our organisation. In some races of men this fact leads to the development of what we call higher faculties and aspirations after nobler pleasures than those of sense, and then the old conception of happiness, which perhaps might have been realised by the help of the newly-acquired knowledge and experience, is found to have lost the power of satisfying the civilised or sophisticated taste. Still the hope of happiness is not at once relinquished; the higher, purer pleasures of art, intellect, and human sympathy may yet, it is thought, give content. But the experience of the nursery repeats itself in the schoolroom; disappointment without, disenchantment within, remind the poet, the scholar, the lover, that the world is not made for man, nor man for happiness. Men not only want pleasures they cannot have, they want ampler, more unwearied powers of enjoying the pleasures that are theirs; and these inward and outward limitations, like all the other fixed conditions of life, modify the human rule of right, or the practical best for men.

Human nature, however, has one last protest to make before the gospel of renunciation is accepted with all its inevitable moral corollaries. As Utilitarians when hard pressed will talk about the pleasures of virtue, Eudæmonists turn with well-affected indifference from the thought of vulgar enjoyment to the praise and worship of the ideal. To live for art, for science, or for self-culture, that is, to create beauty, to discover truth, to cherish and strengthen the power of descrying every present beauty, of apprehending every latent truth, may well seem enough to occupy our pitiful powers, to satisfy our greediest cravings through the short span of a human life. Such an ideal is better than pleasant, and the hope of approaching more and more nearly to its perfect attainment may well carry its votaries through the seasons of physical exhaustion and mental langour which await the strenuous artist, the persevering amateur. But one thing is wanting to the ideal life of æsthetic contemplation and intellectual perception, and this one thing is Necessity. The lovers of art, who are not as a rule famed for their science, count it a praise that no moral sanction compels men to lead their life. The elect will do so; the many are but as swine before whom no pearls are to be cast. And yet it is a flaw in this, the finest conception of human excellence which has been reached by the consideration of man's nature alone, out of relation to the universe, of which the whole human race is but a dependent fraction, that the mass of mankind cannot share it, and that it does, as a fact, lose its hold even upon some of those who have felt its charm, when experience shows that a life spent in pursuit of the ideal is not itself ideal, but penetrated with a thousand human, arbitrary, accidental imperfections. Why, we ask, and ask in vain, should we toil to keep our minds open and our senses clear to receive the impressions of perfect truth and perfect beauty, when we know that so far from finding them we shall learn to bear the frequent pain of failure in their quest at the cost of apathy to rare success? We call it duty when the will is bent to any action by other considerations than spontaneous natural desire, and the will of man is not habitually bent, or consciously self-compelled, towards a life of mere receptivity or self-contained power — however various — of passive perception. This is especially true of the present day, when there is no living national art unconsciously educating the tastes of individuals to healthy enjoyment of contemporary production, for when the Hedonist and the world are, so to speak, *tête-à-tête*, if the former wearies in his task of well-feeling, there is no power behind to secure his constancy, all his excellences are unconditioned, which to us means accidental, and at the mercy of accident. Action is a process, the tendency towards which may be conscious, and consciously dictated by a rational anticipation of ends; but feeling or passion is a state to which the transition from other states is inevitably unconscious; and though one passion may succeed another in a more or less constant order, they have no vital productive force, and their duration or pleasurableness is at the mercy of whatever contingent influences may be brought to bear upon them from without. The impossibility of calling up at will the mental affections which have been found pleasurable in the past, is reason enough by itself why it should not be felt as a duty to revive either the affection or the pleasure; but, because they cannot be revived at will, the happiness of those who follow art for its moments of rapt delight is but insecurely placed.

The despair which follows upon discoveries of this kind is apt to solace itself with irreligious complaints. Young poets suffering from that combination of their own private passions with sympathy for the wrongs of the universe at large, which goes to form the disease called *Weltschmerz*, are apt to acknowledge a God that they may have somewhat to curse and wherewithal to blaspheme. But if we assume, as has been done hitherto, that there is neither God nor devil *in rerum natura*, resentment against the order of the universe seems as absurd as the passion of Xerxes lashing the waves, or of the baby that hurts its knuckles by beating the ground it has fallen down upon. Our ills are real, but it does not follow that they have an author: we are not happy, but it does not follow that we have a jural right—against things in general—to the materials for happy life. The thing is naturally impossible, and after spending a few years in convincing ourselves of its impossibility we cease to think of the fact as more unreasonable than various other inconvenient natural dispensations.

The moral tendency of this discovery (the impossibility of happiness) has been recognised in many religions, notably in Christianity, and empirically formulated some-

what to the effect that "the happy may be good, the melancholy must." But the logic of this inference is not quite apparent so long as we consider the existence of the acknowledged moral law, so to speak, from outside, as the rules by which people in general are objectively bound to act, instead of from within, in relation to the personal feeling that moves each man separately to acquiesce in the necessity of certain acts and forbearances, in view of other qualities than their pleasurableness. To the natural man, whose impulses and likings are the natural and necessary rule of his conduct, it appears monstrous, anomalous, that he should have to do what he does not like, and he only does it under material compulsion. Even when we are too wise quite to expect the laws of nature to perturb themselves for our convenience, it still does not seem to us quite reasonable that we should do what we do not like unless we have something to gain by it—in this world or another.

The grand moral lesson, which brings with it the prospect of release from the bondage of personal desire, is the discovery that we *must* do what we do not like, if we are to live at all; first, because the world has so determined, and the world is stronger than we are; and secondly, because, even if our will were supreme upon earth, there is nothing in life that seems to us quite worth liking always and altogether. And this we must do without reward, since the universe owes us no gratitude, though we pay its laws the compliment of not expecting stones to fall up hill or ice to boil a kettle, not even though we cease to wish that the moral law, of which we feel the pressure, should be less inevitable than the laws of heat or gravitation. This experience of involuntary, inevitable endurance is the first step in the natural discipline by which men learn in case of need to prefer a natural to a moral evil. The power of endurance itself becomes a natural good, because in our imperfect world some evils are absolutely unavoidable, and others have to be endured as the price of a counterbalancing good; and the same power, after meeting us in such homely materialistic virtues as temperance and honesty, furnishes the foundation for every higher effort of zeal and devotion. We do not freely choose the life that offers us most pleasure and least pain; we necessarily accept the proportions of both determined by outer circumstances, and the wide, far-fetched influences which have given the bent to our choice.

If it were true that men lived only for pleasure, and that as long as the slenderest rag of enjoyment fluttered before their eyes they had no choice but to follow the bootless quest, piety would be impossible, for the position of the race would be one of chronic hopeless antagonism to the laws of nature, which are not framed with a view to their greatest happiness; and the fullest knowledge of those laws, while enabling them to make the struggle as little disastrous as possible, yet must aggravate their sufferings by showing the inevitableness of final defeat. The egotist's life is a losing battle. Except under the pressure of necessity, physical or moral, no one would spend his days in chasing a meteor, and there is no physical necessity, no moral obligation upon us, to go on pursuing pleasures that have lost their charm, and happiness, of which we doubt the existence. If there is any course fully acceptable to the disinterested judgment, anything right, necessary, and duly to be done, it is not this.

If man were altogether a rational animal, it is impossible to say what he would do after the discovery of these and kindred truths. The most rational of writers,[1] indeed affirms that action follows necessarily upon the full and certain apprehension of a truth; but this sequence cannot of itself be considered strictly logical. Action is only rational considered in reference to an end; the function of reason in practical life is to show what intentions are compatible with fixed natural facts, but there is

[1] Spinoza, Ethic., iii. 1.

no absolutely reasonable conduct, unless we assign that name to the broad rule of duty, the pursuit of perfection conditioned by the general laws of the universe, of which human reason is the highest exponent. No conduct can be called reasonable which ignores facts essential to the problem awaiting solution, and it is simply a fact of our nature that action may be determined by other motives than passion, or the suffering of a desire.

Loose thinkers, to whom the notion that every being is ruled by the laws proper to its nature is naturally abhorrent, may ask *why* the will accepts an unpleasant necessity, *why* the intellect affirms a painful truth: why not deny the troublesome necessity and disbelieve the unwelcome truth? Certainly this is possible, since it is done, perhaps by the majority of mankind, but it is not done, because it cannot be done, by those who know of their own knowledge and experience that the truth is true and the necessity binding. Considerations of expediency are absolutely out of relation to such matters; it is a rhetorical exaggeration to say that men would believe that two and two made five if the hallucination were for their pecuniary advantage. No doubt they are most anxious to discover truths that have a pleasant sound, but it must be remembered that the facts of nature are not always pleasant, and that facts have a way of forcing themselves upon our knowledge to the destruction of all but the one true theory of their nature and history. If we have nothing else but the clear consciousness of our place in the relations of the world, of that we cannot and need not wish to be bereft—the rather that forces which are too strong for knowledge are not likely to yield to ignorance.

Morality begins with the consciousness of opposition between the nature of the individual and its environment, or rather with the reaction of the nature against the external force which oppresses it. The material conditions of life are the cause, human sentiments, such as ambition, sympathy, love, are the motives, which make moral conduct necessary, and if the sentiments themselves are traceable at last to natural physical causes, this is only a fresh instance of the way in which every natural tendency reacts upon and reinforces itself. But, as the existence of *jus*, or the conception of law in general, can be kept separate from questions concerning the common qualities of just and lawful acts, so the mere existence of a moral law, or rule of right of some kind, is independent of the nature of its injunctions. The fact that the normal man feels obliged in conscience to acts and forbearances of a class does not tell us to *what* classes of acts or forbearances he will feel obliged; and before coming to that further point, it would be well to have the source and character of the feeling of obligation itself, if possible, more clearly established.

It will be admitted that men's actions are determined by their will, whatever opinion may be held concerning that which determines the will, a vexed question that we are not called upon to resolve. Jonathan Edwards, perhaps, after Spinoza, the ablest of Necessarians, says that "philosophical necessity is really nothing else than the full and fixed connection between the things signified by the subject and predicate of a proposition which affirms something to be true"—*i.e.*, is nothing but the formula of natural fact: and again, "The will's beginning to act is the very same thing as its beginning to choose or prefer." It is allowed that the will *does* choose or prefer; which is the same thing as asserting the necessary freedom of the will or active nature of man to be itself. Nothing is entirely within the power of our own will but our actions; we can do as we will (indeed we cannot well do otherwise), but whether what we do shall produce the effects we desire to produce may depend upon circumstances altogether beyond our control. But the disposition of the will, *i.e.*, the nature of the active impulses, is the only possible source of that self-imposed and self-accepted rule of action whcih we call moral, or duty—the only source, that is, of the obligation, or of the consent, which gives to natural necessity the force of law by ensuring its habitual, conscious fulfilment; for this subjective disposition alone is permanent, and ready at any moment to become conscious, whereas the existence of external motives or inducements is accidental; even when they are present, it is the choice of the will that makes them effective; when they are absent, the will generalises its own impulses; and we call the result acting upon principle. If the will were entirely plastic, and followed unresistingly the variable impulsion of external motives, there would be no such thing as morality, for there would be no consciousness of constraint; in matters held to be indifferent there is no such consciousness, because the will is in itself equally ready to adopt either of the indifferent alternatives before it, and suffers nothing if one of them becomes accidentally impossible. In the same way, the sense of moral obligation is in abeyance if an absolutely irresistible external force impedes the natural action of the will; where no choice is possible, the reluctant will does not act, it is passive or suffers. For the will to feel bound to do what it cannot do is a contradiction in terms; the moral law has no impossibilities, which—according to Kant—is the proof that morality cannot lie in the pursuit of anything so unattainable as happiness.

Moral choice is to adopt the one of two physically possible alternatives which that unalterable residuum of will, commonly called conscience, adheres to as involving the least departure possible under the adverse circumstances, from the general course of conduct which the organism would follow instinctively if circumstances were propitious. All the actions of a perfect man in a perfect world would be subservient to his continued existence in a state of perfection. Men, who are not perfect, find pleasure in some acts which do not contribute to their general perfection, and the world, which is not perfect, makes some acts painful which do contribute to their general perfection as men. Nevertheless, upon the whole, and especially when the present seduction of an easy pleasure is removed, the will takes counsel of reason, and resolves, not quite unnaturally, though with a sense of moral effort, to be itself—in such perfection as limited strength and intelligence will allow.

At this point the argument brings us very near to Kant's categorical imperative, without, however, an exact coincidence. His precept, "to act always according to a maxim that might serve for a universal rule," does not indicate a motive for modest persons who feel no vocation to legislate for the universe, while his own legislation depends upon theology for its sanctions; but we find it to be true, *a posteriori*, that that conduct only is thought right which those who think it right hold it would be good to have universal. We do not eat our dinner *because* of certain biological laws—of which most probably we are ignorant—but the biological laws express one side of the natural tendency of men to dine once a day if they can. Similarly any one who endeavours to lead a virtuous life does not do so *because* he thinks it right to realise the highest possibilities of his nature; but the moral law formulates the natural tendency of men towards such realisation. There is no optimism in this; for we do not deny that, tried by the general standard of what—as we say—men *ought* to be, the highest realisation truly possible to most men is discouragingly low; while of those by whom a higher ideal is conceivable, and therefore, in one sense, attainable, but few have the superfluity of virtuous strength required to overcome the material obstacles which the world and the flesh offer to the leading of a perfect life. We have not undertaken to justify the ways of the world to men; and though it is not for naturalists to say that a better world than this was possible, we may without blasphemy admit that this world is not *very* good.

Most of the obscurity in which the question of liberty and necessity is involved may be traced to a confusion in the use and meaning of the word *possible*. The will is free to choose between possible alternatives, but the number of possible alternatives may be rigorously limited;—limited, a fatalist may add, to one—but if the will voluntarily adopts that one, the objection is scarcely significant. If half a loaf is put before a starving man, he does not eat it the less voluntarily because he may wish that it were whole, or buttered. If there are such things as moral struggles, which the advocates of freewill certainly do not question, the subject of such a struggle has to face a difficulty from which there is no escape; the necessity either to yield to the difficulty or to overcome it is absolute; there is no *via media*. Many of those who talk most of liberty as something essential to the dignity of humanity, seem not to understand the difference between supposing men to be free to do as they choose, and supposing them to be free to do as they would like to choose, that is, perhaps, to adopt an alternative which does not naturally exist, made on purpose to suit their fancy. Life would be intolerable if the will were not free to adapt itself, within moral limits, to the possible; but life would be impossible—would not be at all—if the will were free in some inconceivable manner to alter the nature of things by arbitrary *ex post facto* decrees.

To explain how the will should ever seem to be divided against itself, we must remember that the real, conscious man is not a pure spiritual unit, without parts or form, an undivided, homogeneous whole, but the subject of impressions and faculties as various and manifold as his nerves and muscles; yet, though he may feel in many ways, he can only really act in one; and these alternative necessities, the necessity of choice when inclination is divided, gives the moral sense of deliberate will, acting freely, by—or perhaps against—inclination, and not only free, but *bound* by the laws of its nature so to act.

"To make a virtue of necessity" is one of those popular phrases in which much deep philosophy lies hid. The scientific explanation of the real process so described, lies no doubt in the principle of accommodation, the way in which every organism adapts itself to the *milieu* in which it is placed; but this is only restating the fact of necessity in fresh terms, for if the organism cannot adapt itself, it perishes as an organism—and its elements are absorbed in fresh combinations. The human race could not subsist, increase, and develop—which are the natural tendencies of every organism—without virtue, that is, the disinterested co-operation of individuals for the natural good of the kind; those who withhold their co-operation are eliminated by the very fact, and count only as negative quantities, by which the race is *minus* so much active progress. But wherever there is positive vitality in a species, it is impossible that the vital impulses of the individuals of which it consists should, as a rule, be antagonistic—should not, as a rule, be subservient—to the preservation and vitality of the species as a whole. It is the imperfection of real existence that makes the power of self-sacrifice a necessary condition of organic, and still more of social life, but as social life is a fact, the absence of the power would be as inexplicable as its presence is necessary. We call virtue good, because we are animals of a species that subsists after its kind thereby; but when we say that virtue is necessary, we only mean that it is necessary to man: there is no reason to suppose that man is necessary; he is as capable as morality of becoming extinct.

But, it will be said, if everything that occurs, occurs by an equal natural necessity, what is the significance of our moral judgments? Why do we condemn, or at least regret and resist some things? To which the only possible answer is: By nature, which reasserts itself after every accidental disturbance of the normal order, and tends to restore the broken harmony. Good and evil are words that mean— what we mean when we use them—namely, results which our whole mind and feeling deliberately admires and approves, or condemns and rejects; and though liking the pleasant and approving the good are not identical mental operations, one is to the full as natural as the other. Our moral judgments are compounded of a perception, that such or such conduct is good or bad, sanctioned by a feeling about goodness and badness, in the abstract and in the concrete, which is as rational as any other normal reaction under stimulus. The disposition of the will, as the ultimate exponent of the individual nature, is the sole source of moral obligation, but that does not interfere with the fact that some natures are more fortunately organised than others : and there are moments in the history of every individual when the tendencies of the true nature cannot attain their full realisation without conscious effort and sacrifice. The power to effect such sacrifices upon occasion is a part of the natural good or specific perfection of men, and we call those natures fortunate in which it is most pronounced. But if we are asked—since it is only a misfortune to be wicked—by what right we blame people who do wrong from natural infirmity, the reply is, certainly, that man is not to blame, any more than providence, for the misfortunes that afflict him. We call a malicious man bad, as we call a humpback deformed ; and, moral censures apart, we look upon it as evil fortune to be infirm, whether morally or physically. It is not exactly wrong to be humpbacked, but we would decidedly rather that our spines should not curve ; though, indeed, if they manifest a tendency in that direction of their own accord, it may be a question—as it often is with our moral deformities—how much or how painful surgical treatment we are prepared to undergo in the attempt to straighten them.

Objectors of the same class sometimes put, as trying to the practical efficiency of naturalistic morality, the case of a man inclined to be moderately virtuous, who says, Why should I take the trouble (if there is nothing to be gained by it) of being more virtuous than I feel inclined ? which again is an unanswerable question, the rather that no one but the person most intimately concerned can tell what his own inclinations are. But inclinations fluctuate and compete, and it is hard to be certain that any given disputant who, for the sake of argument, represents himself as a cross between La Rochefoucauld and Sardanapalus, may not really be as much disinclined as the most austere moralist for a life of sensual indulgence and emotional isolation. If actual vice is considered to be out of the question (a large concession, which would not have been made to free-thinkers a century or two ago), and the degree of virtue to be practised is the only doubtful point, the case for the naturalistic theory of morality is that every inclination gains strength by indulgence, and that it is a question of degree how much, rather than how little virtue a well-natured person will find himself entrapped into finding desirable. It is not pleasant to be as virtuous, or as vicious, as we are naturally inclined to be; in other words, the world is not constituted so that we may be happy by following our most natural inclinations. But there is nothing paradoxical in maintaining that in the case of any individual choosing between two courses, one of which he sincerely believes to be right and the other wrong, it does not on the whole conduce to his happiness to give the preference to the supposed wrong. Other things being equal, a man will do what he thinks right; when other things are so far from being equal that the normal preference for virtue is overruled, the victim of circumstances suffers, from the violence done to his true nature, which it is happiness for the individual to be able to follow unimpeded. Cases are abundant, however, in which the scale of decision is turned, not by the objective pleasurableness of one alternative as compared with the rest, but by the strength of the man's inward bent towards noble, rather than easy living. Every power we have limits our liberty to be content without giving it exercise, and every power we exercise awakens sensibilities and tastes which make us subject to all the conditions which regulate this indulgence. Mr. Spencer notices the existence of "a connection between progress in the impressibilities and progress in the activities," and if man found no stimulus to fresh action, in the necessities he recognises, it would not be true that "the advance of either involves the advance of both;" but the powers which bring us under the sway of new rules are such as by their normal activity serve to enrich our life and perfect our nature.

Dropping the ancient associations which bias the judgment when we speak of virtue and vice, the simple fact is that we have conflicting, incompatible impulses, and that the sacrifice of some is necessary when the reconciliation of all is impossible; that the sacrifice of one class of impulses is as painful as that of the other; but the one sacrifice habitually appears, to those acquainted with all the circumstances of the case, as good, eligible, and to be accomplished, the other as, if inevitable, essentially deplorable. Every one is as good as he can be; and though it is a serious misfortune to all parties that men in general have not been able hitherto to be better, there is no reason in the nature of things why additional knowledge and wider experience should not have the same effect upon the mind of any particular sinner as the same influences may be supposed to have had upon his self-elected censor. It is true that we are most of us stupid—or society could never have got into its present lamentable entanglements—but we might all without much difficulty be just a little wiser than we are, and the aggregate effect of a number of such small improvements would be considerable. After all, the human race is of one kind: fools are rudimentary philosophers; philosophers are developed fools; and with the development of philosophy we may learn that it is not a law of nature for the lives of men to be made miserable by man. Human conduct is determined by many fixed conditions, but the conditions are not all discoverable, and the problem of what it is fated that we shall do, cannot be solved prophetically even by ourselves, much less by any one else; we learn our fate in fulfilling it, but we are unfortunate if it is a part of our destiny to fulfil the most melancholy of all the various destinies we can conceive—that of an evil liver; there is no natural connection between such a misfortune and necessarianism.

It might still, however, be objected by a Utilitarian critic, that to prove morality to be necessary does not prove anything against its being conducive to the greatest happiness of the greatest number, and that if it is so, this fact, and not its necessity, will be the motive, as distinct from the cause, that leads men to act morally. Granted that it is not possible to live by inclination and be perfectly happy, if we have seemed to maintain that the best (of many bad) chances of happiness is to indulge the virtuous propensities at the expense of all others, is not the theory utilitarianism in disguise? And here it may be admitted that we have no reason to suppose that persons who are born with, or who have acquired such a temper as to find it habitually impossible to choose the worse of two alternative courses, are, on the whole, less happy than those with whom the possibilities are reversed or vary intermittently. The surest way of escaping the disappointment of self-regarding wishes is to have none, and the power of sacrificing inclination to a disinterested apprehension of what is good is attended, like the exercise of every other natural faculty, with a slightly pleasurable consciousness of vital force. Nevertheless, if the impulses are only sacrificed as a matter of calculation, and to secure a calm, passionless old age, the sacrifice may be regretted, and the ancient egotist find himself of all men most miserable. To calculate upon the pleasures of virtue, the answer of a good conscience, the relief of duty done, is neither moral nor wise. It is not prudent to look forward to the few and distant moments of comparative ease that may no doubt be theirs who can say, after a lifetime of unprofitable service: We have done that which it was our duty to do. The pleasure would not pay its cost. To do the painful right because we might in time come to find it pleasant, is like starving as a precaution against poverty; and if we once admit that men are capable of feeling a moral necessity to sacrifice, not only happiness but life itself, to the natural good of humanity, the existence of a stronger motive than the instinct of self-preservation becomes apparent.

Self-preservation is the natural good, the necessary motive of every isolated organism, but men are members of a social body, and we know by experience that the preservation of a whole frequently involves the immolation of its parts. Conscious acquiescence in this common necessity is the only peculiar prerogative of man, the only distinguishing characteristic of his share or co-operation in the eternal scheme of the universe, that which constitutes him in an especial sense a moral agent.

Under favourable circumstances, the habit of well-doing forms itself by exercises which cost nothing but a healthy effort; but the moral bias, hereditary or acquired, ends by becoming so strong, in a few chosen natures, that the passion for perfection outgrows the natural love of life and ease and fame, and rather than give his sanction to a wrong, the righteous man will dare an unhonoured, painful, fruitless death. "Skin for skin, yea, all that a man hath will he give for his life"—but if it *is* a man's life to do well and endure wisely, and the choice lies between death and ill-doing, how can it be otherwise than naturally easiest to him to die?—or, living still, to endure any other natural ill rather than the moral death of hateful action—of action fraught with natural evil to the unoffending sons of men? But the mental attitude of the man who deliberately resolves to follow his own highest impulses, at whatever personal cost, is altogether different from that of one who resigns himself to paying the needful price for a desired pleasure.

We are nearing the confines of the practical question.

Morality exists. What, then, is the conduct men praise as moral? Hitherto we have considered morality from the subjective side, as the sense of duty or obligation incumbent on the self. But most of our moral conceptions include the idea, not only of a duty binding *on* some one, but of a duty *towards* some one else. The fact that men have duties follows from the fact that their will acts under conditions not of their own making. The fact that most of these duties are imposed by consideration for other interests than their own follows from the fact that the life of men in society is mainly conditioned by the acts and feelings of their associates—in a word, that the many weigh more than the one, and that each Self, in proportion as its acts and desires involve it in relations with other Selves, must act and wish in conscious reference to their acts and wishes.

This is so much the case that the words altruism and egoism are used without much straining to denote moral desert and its opposite, as if self-indulgence were habitually bad, and the indulgence of any other self than the agent habitually good. And this is really the case, if we emphasise the "habitually," because in the shorthand of thought we understand by indulgence the giving of pleasure without effort; and it is easier to give ourselves noxious pleasures than it is to give noxious pleasures to other people, at least we have more temptation to do so, not only because in their case we may ourselves be the victims of the noxiousness, but also because our judgment is less biassed by private passion, so that we can estimate consequences more exactly. Still the standard of right in particular cases is no more to be found in the likings of my wife or next-door neighbour than in my own: it is simply an empirical generalisation that I am more likely to be seduced into wrong-doing by my own inclinations than by theirs, though the latter also is possible. Strictly speaking, my duty towards them is the same as my duty towards myself—*i.e.*, to minister to their wellbeing; but without accepting the dictum of those social philosophers who deny the existence of self-regarding duties, it is clear that the peculiarly moral element of self-devotion is necessarily least conspicuous in such acts, for by self-interest, rightly understood, we mean the pursuit of natural, not merely sensible good, and the attainment of a natural self-regarding good never results in a predominance of sensible evil in its consequences.

Hence the definition of moral conduct seems almost to narrow itself to the satisfaction of claims for social services. But it still remains a question whether this is the widest synthesis of motive attainable. Is Humanity the supreme lawgiver, because our chief duties are to men? Is there any other God, and have we duties to Him? or is our life conditioned wholly by the natural forces, among which our susceptibilities of passion, impulse, and reason are the chief? And if our life is conditioned by nature, what is our duty to—and in—this natural world ?—and whence the feeling which makes us accept with something more than resignation the laws which bind our will; and is our obedience to these laws—if indeed we do obey—due after all to this vague, unexplained sentiment of piety that makes us imagine, before we know, obedience to be the better part?

IV.

RELIGION.

"Sed humana potentia admodum limitata est et a potentia causarum externarum infinite superatur; atque adeo potestatem absolutam non habemus res, quæ extra nos sunt, ad nostrum usum aptandi. Attamen ea quæ nobis eveniunt contra id, quod nostræ utilitatis ratio postulat, æquo animo feremus, si conscii simus nos functos nostro officio fuisse, et potentiam, quam habemus, non potuisse se eo usque extendere, ut eadem vitare possemus, nosque partem totius natura esse, cujus ordinem sequimur. Quod si clare et distincte intelligamus, pars illa nostri, quæ intelligentia definitur, hoc est, pars melior nostri in eo plane acquiescet et in ea acquiescentia perseverare conabitur. Nam quatenus intelligimus, nihil appetere nisi id, quod necessarium est, nec absolute, nisi in veris acquiescere possumus; adeoque quatenus hæc recte intelligimus, eatenus conatus melioris partis nostri cum ordine totius naturæ convenit."—SPINOZA.

"Look straight to this, to what nature leads thee, both the universal nature through the things which happen to thee, and thy own nature through the acts which must be done by thee."—MARCUS AURELIUS.

"Magna res est amor, magnum omnino bonum, quod solum leve facit esse onerosum et fert æqualiter omne inæquale; nam onus sine onere portat, et omne amarum dulce ac sapidum efficit. Amor Jesu nobilis ad magna operanda impellit, et ad desideranda · semper perfectiora excitat. Amor vult esse sursum nec ullis infimis rebus retineri. Amor vult esse liber et ab omni mundana affectione alienus ne internus ejus impediatur aspectus, ne per aliquod commodum temporale implicationes sustineat aut per incommodum succumbat. Nil dulcius est amore, nil fortius, nil altius, nil latius, nil jucundius, nil plenius, nil melius in cælo et in terra."—DE IMITATIONE CHRISTI.

The natural history of emotion—All human knowledge, belief, and perception natural, because all received through the natural faculties of man—The existence of religion, if not otherwise explicable, *might* have to be referred to an otherwise unknown principle, the existence of which would, however, even then be known naturally, as that of an unseen planet, by its action—Men find themselves affected by forces that are Not-man, and do not at once conceive any of the forces as unconscious—Natural religion, *e.g.*, of savages, dread of uncontrollable power to injure. Later stages, apprehension of uncontrollable power not irrationally malicious, and personification of the moral influences of the Not-self in man—Agnosticism and the Cultus of the Unknown—Personification of the imagined cause of a felt impression—Spiritual religion the sentiment called forth in the individual by the apprehension of the Not-self in its most general aspect, as the one real, irresistible power in which the self is included; or by the apprehension of as much of the moral influences of the Not-self as can be personified or interpreted by personal agency—Dualism unspiritual because the sentiment towards the Not-self is weakened by division—Comte: Humanity great, but not supreme; does not inspire the true religious devotion—The religious sentiment one of complete (yet dynamic) acquiescence in the tendencies of the whole by which the tendencies of the part are now consciously conditioned; the two tendencies are identified, but without any sense of obligation or effort in the weaker, for feeling is naturally free, and supposing the religious conversion of the will or nature to be complete, co-operation with the "stream of tendency" becomes truly voluntary and spontaneous—Query, whether the religious sentiment is equally reasonable in all ages—Strong piety most rational when human aspirations after the Best possible find themselves most nearly in harmony with the spontaneous course of things—Rational faith only belief in the reality and trust in the power of goodness—Unequal strength of natural power and natural aspiration—Atheistical religion.

IV.

RELIGION.

LAW sanctions what men are; morality sanctions what men wish themselves and each other to be; religion, as commonly understood, might be described as sanctioning what God wishes men to be. Waiving theological controversy, it will be apparent that law and morality, as above described, account for all that part of men's conduct which consists in the discharge of personal and social duties, or actions performed with a consciousness of constraint or obligation; and that the sphere of religion, as a binding force, is therefore restricted either to the actions which men perform spontaneously, with a sense of freedom, or to their emotions, which are not properly susceptible of constraint at all: in other words, we have here done with law and enter upon the field of religious liberty.

The only way in which we can conceive a law to exist without its being felt as constraining is for the constant relations between different things formulated in the law to pass into the consciousness of the one conceived as more peculiarly subject to the law, not as a necessity compelling to acts and forbearances of a class which would not have been performed voluntarily, but as a necessary release from other irksome, arbitrary, or accidental compulsion. Such a release we have seen to be afforded to men by positive law from the caprices of other men, and by morality from the bondage of " chance desires " of their own; if their subjective emancipation is to be completed, religion must release them at once from the sense of bondage to the natural conditions and accidents of human life, and from the sentiment of reluctance which may, and usually does, attend the deliberate submission of the will to law. But since religion does not affect the objective validity of the other laws with which we have been concerned—the laws of nature, of society, and of human morality—whatever change it effects in the consciousness of the human subjects of such laws must plainly be immaterial and emotional.

There are two parts in every rational action, the will and the intention, or the act and the desire, and the natural, normal agreement between these two may be disturbed; but any form of passion, suffering, or emotion is in its nature simple, irrational, and where there is no consciousness of division or antagonism, the first element of law, or constraint, the juxtaposition of two natures in a necessary relation, is wanting. No one feels bound to feel otherwise than he does feel, any more than any one feels bound to be something entirely different from what he is. It is easy for a real, slight feeling—as of gratitude or affection towards a person plainly deserving of such regard —to be mistaken for, or concealed by, a non-natural, second-hand remorse, produced by the impression that other people, under the circumstances, would have a stronger feeling of the same kind. But though people may vaguely wish that they were as good specimens of their kind as somebody else, they do not really feel bound in conscience to be other than they are, namely, the subject of moral aspirations of such and such a degree of strength and efficiency, though the aspirations may be regarded as an incipient tendency towards advance to a higher stage of moral development, at which fresh tendencies and aspirations would become both possible and necessary. Still, no criticism of the emotions in their actual development at any given moment is possible : if we attempt to judge whether a feeling is wise or right, the feeling vanishes at the very moment, at least until the critical mood is over. The emotions begin and end with themselves, or rather with their conscious subject; there is no room for wisdom in states of consciousness that can only exist in one way

—as they are involuntarily felt to be. Yet all the more complex emotions are feelings towards or about some other object, by the nature of which they must be in some manner conditioned, if the relation is to be orderly and observant of perceptible constant laws.

In the absence of precise knowledge concerning the physical basis of consciousness and the different physical conditions of sensation, emotion, and thought, conjecture involuntarily takes the form of hypothesis, and we compose our minds with the expectation of finding hereafter proof of the opinions which now impress us as most likely to be true, or if not exactly true themselves, yet most like what the truth must be. There is not yet proof to go before a jury upon, and yet it seems both credible and probable that sensation is the subjective side of certain objective molecular changes in the organism produced by outer, material influences. Sensations by repetition accustom the organs of sense to certain modes of vibration or molecular movement, which, thenceforward, may be excited by the faintest touch suggestive of similar movement, or may even continue automatically without stimulus. We believe Mr. Lewes is parent of the suggestion, that these normal sets, or patterns, so to speak, of vibration, do as a fact fall into other patterns or groups among themselves, and that feeling or emotion is the consciousness of such more elaborate groupings of set forms of nervous agitation. This is not proved, but it is eminently provable as well as probable; and it is only by some such explanation as this that the growth of feeling can be made thoroughly intelligible to the reason.

The character of normal human feeling, as of normal human conduct, has been systematically explained as the outcome of personal and inherited experience of pleasure and pain; the emotions are supposed to be favourably affected towards felicific influences, and unfavourably towards whatever causes or is associated with pain. We have already attempted to show that this is virtually trying to explain the whole by a part, for the very sense of pleasure and pain itself must, on our view, be the consciousness of opposite kinds of relations, some jarring, some concordant, between groups or patterns of moving molecules. But this sense of discord and harmony is only one of the secondary feelings about things which grow from the repeated feeling of the things themselves. The eye rises from the sensation of form and colour to the perception of grace and beauty, but we have no *a priori* notions of beauty which would guide our judgment towards received canons of taste, even though all the present laws of optics were reversed or confounded. Similarly with our loves and hates; we have no preconceived theory of what should charm us, but we grow by degrees into a mental habit of sympathy with every act and symbol of gracious goodness and loving power, and these affections become a part of ourselves, so that we interpret every new sensation by their light. Thus the feelings, like the impulses, attain to an independent life of their own, not at the mercy of momentary inducements.

The origin of each mental feeling, its true antecedent *sine qua non*, is seldom if ever another mental feeling, it is the existence of a certain group of more elementary sensations which become articulate in the consciousness in that particular form by virtue of their combination. We are not at present concerned with the development of feeling into thought, which may be conceived as the appropriate consciousness of still more complex relations among composite groups of sensation and feeling—or a sense of the grouping of groups; but this would be the logical continuation of the former process, and unless the whole of it has been misapprehended, it would follow that, barring casual fallacies, thought and feeling are alike based on rational reality, so that knowledge and passion, instead of being antagonistic, appear as both alike the creation of the objective fact which, when created, they serve to reflect.

Thus it is that while single movements of feeling are

almost completely independent of the reason, human feeling is on the whole rational and trustworthy, and the habitual inclination of feeling as respectable as the habitual inclination of the will. Enthusiasts for the religious emotions and the impulsive side of human nature are not content with this admission, but wish to have religion exalted above morality, and feeling more trusted than thought. To find a partial justification for the common order of arrangement (which we have followed), which treats the broadest facts of feeling as a kind of climax, as possessing for mankind a higher, more indefeasible kind of authority than the judgments of pure reason, we must remember the double character of all human experience. If thought is a development of feeling, feeling is not the higher product, but it is the deeper root, and it is more possible for a concerted change of fact and feeling to modify belief than for additional knowledge to alter the spontaneous affection of the mind towards the things known about. The most general conclusions of human feeling at any period are a degree more necessary and immutable than contemporary beliefs of the *same* degree of generality, a degree less necessary than a theory of which the special truth is conditioned by broader, more elementary feeling.

The comparative authority of feeling and reason as a guide for conduct depends, however, on another set of considerations. A present feeling is or may be a direct motive, thought only suggests action through the medium of an associated feeling. Also feelings are in relation with present, concrete realities; thoughts only with generalisations about permanent qualities, which by themselves suggest no action or wish; hence the true or real motive for present action may be more discernible to feeling than reason. But, on the other hand, should a doubt arise as to which motive—simple feeling or feeling grown into thought—had better be allowed to prevail, the thought which is conditioned by all the facts of the past is more infallible than the feeling or desire which is conditioned by those bearing on the individual at the present moment. But the general disposition of human feeling towards outer influences is, after all, the result of broad conditions, and the conscious intellectual generalisation which grows out of the unconscious emotional one would itself be worthless unless this also were in normal correspondence with the real relations of things.

The intensity of a passion depends upon and varies with the susceptibility of the subject, or person by whom the passion is felt; the occasion, or as in merely personal relations, we should say, the recipient of the affection, influences its character as compared with other affections of the same subject, but within limits that cannot but be fixed by the nature of that subject. Religion, as it does exist, or as it ever has existed, cannot be regarded as anything supernatural while it deals only with that which real men have actually felt or done under the influence of feeling. The notion of early rationalists that religion was invented by priests to serve their private purposes may be considered as exploded; but even at the present day it is not unusual to hear religious or superstitious beliefs spoken of as if reason had no concern with their existence as soon as they are proved to be unfounded, which is not often a task of much difficulty. But if the belief as it stands is entirely unfounded, while the belief is nevertheless commonly held, the phenomenon is one that calls most urgently for rational explanation. Most vulgar errors arise either from a natural and easy misinterpretation of real occurrences by a false analogy, or from something peculiar in the phenomenon itself, which makes familiar analogies misleading and ordinary methods of interpretation an unsafe guide in dealing with it.

The common belief in the existence of supernatural beings would be entirely inexplicable if there were no real foundation in nature for the impression which men have (and to which religion is the answering sentiment), that their lives are controlled by some irresistible, impalpable, superhuman force or forces. More than this general apprehension of a mighty Not-ourselves it would be vain to seek as common to all mankind in its religious moments, and if the more elaborate religions which have prevailed in historical times were strictly accurate in their doctrines, this fact would be as mysterious and unaccountable as the existence of any religious sentiment at all is on the principles of an intolerant, supercilious scepticism. On the one hand the very common diffusion of the religious sentiment, on the other its usual weakness, and not infrequent absence have to be accounted for, and if that general apprehension of the Not-self, which we have supposed to be the basis of religion, takes place by means of the ordinary human faculties, this result is exactly parallel to the tentative progress towards approximate agreement between consciousness and fact which characterises human science and morality. In spite of the palpable errors of all systems of religion, the religious sentiment survives, because in all, or nearly all religions, it has been possible for religious minds to ignore the false formula, and only be really moved by the spontaneous feeling of loving awe which makes obedience to the natural laws both of life and society not only voluntary but easy and contented.

One of the points in which primitive and scientific thought agree is a tendency to regard all the external forces amidst which the individual moves as substantially of kindred nature. In early society when law and morality are still undistinguished, religion unites with both, and the general sentiment, of resigned acquiescence in the will of a higher power, in which it consists, supplies the place of whatever is wanting to the logical completeness of the natural sanctions of customary morality. Society, nature, and conscience are all dimly conceived together as something different from the unit of conscious will, which performs one simple action at a time at their united bidding. When a distinction corresponding to that analysed in the preceding chapters between law and morality, or objective and subjective checks, has become a reality, the sphere of religion becomes either more contracted and intense, or wider and less practically important, according as natural forces, or the tendency of natural forces, are personified and idolised—in astrolatry, fetichism, and anthropomorphic mythology—or as the relations amongst natural forces, human and otherwise, are viewed synthetically, and produce a particular sentiment in the comparatively limited number of individuals capable at once of the wide view and the emotional response. There is ample room for religious error or misbelief in religious developments of the first kind, but mistakes that have a merely natural origin may be depended upon sooner or later to die a natural death; there is a limit to human powers of believing the thing that is not, and whenever that limit is reached, the system of false doctrine or imaginary facts either collapses at once at a vigorous denial, or is tranquilly ignored by more and more general consent.

We are only concerned with the historical phases of religious development so far as is necessary to show that, as soon as law and morality came to be distinctly conceived apart from each other and from religion, the course of all three became independent, though not necessarily divergent, and that religion, so far from serving as a basis to morality, can only attain to its fullest development when the moral education of the race has reached a point that makes religious reverence necessarily include sentiments of moral regard and admiration for the object of worship.

Most recent writers agree in holding the religion of the savage to consist of unintelligent, uncritical terror. Even to the civilised man there is something mysteriously impressive in power of which the seat is altogether inaccessible, and there have been ages when the simplest natural fact, if it was reflected upon at all, would be unintelligible enough to be awful.

Most of the apparently meaningless superstitions of savages refer to the region of the unknown, the unverifiable, and the unreal; but most of them are either rational from the savage point of view, or the remains of custom which had once some reasonable motive or suggestion; that is to say, though their rise may have been (and probably was) irrational as a consequence of the given premise, still they did not arise in the first instance without *some* cause or ground. And even these first aberrations of the human imagination have a claim on our respect, if we are content to recognise in them the first independent workings of the subjective element in man, the first result of the dawning human power to see things not only in their sensible relations among each other, but in the new light shed by human feeling on their ideal existence, as having a distinct, peculiar relation to man. Now it is certain that many natural objects *have*, in addition to their sensible qualities, an influence of a purely immaterial kind upon the lives of men, and though, except in a religious reverence for fire, and the fantastical scruples which regulate his dealings with certain animals, the savage rarely betrays any perception of the real influences to which he is subject, yet the faculties which are capable of rising to such a recognition may be used meanwhile to believe in influences that are not real, and in causal chains every link of which, except the first or last, may be imaginary.

A subjective connection between two phenomena is established merely by their being thought of together, and unless we suppose all the impressions of the savage to be literal reproductions of the facts of nature in their historical order, the connection will sometimes be mistaken.[1] The most common source of error is perhaps the

[1] What Mr. Tylor says of magic might be extended to most forms of superstition—that "it is based on a delusive tendency arising out of the association of ideas, namely, the tendency to believe that things which are ideally connected in our minds must therefore be really connected in the outer world."

conjunction of a strong hope or fear with the thought of some untried, or the memory of some effective means for producing or averting the result anticipated. "To see how an effect may be produced is often to see possible missings and checks; but to see nothing but the desirable cause, and close upon it the desirable effect, rids us of doubt, and makes our minds strongly intuitive." This way of establishing sequences, as a modern philosopher has observed, is too common even at the present day to be counted as a peculiar folly in those found guilty of it. The desirable cause is, of course, the present possible act that suggests itself to the mind; no sooner has it been performed with full and earnest intention than expectation of the desired result begins; supposing the act, as may be most often the case, to have no influence either way, expectation will continue, if its gratification in the course of nature is an even chance, until it is either gratified or disappointed, but the habit of expectation leaves so much profounder traces on the mind than the moment of disappointment, that the strength of the subjective connection may become thoroughly established as a superstition without even the crudest kind of inductive inference for its support.

It may be doubted whether, without this power of believing the thing that is not—or rather of believing *something*, till the thing that is can be known—the human mind would ever have taken courage to grapple with its own ignorance, or would have contracted the habit of believing in causal sequences at all, for those which are clear and undeniable do not invite analysis, while those which are longer and more remote escape notice altogether. In this way religious speculation becomes of vast importance to the early history of progressive races, while in others it stops short at the establishment of arbitrary and meaningless ceremonies. What has been said of the effect of expectation might seem sufficient to account for the practice of prayer, to fetiches or other unknown powers, because prayer, or concentration of the mind upon a desired end, both heightens expectation, and, if it appears as an antecedent fact to the realisation of the desire, would naturally, and even reasonably, be regarded as its cause, while primitive man could in no case regard the prayer as the cause of so unlike an effect as his disappointment. In most cases, too, there is probably a little half-unconscious self-deception, like that of the Mandan rain-makers, whose surprising success in their art is explained by the statement that they always go on with their incantations until the rain comes—as it must soon or late—while the man who has once made rain with *éclat* is careful not to risk his reputation by trying a second time.

But beside prayers, which cost nothing (unless offered by deputy), most savage religions, if they can be called by so respectable a name, abound in prohibitions and commands which are useless as natural means towards their professed end, and yet continue to be observed disinterestedly, as well as observances of which the first and only attraction seems to be their positive painfulness. The explanation is partly mental and partly physical. An unoccupied mind finds stimulating suggestion in a prohibition, when natural impulses that really need ruling are still too few to engross the thoughts. The typical savage looks upon the objects familiar to him in the same spirit in which the writer overheard two civilised children call upon each other to read the regulations printed outside the gates of a suburban park. "We had better read this," said the elder, who was still young enough to find reading a new and exciting enterprise, "or perhaps we shall be doing something that we oughtn't:" to a child or savage in this "law-thirsty" mood even an injunction "not to walk upon the grass" is welcome, and certain to be repeated with authority. Many rules of barbarous etiquette are to be explained by this intellectual craving after regulation for its own sake, and the craving assures the permanence of any other custom that has the semblance of an independent foundation in reason. In the Chinese classics morality and ritual are even comically indistinguishable, because both are made to rest upon the same sentiment of material propriety; and even in societies as civilised as our own, most sincere, unintelligent religion might be explained, or described, as inherited feeling attached to an abridged formula of duty and ritual, which, if once pulled to pieces, could certainly not be restored, by any rational process, to its present form.

Religion might continue to consist of dim fear and fear-born rites as long as fear of the unknown was a motive habitually determining whatever part of the conduct was neither rational nor automatic; but religion of this sort, though as absolute as the power of a mad tyrant over a barbarous people, is not capable of surviving the natural tendency, which it shares with most things earthly, to develop its leading characteristics with self-destructive consistency and zeal. Early fetichism supposes every action of natural force which affects the individual to be in that final and composite form, the result of will; but from this point of view the various necessities personified become so numerous that it is impossible to class any as invariable, and the human mind, which would be incapable of acting at all in the chaos it has over-hastily imagined, begins in self-defence to introduce order and measure into its pantheon. As this process advances, the difference between the religion of the few and of the many begins to make itself felt. In religious cosmogonies, the attempt is made to unify the conception of the Not-self, at least so far as to allow of its history being told intelligibly to man; while in popular religions, when the number of gods acknowledged has been brought within manageable limits, separate divinities, each of whom we must suppose originally to have represented some one real aspect or influence of the Not-self, engross all the limited capacity for religious feeling of which the average idolater is possessed.

Theosophies and mythologies preserve the tradition of a relation between man and that which is not-man, but they do not rationalise what is real in the relation, or spiritualise the human sense of its existence. Gross misconceptions of the nature of the Not-self in its relations to the self will be corrected by prolonged experience of those relations as they really are; but if those relations are less close, concrete, and immediate than they are generally conceived to be in idolatrous religions, we need not be surprised at finding, as in fact we do find, that religion, in shaking itself clear of mythology and superstition, comes to occupy less space in proportion in the consciousness, and to exercise less influence on the conduct of the generality of men. An amount of intellectual power which is not common by itself, and which is still less commonly combined with highly developed emotional sensibility, is necessary to make religion at once vital, rational, and spiritual; and though a very beautiful development of the moral nature, such as is sometimes to be met with in the uneducated classes, or amongst women, may to some extent supply the place of intelligence, it is generally true that religion is spiritual in proportion as it is rational. Accordingly spiritual religion is even more rare than rational thought, indefinitely more rare than a simple obedience to the dictates of law and morality.

We may assume every human thought or feeling to have some cause, occasion, or counterpart in nature, without supposing that the thought or feeling is necessarily adjusted so as to correspond in all points with the thing that suggested it. True wisdom and happiness (of which religion has often been thought to have the secret) lie in an effective coincidence between the power that is real and the influence believed in and acknowledged—that is, between human feeling and the permanent conditions of human life; and the tendency of human development is towards such real and conscious harmony, if only by clearing away the confused ideas and factitious impressions of which false religions are compounded. With the advance of natural, or as it is now called, positive knowledge, religion becomes more entirely subjective, that is, more concerned with the feelings of man towards the Not-man, and less with the direct action of the Not-man upon our race; and while one source of error is thus diminished, another is opened by the possible misdirection of the religious feeling already in existence. A sentiment good and natural in itself may fall wide of its supposed object, and it would be easy to show that the only cases in which religion has been clearly injurious to human progress are those in which fine, unpractical emotion has been either simply wasted or dangerously misapplied. Both of these results may follow from the confusion which is not unfrequent between religion, or matters of sentiment, and morality, or matters of conduct. It is a psychological impossibility to feel to order, but people may easily believe that it is their duty to act as if they felt something which they do not feel, and such a course is extremely likely to react upon their real feelings, much to the detriment of their perfect religious spontaneity. And if religious feeling, which, for the reasons indicated, is much more variable than the sense of moral obligation, should happen to be amongst the motives by which conduct is determined, in cases when the sentiment was itself mistaken, effects as disastrous as any of the incidents in religious persecutions may easily ensue.

It is difficult for criticism of the religious sentiment to go into much detail without running the risk of arousing the *odium theologicum*, which is the more unnecessary in the present case because the theory of religion here suggested is too far outside the current creeds to come naturally into collision with them. As in the case of law and morality, the existence of a constraining influence must be distinguished from its nature or effects. Religion exists because the life of man is conditioned by other than human forces; the operations of nature are independent of human law and human morality, and human life is not independent of the operations of nature; nay more, even human law and human morality, the steps by which man rises to a height from which he surveys, as a critical superior, the operations of natural law—these steps are themselves only the supreme expression, the last development of the all-pervading, unbroken sequences of nature.

We have no reason to suppose that the elements of the inanimate world are conscious of the influence which their orderly persistence exercises upon the generations of men who fall under it; and the loose mysticism which talks of the universe attaining to consciousness of itself in man is unscientific as well as unpractical, for it is but a fraction of the universe that so becomes conscious, and it is only conscious—and that but imperfectly—of itself and such other fractions as lie nearest to it. But the influence of the universe upon man is not the less real for being unconsciously exercised, and being real, man may become conscious of it as affecting himself, which it does in two ways: first, by physical causation—for it will be admitted that the bodily nature of man is conditioned by the material circumstances of the world in which only organisms of a certain kind can lead the life for which they are fitted; and secondly, as an object of perception and more or less adequate knowledge, and the occasion of such feelings as arise in the human subject when it becomes conscious of the impressions and thoughts thus received from without.

As has been said, a confused apprehension of the first kind of influence is the source of most gross religious misbeliefs; men promptly become aware of effects produced upon themselves or their circumstances without their own co-operation, but the identity of the natural cause or causes which produce the effect and their *modus operandi* are not distinguished till later, are not to this day always distinguishable. Idols are made by premature or inaccurate reasoning from effects to causes, and the religious feeling which they, so to say, intercept, can never be as profound or lasting as that which is awakened by a true sense of real power. More rational, spiritual religion is not confined to the recognition only of such agencies as immediately affect the subject, and anything that can be perceived or known, but not produced or materially modified, may become the object of disinterested religious regard, as a part or aspect of the Not-self. Periods of theological controversy and perplexity are only to be expected when the apprehension of real facts and relations in the Not-self is clear enough to call forth feelings of religious strength in the self, while it is not yet understood that the significance of the facts and the very existence of the relations is itself altogether relative to the emotional nature of the percipient man.

Laws, scientific, political, and moral, state the true relations of real things, but in so far as these relations are conditioned by unconscious being, they cannot be supposed to have any intentional bearing upon the individual perceiving them; the effect upon his mind of the perception is and remains subjective, and any attempt to account for the impression produced except by the relations which produce it, or for the existence of the relations except by the existence of the things related, by introducing an imaginative, uncogitable element, favours the notion that religion deals with things supernatural, not merely with things superhuman. But things supernatural and uncogitable, of which the existence cannot be perceived nor the efficiency calculated, are to reason non-existent. It is only that which, at some point or other, comes in contact with some sensibility or faculty of the human mind that has any existence at all for the human mind; the contact may be indefinitely slight or indirect, but without such contact the existence is not even thought of as possible, except in the way that any arbitrary combination of terms is possible.

The association between theological or theistic belief and

any kind of religious feeling is so close at present, that to most people the question, Has religion a natural, necessary, and reasonable existence? virtually means, Is there a God or no? Positive convictions of all kinds are intolerant, and to any one who has a definite theory of how, or by what means, the moral order of the world is secured, all the other hypotheses of theological science or metaphysical nescience, are subject to the one common, fatal drawback—that they are not true. It is possible to hold an opinion so confidently as to *believe* every other opinion to be false, and yet to know, with at least equal strength of conviction, that we ourselves are at least as fallible as the rest of the world. We believe in the possibility of our own view being mistaken, but meanwhile it *is* our view—that the mistake lies with those who differ from us. And though, from some points of view, it may be more useful to dwell on points of agreement than on points of difference, as was said, every positive construction is intolerant, and the outline of our own convictions forms a sharp line of exclusion against the opinions which we hold to be false or confused.

The opinion which we feel impelled to exclude in this way at the outset is that which rests on an unholy alliance between ignorance and faith—the compromise which allows men to believe anything they like, provided they know no reason to the contrary, and encourages them in not knowing what they prefer to ignore, by treating ignorance as a coequal ground of inference with knowledge. If there is a true scientific faith, agnosticism must be heresy, and the term includes alike the quasi-orthodox who appeal to the ignorance of opponents, and claim licence to believe anything that the said opponents have not wit or courage to disprove, as well as the half-fledged rationalists who claim tolerance from dogmatists because they are too modest to say anything worse of a dogma than that it has not yet been proved to their satisfaction.

If we have a clear and adequate apprehension of any

truth, its opposite is not conceivable to us as true, and both religion and philosophy would gain if the issue between theism and natural philosophy were more clearly defined, and the rival alternatives more courageously faced. The real question is, Have we reason to believe in the existence behind or above the Knowable Not-ourselves, of a person, or power, to whom, or which, we can and must stand in a spiritual relation? Does philosophy prove the existence of the (or an) Unknowable? and does religion prove the Unknowable to be God? It is scarcely intelligible that those who answer this question in the affirmative should be content without further illumination, as if the modern race of men had attained to the Olympian calm of Epicurean deities, and gods might be, and yet men have no care for things divine. Those who answer in the negative, at any rate, are concerned to show that they do not thereby propose to sacrifice any positive result of human development, only to give a different interpretation of real fact, and eliminate from the region of belief doctrines to which no answering realities can be discovered.

There is nothing known, felt, or imagined by man, except that which human powers can know, feel, or imagine. The counterparts or occasions of these human experiences are real, sensible, conceivable, to be cognised: for, if we consider, knowledge or perception of a cause is only knowledge or consciousness of an effect produced under conditions which are also known or perceived, and the consciousness of the relation between the effect and the condition is itself only an affair of knowledge and perception; and we cannot distinguish one part of our knowledge as less essentially authentic than another part; it is all susceptible of the same kind of verification, and is distinguishable by the same kinds of test from corresponding varieties of human error. Before forming an opinion as to the possibility of metempirical or supra-sensible knowledge, we should require to know precisely what is understood by the terms. We may assume sensation, emotion, and thought to be invariably attended (if not caused) by certain modifications of nerve and brain matter; but, if all our knowledge of things consists of inferences to the effect that there is an objective reality answering to our varying impressions, how can we infer the existence of something to which we have not had, and are not supposed to be capable of having, a corresponding impression? If some kind of physical affection attends every act of consciousness, what kind of physical affection attends the cognition of the supra-sensible? Is it distinguished from natural knowledge by having no physical conditions at all, or by having no immediate objective condition beyond the state of the subject's mind?

The two questions: Does the Supernatural exist? and, Can it be known to exist? are really different aspects of the same, because an affirmation that the supernatural may exist, or that it cannot, is in itself a profession of knowledge respecting it, and that respecting which natural knowledge is possible, is, by the very fact natural, as natural—in the wide sense in which Comte and Spinoza use the word Nature—as any single sensible intuition. If we examine and compare the different conceptions of the supernatural entertained by philosophers and the vulgar, we shall find that all agree more or less clearly in regarding as supernatural the existence of disembodied spirits and the modification of human consciousness by purely immaterial agencies. There is nothing else to which the word supernatural would be certainly and unanimously applied by believers in the supernatural. Now it is evident that real modifications of consciousness, even though produced by other than physical and intelligible causes, must be felt or perceived if they exist; their *esse* is *percipi;* if they are perceived to exist, the perception itself must be natural or supernatural; if the perception is supposed to be supernatural, that is, unaccompanied by normal physical modifications or nervous movement, most physicists will simply deny its existence; if the perception is natural—and it is a simple fact of experience that men have believed and do believe in the existence of ghosts, of God, and of the Unknowable—the natural antecedents or conditions of its production can be investigated.

The problem to be solved is: Do they believe for good reasons—natural or supernatural—or for bad reasons—natural or supernatural? There may be a perfectly natural and accountable state of mind consisting of false belief in supernatural entities; this is admitted on all hands, and only amounts to saying that the errors of the imagination may include the nature or existence of things as well as their relations and manifestations. Similarly we can imagine a natural and accountable state of mind consisting of true knowledge of God, as a moral governor of the world, which might be attained by man if the world really were perceptibly subject to such government, in the way conceived by such writers as Butler and Paley. The permanent and orderly production of a class of effects, with no other assignable constant antecedent than the will of a person otherwise unknown, is inferred with considerable plausibility to follow from such a cause, if that and no other appears naturally adequate. Such inferences may be mistaken, like any other conclusion, but the method is not self-evidently faulty. The hypothesis of a supernatural ground of error, such as the deceptions of evil spirits, need hardly be considered seriously; and the last remaining alternative of a valid supernatural ground for human belief in and feeling about things supernatural, is the one in which most shades of confused thought have finally taken sanctuary.

The reason that Spinoza's definition of passion, as a confused or inadequate idea, has not been more generally accepted, is probably that he has been understood as meaning that emotion and thought are the same thing, only one good and the other bad of their kind. *The same* is a dangerous phrase, but the real distinction between thought and feeling would not be affected by the historical identification of the final stage of the one with a transitional or introductory passage in the growth of the other. The thronging groups of impressions which are just upon the verge of crystallising into the new and lucid form of an intelligible proposition, fill the consciousness meanwhile with an inarticulate murmur which the uncritical ear may easily mistake for revelations of an unknown tongue. If we take as the premise of reasoning the consciousness of a man in whom the sense of such confusion is at its climax, the objective reality answering to his impression may be inferred to consist of Impenetrable Mystery, but this is only a reproduction of the primitive blunder which infers a numerically distinct original for every subjective impression, whether it be a correct intuition or a fallacious inference.

With regard to the natural sense of mystery—begotten by Ignorance upon Curiosity—the inference is certainly premature. We are assuming all states of consciousness to be the product or accompaniment of definite physical modifications, or conditions; and from this point of view, ignorance, the being without a particular piece of knowledge, is not a mere negation. The nerves of a person, who does not know this or that, exist as positively as the person who does know or the person who erroneously believes himself to know, they are only differently affected. Before admitting that science can demonstrate the existence of an Unknowable, we should want to have it made clear how the organs of perception are affected when the mind is convinced of the existence of something imperceptible. When, however, we pass from the unconscious but perceivable conditions of thought to thought itself, we cease to regard ignorance, or the want of knowledge, as anything real: the word only denotes the negation of scientific belief caused by the absence of some or all of the elements essential to the constitution of positive knowledge. But this negation is concerned with thought not with existence. That *we* do not know whether a chimera buzzing *in vacuo* can devour second intentions does not prove that chimeras and second intentions are unknowable entities. The realism lurking at the bottom of most thinking would make this a dangerous way of expressing our sense that the problem is an amusing absurdity.

To say that a thing is unknowable is to say less than nothing about it, because unknowableness is not a property of things in themselves, but of things in relation to a mind with faculties subject to such and such limitations. To say that something unknown is, may be true and significant, if the word *unknown* is held to mean nothing more than that existence is the only property which can at present be ascribed to the thing in question. To say that we have a knowledge of unknowable existence is a contradiction in terms; but we may have a tolerably clear and adequate idea of the limits of our own positive knowledge, and beyond those limits it is certain that *we* know nothing. We have valid reasons, physical and metaphysical, for believing that the limits of thought are not coextensive at any given moment with the limits of existence, and we therefore infer the existence outside our knowledge of a more or less thinkable unknown. But this speculative inference is homogeneous with the rest of our knowledge or thought; it presupposes no supernatural factors either in the unknown or in the state of consciousness in which existence of the unknown is conditionally affirmed. The unknown is the conceivably knowable, not something generically different from the known and only conceived by contrast or opposition to it.

If all knowledge is transformed and organised sensation, what sensation, we ask, can give the knowledge of something the essence of which is that sense cannot perceive it, and that the organised conclusions of sense in thought affirm nothing respecting its qualities or relations. The fact that we have not had a sensation of an entirely new order does not prove that something exists capable of producing sensations that we have not had, and yet such an inference is hardly more imaginative than the argument that when we have come to the end—or the beginning—of our knowledge, we necessarily assume in thought the existence of an objective substratum or boundary, a personification, so to speak, of the idea of limitation, external to the thought which, by the hypothesis, we had come to the end of.

The mental state answering to the perception of an unconditioned unknowable is one of simple, blank unconsciousness, not a positive consciousness of the presence in nature of a mysterious blank. No naturalist denies the existence of mysteries in nature, but the sense of mystery, the oppressive feeling of excited, unsatisfied curiosity, does not carry us a step beyond the point of positive knowledge previously attained; it discloses no new property of things, only the relative proportion of the mixed knowledge and ignorance possessed concerning the things felt to be mysterious. The attendant sense of awe or perplexity is best explained as the mental consciousness of imperfect or confused knowledge; and this consciousness shows no tendency to disappear with the progress of knowledge, of which one chief result is the increased development of curiosity, by the suggestion of new things that might be and are not known. But rational inference proceeds from knowledge to knowledge; from the contemplation of our ignorance we can learn nothing but its extent, and though this study also may have its moral use as a discipline of humility, we can hardly expect to learn what constitutes moral perfection from experience of what constitutes mental imperfection. Edification is even less to be looked for than instruction from the philosophy which brandishes the conception of a mighty x as a sort of two-edged muzzle for science and religion.

Hitherto we have only considered what may be called the external evidences (real or supposed) for the existence of some spiritual power in the Not-self; but as religion gradually frees itself from accidental historical encumbrances, and assumes its permanent emotional character, we observe a not unnatural tendency to attribute mere subjective changes, variations in the mood of the self, when no other cause for them is known, to the direct, immediate action of the Not-self, making itself felt by the mind in some altogether peculiar, supersensible manner. When the extreme closeness of the connection between the modifications of the mind and those of the body was less apparent than it is now, there was nothing absurd in the belief that one mind or will could directly influence another, the only mistake lay in assuming that the process, supposing it to be real, must be called supernatural, because it was rare or peculiar. Even now, if we suppose the physiology of thought to have made all the progress it presumably will, it is perfectly conceivable that some Force, not otherwise perceptible, should be found to have the property of traversing or correcting the ordinary course of mental processes by inducing fresh modifications in the molecular composition of the brain. The existence of such a force would be sufficiently proved by its action, and its nature would be known and described by the effect it produced, as there are chemical substances of which the presence is inferred from some unexplained effect, before they have declared themselves directly to either of the senses; or as the existence and position of an unseen planet may be determined by perturbations in the orbit of those already known and observed. Of course in scientific investigations every possible hypothesis is exhausted before the presence of a new element or power is assumed, and no attempt has ever, so far as we are aware, been made to prove the existence of a deity in this mechanical, *a posteriori* manner.

Inferences drawn merely from the emotional vicissitudes of religious experience scarcely bear the test of impartial reason, and are not, as a fact, chiefly relied upon by the ablest religious doctors in ages of more faith than the present. Common experience shows how feeling towards or about an absent person, or about an action past or contemplated, will vary from day to day, perhaps from hour to hour, while the real circumstances are the same, even in our thought, and the real qualities of the person or the action do not, we know, fluctuate with our opinion. It is only in religious experiences that such changes of mood are supposed to have an immediate objective cause, so that the intelligible effects of physical or pathological conditions may be treated as ultimate facts of the spiritual consciousness, serving as a foundation for inferences respecting antecedents of the same spiritual order.

It is generally admitted that the most vivid and seemingly realistic temptations and consolations of men like Bunyan, Luther, or Loyola are half-hallucination, the work of an inward voice, the echo of the soul's own mood, and every authoritative manual of devotion contemplates for the believer periods of trial and desolation in which his most sincere efforts may fail to recall the living sense of spiritual communion with the powers invoked, failing which he feels himself to be a castaway; no one but the person concerned really believes that there is any objective process going on outside the mind of the saint corresponding to the (real) experience within, most describable in the phraseology of the penitential psalms. Even pious Christians are willing to admit that the sense of answered prayer, in regard to spiritual blessings, is vivid in proportion to the strength of the desire felt for their possession, and it is hard to convince a naturalist that faith strong enough to believe in the answering of prayer is too weak to be its own reply, when only spiritual or subjective consequences are required.

Comparatively few persons are sustained in their religious convictions by the higher, more intimate and imaginative phases of religious experience: but many who believe, in a more or less perfunctory manner, that there are gods (three in one) who concern themselves about human affairs, do sincerely think that the most important incidents of their outer life (after they have happened) were ordained to happen by a moral governor of the universe. Every one instinctively and in a manner necessarily regards the incidents which concern himself as really grouped in the manner in which they present themselves to his feeling—as of course they really are—though not less really in a thousand different ways, visible with equal clearness to other centres of consciousness; while to the dispassionate eye of reason, each several mode of stringing together the actual occurrences is true—from an arbitrarily narrowed point of view, but worthless as a formula for the general relations among all the things concerned. We may cover a sheet of paper with circles described from equidistant centres, and then take every point of intersection as a new centre with an indefinite number of radii. Each spot may conceive itself as in the midst of nearly any geometrical pattern it pleases to see or to invent, but no description of these visionary stars or rosettes will give us the key to the method by which the confusing network was arranged; and so it is also with the network of natural chances in which men are entangled.

People as a rule are only vividly conscious of incidents that concern themselves, and out of the whole number of these incidents it is practically certain that a considerable number will not merely be naturally connected amongst themselves, but will also admit of being classed together in consciousness as tending the same way, or working together to produce the same effect. If a man has fully formed plans and wishes, which one accident after another prevents him from realising, he generalises his experience, and calls himself unlucky, as in the opposite case he learns to have faith in his star. But supposing he has had misgivings as to the moral rectitude of his purpose, the checks he meets with may seem designed to warn him from the path of error; and conversely, if his ruling intention is to follow the call of duty, not inclination, every objective possibility or opportunity of doing the duty which he recognises, appears as a "leading" or direct indication of the will of Providence concerning himself and his conduct. To most people, however, the greater part of life is no more taken up with the conscious deliberate pursuit of duty than with that of happiness, and it is only in the more serious crises of life, when one difficulty more or less may turn the scale of failure and success, when one more loss may turn courage to despair, or a single act of help make effort hopeful and strong,—it is only then that trifling incidents become so pregnant of consequences that few men can resist the temptation to feel that the mighty accident must have a cause proportioned in power to the importance of its effect—on themselves. If they are theists by profession, they see without difficulty the will of God concerning themselves; if not, they ask in perplexed wonder, what have they done to the universe that it should deal thus and thus with them? why should they of all men have fate meddling with their affairs? whence the mysterious power of the Not-self over the sons of men?

The belief in God is kept alive much less by the belief in actual miracles—which must have a supernatural cause, since, by the hypothesis, no natural cause is equal to their production—than by this other belief in what we may call facts of the mind, arbitrary constructions built out of real materials, but with a connection that is only subjectively real. The bankruptcy of A may be caused by the dishonesty of B, and cause C to emigrate instead of marrying D, to whom he was engaged. D calls her disappointment a "cross" or a "trial," and enters a sisterhood, and in the placid middle age of religious women, with small amusements, small agitations, abundant routine, and complacent conviction of having chosen the better part, she looks back gratefully to the Providence which led her to this happier state. But if this method of interpretation were consistently followed—and no theory is true that will not admit of consistent application—every motive, opportunity, or desire might in the same way be ascribed to the working of the Divine will, thus made a party to everything that occurs, as in the purest extravagances of pantheism. It is hardly necessary to fill in the outlines of an opposite case to the last. A girl or boy has exalted dreams of self-sacrifice and religious consecration; trivial accidents of time and place favour the growth of relations that point to another vocation, and it is quite within the limits of probability for the sober father or mother of a Christian household to thank God for having been providentially saved from the ill-advised ambition of their youth after saintliness or martyrdom.

It is evident that those in whom religious feeling and faith are intense will have more abundant demonstration of the existence of the powers they believe in than the worldly. Those who have learned to see the hand of God in the changes of their own mood, resulting from physical or moral causes of the most personal nature, are sure also to be quick at imagining the outer circumstances which affect their spiritual life to be controlled in the same way and towards the same ends as the vicissitudes of their spiritual life itself. And since people are inwardly moved by the influences present to sense or imagination, a felt influence becomes the stronger for being associated with an imagined cause, all the effects of which are preconceived as supremely potent and good. Those who have made it their chief object to do the Divine will (as they understand it), and have a general outline of belief as to what this will must be, are more susceptible than others to leadings or opportunities afforded from without for more and more complete conformity to the same will. It is difficult to uproot old associations, and we may even go so far as to say that for minds thoroughly impregnated with theological ideas, the familiar formula really expresses a larger portion of truth than a perfectly correct scientific statement, say, about the "stream of tendency," to which they would attach no meaning at all, or a quite mistaken one.

It is for the many who find the theological hypothesis meaningless and incredible that we offer the above account of the facts innocently distorted by the undisciplined imaginations of virtuous persons, whose egotism, banished from the heart, has taken refuge in the brain. We do not say that the patterns in the diagram are unreal; they are real to the feeling of centre A or centre B, who are conscious of no influences except along just these converging lines; but the true statement of the relations in space of all these points is infinitely more general, the full statement infinitely more complicated than anything we can get at, even by adding together the impressions of the various centres. It would baffle a mathematician to find terms for the number of positions which each centre might occupy in the innumerable figures which may be described from each of the rival centres, all constructions being equally possible, from the single point of view adopted, equally true in reference to the consciousness which accepts them, and equally inadequate to a mind accustomed to class its intuitions impartially in accordance with the objective proportions of things.

If we agreed with those writers, religious and otherwise, who hold religion to be of its nature supernatural, we might perhaps be tempted to see nothing but supernatural imbecility in the elaborate "exercises" of the heart and mind undergone by our pious forefathers. But if we believe religious ideas and feelings to be entirely natural in their growth and origin, we shall expect to learn much about the natural working of the human soul in its emotional apprehension of things not human from the great writers who have made such processes the study and employment of their life. A theory of what religion is now, or may be in the future, is hardly susceptible of more precise verification than what may be afforded by its adequacy as an account of what religion actually has been, according to persons eminent for religious gifts and entirely innocent of rationalistic bias: though, at the same time, it must be remembered that the foundation of primitive theological conceptions depends on rather different conditions from those which enable their application to survive into a state of things in which they could not possibly have been formed anew.

As soon as the stupid terror of the savage is spiritualised into a reasonable awe of transcendent, superhuman power, the mind rises to a confused intuition of the Not-I as a moral force, which it then for the first time becomes, when this natural and reasonable awe is found to control the will and moderate the passions, partly by the mere spectacle of a stern and lofty impassivity, partly by the unconscious development of an intuition that the stars in their courses do not fight the battle of evil and self-indulgence. Consistent belief in divine intervention in human affairs comes, as was observed, practically to the same conclusions as the courageous pantheism which ascribes all that is done to the life and will of the one living substance. And even though we refuse to personify the All, we must admit that it is from the All, the real universe in which we live, that all those influences proceed of which we become conscious as ruling our moral as well as our bodily life. And if we, whose habitual mental attitude towards the natural world is one rather of observant criticism than of reverence, are nevertheless constrained to such an admission, it cannot surprise us that primitive religion should have instinctively recognised the presence of some such authority. The vital consciousness of a real omnipresent power which prompts the Psalmist's complaint, "If I go down into hell, thou art there also" —though it has disappeared, or nearly so, with the elaborate anthropomorphism of modern Christianity, and the partial, familiar explanations of scientific analysis, may yet revive in a quiet literal way when the sceptic or atheist, after mentally denouncing several of the laws of human and material nature which hamper his wishes, sees at last, in these or other laws, the necessary explanation of his own discontent, and really and finally discerns that his revolt, if he does revolt, is still a fatal submission to the necessity which made him incapable of the wiser, earlier, voluntary acquiescence.

But the fear of the Lord is only the beginning of wisdom, and the mere recognition of an external supreme power is scarcely of itself religious; for it to become so habitually or normally there must be some natural constancy of sympathetic relation between the self and what it acknowledges as its superior. The religious sentiment which consists in the going out of the whole emotional nature of the self towards that which is Not-self can only have a natural and necessary existence in human experience if it is possible for the whole being of man to become conscious of itself as subject to the collective influences from without by which it is really modified. We began by describing religion as the sentiment which arises in the human self, when it becomes conscious of its own relation towards the apparently infinite Not-self. That relation is primarily and chiefly one of dependence, but religion does not lie in the sense of that dependence, but in the emotion, whatever be its nature, which arises after a clear and adequate apprehension of the relation has been attained. Such an apprehension does not imply an exhaustive knowledge of the Not-self considered absolutely, to which human faculties are by the nature of the case inadequate, but the relation of a conscious being, as such, is only real so far as it is conscious, or potentially conscious, and the only condition of the emotion is that the consciousness should be complete.

It is through the moral and intellectual powers of his nature, as knowing and acting, that the individual man for the most part becomes aware of the collective influences from without in which his own native tendencies and instincts are, as it were, swallowed up. The scientific laws of nature (including human nature) and the moral law of conduct determine between them the fashion in which he will think and act, and the effect which his actions will produce; but we must remember that these laws, that is to say, the real relations amongst existing things, only systematise our knowledge of those things by formulating the methods of their existence; they tell us *how* things are, but they do not account for the fact *that* they are. Of course this is one of the points at which a theological solution is frequently offered with great confidence, but if it is offered to reason, it must be rejected for want of terms in which it can be intelligibly expressed, for we have had no experiences qualifying us to form any idea corresponding to such a process as the creation of things in themselves; and if it is offered to faith and the religious emotions, it is unnecessary, because they find no difficulty in the existence of that which they themselves only exist to acquiesce in. By knowing the laws of the nature of perceptible things, the self is enabled to modify to its own advantage some of the effects to be produced by the things actually existing at any time, but the number of such things and the laws of their manifestation are at any given moment capable of being apprehended as the really supreme and controlling influence by which the being of the self is conditioned.

The intuitions of pure science produce an acquiescence in truths or facts of relation which is scarcely religious, because it is not concerned either with the causes or effects of that which is known. To know a thing is to assent, to acquiesce in its reality, and the exercise of the faculty of knowing is attended with a natural pleasure that almost overflows into enthusiasm for the truths known as real. But in the pursuit of special sciences, the student, though he sits with pious attention at the feet of Nature and receives her instructions with docility, reserves the right of interrogating her upon one subject rather than another, and is guided in his choice more by the knowledge which he himself wishes to possess than by the claims or influence of the Unknown as a whole.

The difference between science and the philosophy which we maintain to be religious is parallel to that between mere morality and the true, purely subjective religion of the regenerate or "converted"—the feeling which, whether reasonable in its origin or not, comes into being somewhence, and, we suppose, by no supernatural means, but which, when it has come into existence, is only feeling, perfectly disinterested, unpractical, uncritical, self-contained emotion. Any less massive power than this fails to overcome the real difficulty in the way of conceiving as an object of proper religious emotion a sum of forces which are independent of any associations of sanctity, independent of personality or consciousness, of purpose or intelligence, of love or will—in brief, of all those analogues of human faculty which even pantheists and mystics implicitly attribute to the divinities of their imagination. What at the present day generally passes for religion, as the religious themselves acknowledge and deplore, is a more or less unintelligent acquiescence in a few theological formulæ, more or less infrequent paroxysms of sentimental remorse or aspiration, and a more or less confused belief, very seldom present as a controlling force, in the existence of a higher power than the self with its small aims and wishes. An edifice of this kind collapses when the rottenness of its foundations is exposed, but there have been men, very able thinkers, and by no means of hysterical temperament, to whom religion has been the supreme science, the mainspring of action, the guiding force of life, and the essence of true natural religion, if it can be found anywhere, must lie in a feeling, independent of creed, common to all souls in whom the intelligence of the affections has received its fullest development.

Religious feeling must be distinguished from religious creeds, but creeds may be roughly classified by the importance or propriety of the place they leave for feeling. Monotheism, Dualism, Pantheism, and Mysticism are names that serve to cover most of the hypotheses under which men have conceived their relation to the supreme forces · outside themselves. When familiarity with the action of natural forces has bred contempt for their unintelligent mechanical efficiency, and the vast intricacy and variety of their interaction is not yet apprehended by the intellect, and therefore cannot stir any emotional enthusiasm, men begin to personify the moral influences to which their lives are subject, in the same way that fetish worshippers personify the physical action of material nature. The religious errors to which this practice naturally leads are less dangerous, because the divinities made out of idealised natural forces are not usually more moral in their supposed conduct than the forces themselves, of which the best that can be said is that their influence is altogether outside morality, since it is innocent of intention or consciousness. The moral influences, on the other hand, of which men become conscious outside themselves, can be tried by human standards, and only such of them will be naturally selected for religious worship or idealisation as are really admirable according to prevailing moral ideas. Law, for instance, or justice, are moral realities, and if they are worshipped it is always in a state of ideal perfection, but to worship an abstract idea, or a relation in its native immateriality, is an achievement scarcely to be expected from populations at once imaginative and emotional enough to find some concrete object of worship essential. The transition from deified virtues to virtuous deities is as natural and gradual as that from personified forces to persons whose will is supposed to be a force. Both steps are intellectually retrograde, though the latter at any rate seems to have accompanied a moral advance. As the standard of human morality became clearer and higher, men lost the power of feeling religiously towards imaginary beings that were not even equal to themselves in some important points of reason and morality; and since the religious feeling persisted, the inference took shape—if there are Gods, they must be good. The same generations that seemed to be incapable of reverencing truth, mercy, and justice, unless in the garb of gods of that ilk, by dwelling upon these moral qualities as attributes of real objects of affection, acquired a habit of valuing them more. Men gathered moral courage to call a bad god a devil, and renounce the worship of devils, though their moral faith was not yet strong enough to resist the second inference—if there is goodness, there must be Gods—to make or exemplify it—as if love could not be real unless Eros were a person, or wisdom venerable unless Pallas Athene and her owl embodied it, or justice and holiness divine unless Jehovah was Lord of a heavenly host of winged Seraphim and Cherubim.

As it is from the action of men upon each other, and distinctly not from the action of nature upon men, that human notions of goodness are derived, we find that all attempts to define or describe the divine excellences, or a perfect Not-self, begin by supposing human virtues indefinitely magnified and exalted. An intellectual preference for the simplest statement of a proposition may have had something to do with the advance from polytheism to monotheism, which, however, could hardly have taken place without an accompanying desire to bring together in one object absolutely every power or quality felt to be adorable. The founder of an historical religion, in offering to the adoration of his sectaries, what is in practice only a magnified self, is not conscious of any imposture, he simply yields to the necessities of the case, which have made Bouddha an object of worship in spite of the (traditional) resolution of Sakya-Mouni to preach neither himself nor a god made in his own image. An historical religion lives and exercises more or less control over its votaries for as long as its prophet, or the God he preached, continues to represent or symbolise such aspects of the Not-self as call forth all the power of religious susceptibility in the age. The success of such religions is generally proportioned to the degree of objectivity which has been given to the original revelation, or in other words, to the extent to which its founder has made friends of the mammon of unrighteousness—of unspirituality—and brought the deity so near to the senses or imagination of the worshippers that they find it easy to feel about him as a person.

It would seem paradoxical to say that religions based on idolatry were more moral than those based on theosophical theories, and yet, if we use idolatrous in this general sense to indicate a mistaken concentration of feeling upon imaginary entities, it is true that the mistake may be morally beneficial, provided the feeling which it causes to be cultivated and developed was itself the outcome of a healthy moral state. But each new step of normal development results in the casting off of some fresh husk of natural error, and as moral intuitions become more exact, after the association of duty with religion, an instinctive sense of the conditions of human virtue troubles the simple ideal of divine perfection. Primitive man can imagine gods that suffer through imperfection or defect; idealised Paganism requires its gods to embody the perfection of natural good —they must be perfect after their kind, whether that kind be morally perfect or no—and rejects as blasphemous the conception reverted to by Christianity, of a suffering God, which is the next—and logical—expression of the difficulty, or rather the impossibility, of forming a clear, close, and sympathetic conception of transcendent virtue combined with triumphant power and unbroken happiness. Human virtue, we find, consists in the pursuit of perfection under conditions which give a sense of difficulty, constraint, and self-denial to the pursuit, and we cannot form a clear and adequate conception of superhuman virtue under superhuman conditions, that shall yet affect us as human virtue, carried to an ideal infinity of perfection. Of course there are persons whose state of mind allows them to think that they apprehend as possible the existence of a Being who both is and is not potent to alter the essential nature of things; who might have made the highest good attainable without effort or suffering, but has not done so *because* no human good is so high as that which is attained by painful virtuous effort. But Christianity stands almost alone among religions in having tried to find in theology the key to all that is mysterious in existence after the mysteries had assumed dimensions that made simple religious feeling unable to cope with them; and when religious feeling has to call the intellect to its defence, unless the foundations of the feeling are in all respects rational, the result, as in most unequal alliances, is fatal to the weaker of the two. And accordingly there arises a new generation of moral zealots to insist on a third inference, there is no God—or object of worship—because the works, which must be his if he existed, are not good enough to make their author adorable. Idolatrous religions, or those in which the leading feature is the worship of a person, are naturally more exposed to this kind of assault than more abstract schemes, in which such associated religious feeling as exists is self-centred, and, instead of going out towards an external object, grows by the intensification of its self-consciousness. A religion based, so to speak, on incident, is more easily believed in, and its observances kept up, than one which is only speculative and emotional, but it is also more easily believed in with superficial conviction and emotional unconcern, which really leaves it not religion at all, but common, matter-of-fact error.

The natural classification of religions according to the comparative prominence of the subjective element would be of more importance but for the cross divisions which, in every special age or country, arise from the variations of personal temperament; men who are by nature born mystics inherit narratives and dogma, and those whose natural taste is for the concrete find means of materialising the most hazy outlines of a national mysticism. Still the religion of a people is a tolerably sure index of the set of its strongest emotional tendencies, and in the days when no national creed claims adhesion as of course, the form of belief to which individuals incline is an almost equally trustworthy symptom of mental and moral character.

Dualism, express or implied, though it has a certain plausibility as an explanation of the imperfection and discord apparent in the universe, is not compatible with the fullest development of the religious sentiment; for, on the one hand, the tendency to glorify the good spirit, whose victory over the principle of evil is so obviously incomplete, leads into theological dilemmas of the same sort as those just alluded to concerning the origin of evil, and on the other hand, the spontaneous feeling of men towards the Not-themselves is much weakened if this Not-self is conceived as divided into hostile fractions. Even if hatred were not a peculiarly irreligious sentiment, it would be found impossible to love one object and hate another at the same time with the same fervour as if all the powers of the mind were united in one direction. It is true that new religions always appear most thriving when in a militant condition, while persecution has the power of reviving a waning religious zeal, but the inference from this will be not so much that true religion requires the stimulus of opposition to keep up its vitality, as that the convictions of creeds and congregations which are kept alive by that stimulus do not constitute true religion. Any form of saintliness that requires the existence of a world of sinners to allow its full development or display, wastes away and perishes when an external conformity to the saintly type becomes the rule. But the relation between man and that which is Not-man is unchanging, and though man may not always be distinctly conscious of the relation, and though he may even be conscious of the relation without becoming conscious of any emotion answering to it, the emotion, whenever it does make its way into consciousness, is as unchanging as the relation, and as inaccessible to petty disturbance or casual interruption.

Pantheism, considered merely in its negative form as maintaining the great World-Machine to be the Supreme Being because there is nothing beyond or greater than it, is scarcely religious; a vague sentiment of respect or admiration, as for something very great or powerful, does not control and subjugate the heart and will unless there is some intimate and (on one side) personal relation between the supreme power and the subject of religious emotion. In practice pantheism either stops short with a slight consecration of natural philosophy as a substitute for religion, or else its scientific character disappears, and the world as it is is deified and endowed with soul; or again, the rational element is sacrificed to the emotional, and a result undistinguishable from that of mysticism is arrived at.

Mysticism has at least one note of true religion, it is entirely subjective. A number of definite impressions are conveyed to the mind from without, from sources more or less distinct and separable, and these, meeting in consciousness, give rise to a special state of mind. Sometimes, and this often when the mental state is one of great gravity and earnestness, the subject may be more conscious of the general effect of all these influences than of their origin or of the natural and appropriate expression of the mood itself. When we are agitated by the confused consciousness of many things at once, we may either try to personify them, so that they may come more easily into consciousness, or we may try to lose ourselves in some larger percipient power, to merge our own rational consciousness in an inarticulate impressibility, an affectionate self-suppression, which is virtually an appeal to the not-self to round and complete by interpreting a relation so momentous as to overwhelm the frail personality of the mystic.

The intensity and character of a passion depends certainly upon the power of the subject for feeling intensely as well as upon the qualities of the object felt about, but the character of religious feeling, as the *normal* response of the human soul to the sum of non-human influences, is conditioned by the general nature of these influences, and furnishes in fact, as it were, a reduced image, or echo of their tendency. From the standpoint of pure naturalism, that which men have worshipped as God appears either as the sum of natural tendencies in favour of good [1]—or, as Matthew Arnold calls it, the Not-ourselves making for righteousness—or else as the ideal construction which Feuerbach describes as the shadow of human feeling cast upon the universe. But both these are attempts at a quasi-reconciliation between theistic feeling and positive fact, and if speculation were making a fresh start unbiassed by former hypotheses, we should probably substitute for these formulæ a double statement concerning the influence of the whole of natural existence upon man, and the feeling of man towards natural existence.

In discussing the natural growth of human feelings of moral obligation, we have already had to recognise the existence of a kind of natural selection among the tendencies of individuals, which allows, in preference, those to survive which are conducive to the true good or perfection of things in general, because these are sustained, objectively by the tendency of other individuals towards their own several goods, and subjectively by the sympathy of kindred things with the same goal of natural good, while evil propensities are resisted at once by other evil, as well as by all good. The means for any action, of which the end is perfection, are normally subservient to the good or perfection of other things than the agent, and accordingly

[1] " Daher der Völker löblicher Gebrauch,
    Dass jeglicher das Beste, was er kennt,
    Er Gott, ja seinen Gott benennt."

moral action develops, and moral temperament includes a disposition to approve and sympathise with all the best tendencies in the natural world. These tendencies are not persons or entities, but they are perfectly natural and legitimate objects of feeling, and in proportion to the sensibility of men to those natural influences which "make for righteousness" will be their affection for the powers which have called and chosen them for the service of the Best, *i.e.*, their religious reverence for the Supreme Not-self. The intensity of a passion depends upon the power of the subject for feeling intensely as well as upon the qualities of the object felt about; but human feeling is, as a rule, conditioned by the permanent relations and qualities of things real, and it is certain that men and women have had real and strong feelings about and towards that which they call God. A rationalist would deny that any one ever loved his God more intensely than men and women have loved each other, and it may at least be maintained without offence that the strong and tender love of David and Jonathan is more religious than the affection of a modern rationalist for the *Universum*. We can fill in more or less clearly the steps by which all the normal human affections were developed, and we can understand how, when developed and become part and parcel of the nature of a well-born man, they seek objects for themselves, and in case of need (*sic vos non vobis*) pour themselves out towards imaginary constructions, spiritual entities or abstract conceptions. We may argue that men have more power of reverencing than any living man can fairly call forth by his real merits, that they have more power of loving than can be reasonably exercised upon the general scheme of creation with its manifold unamiable imperfections ; still men and nature have made each man what he is, and he has no choice but to divide between man and nature all the outflow of religious sentiment which he can rationally entertain. Some natures have inherited through a fortunate set of spiritual antecedents almost infinite capabilities of tenderness and charm, but it does not follow that their personal history will be correspondingly happy, and that the material chances of life will bring the finest feelings within reach of ideal objects of devotion. The familiar forms of erotic mysticism, which are rightly condemned as morbid, owe their existence to this combination of a rationally conditioned *besoin d'aimer* with material restrictions on the reasonable indulgence of the want. Men argue that there must be a perfect God because they have feelings that suffer a painful check unless there is : they feel as if they could love infinitely and without reserve, and they cannot accept without a sense of sacrifice the conditions under which alone this power of theirs can be exercised with unmixedly good result. It is easier to a loving nature to love, even though the object is unworthy, than to check the pleasant self-abandonment of affection by a just estimate of the moral qualities of the beloved; but here also the pleasant and the good are not identical, and at the risk of appearing harsh, we should maintain that to love an evil thing well is not conducive to moral sanity. We do not say that the universe is evil, but there is evil in it, and without moral obtuseness or mental obliquity man cannot abandon himself to the rapturous adoration of creative power which assumes all its handiwork to be "very good."

Religion, viewed from outside, might be described as the control exercised over men by their affection for the good ; viewed from within, it *is* the very affection for the good which controls them. The only difference between personal religion—as the term is generally understood— and private saint and hero worship, or even a sufficiently strong secular attachment, is that in the one case the controlling power or superiority which is recognised by affection, is a superiority to the subject in its own kind ; the object of regard is apprehended directly as a moral agent, and is capable of exercising a direct moral influence by ordinary human means; while in the other case of mystical religion, the mind has to supply from its own associations all that is moral in the sentiment with which it responds to the harmonious impression that it receives from the Not-self along a thousand unexplored channels. Why the response is naturally affectionate may be inquired later if the point seems to call for more explanation than the naturally harmonious character of the consciousness of harmony. The issue between religion, theistic or otherwise, and positive irreligion or impiety, is virtually, whether this response of natural affection towards the sum of moral influences in the Not-man is rational or not, whether the inward bent of feeling should be resisted as well as the outer current of its direction controlled? and it is hardly worth while to set up a man of straw, like the atheist of modern theologians, to argue in the face of fact that there is no good, and in the face of reason that men "ought" to be indifferent or adverse in their feelings towards what good there is.

The question why, in merely personal affection, there should be a suggestion of religious infinitudes, belongs, however, to this stage of the discussion, the rather that a satisfactory answer to it would almost amount to a verification of the rest of the theory. Science proceeds from the near to the remote, and if the strongest feeling of men for a known mistress is generically akin to their strongest feeling for the unknown God, the explanation of the more accessible phenomenon will go some way towards elucidating the other. It has often been observed, amongst others by Rousseau, that the enthusiasm of devotion borrows the language of love, as the enthusiasm of love borrows the language of devotion; and unless the language is out of place in one or other context, there must be some real similarity between the conditions which inspire its use.

It is easy to be cynical concerning the physical basis of emotion, and every one of sound mind and sane morals with a normal physical constitution will sometimes observe in himself the working of an organic predisposition to feel, quite distinct from, and perhaps at variance with, the present suggestion of appropriate external stimuli. The so-called *besoin d'aimer* is an obvious illustration, but the remark applies equally to every form of ambition, cupidity, or attachment, in fact to every kind of relationship between the emotional self and its surroundings. The thrill of undefined, unmotived aspiration which is so common in youth—and so commonly starved to death in maturity—is an inheritance of the same kind; there is the developed desire and the latent ability to work towards ideal aims, only the ends are hidden and the openings blocked, and few have strength and insight to clear the path for themselves. But when the subjective predisposition coincides with the external stimulus, there arises a vital sense of wellbeing, which it is unreasonable to scorn because of its composite antecedents. Those who are fortunate in their natural life glorify the physical basis for the sake of its spiritual developments; those who are not fortunate depreciate the development by dwelling on the baseness of its origin; while disinterested science places the goal of good neither at the beginning nor at the end, but in the harmony of the whole process of development, whence the succeeding joys of natural life are born.

And there are not two opinions in the human race as to which is the most intense and rapturous of these joys. The life of the world and the life of the individual go on side by side, but the supreme happiness of the individual is to feel his own life intensified, rounded, sustained, and sweetened by the spontaneous favour of that which is around and above him. It is not easy for ordinary minds to recognise their own most cherished experiences under the terms of an exact scientific description, and many who might be disposed to ridicule, as chill pedantry, Spinoza's definition of the divinest love, yet know no more intense feeling than that "gladness attended with the idea of an external cause" which they are as little able as he was to analyse further. Liking may be reasonable, reducible to motive, just as obedience or resistance to the natural order of the world may be motived, but love and worship include too much to be themselves included in a phrase; the strongest motives may fail to call them forth, and when they have come into being they seem able to defy at least an apparent absence of motive for their persistence. What pleasure is to the senses or to the animal life, that love is to the imagination and the emotional life—an irreducible, final contentment of natural taste; with this difference however, whence perhaps our readiness to apply to the latter feeling alone the epithet religious—that human beings delight in possessing the pleasures of their choice, and in being possessed by the love of their choice.

The subjective element, which causes one person to be affected by one type of physical or moral beauty and another by a different or opposite type, leaves the bare common fact of affection unexplained, and we need seek no further motive for it than the acquired susceptibility of mankind. The utmost we can do is to find a quasi-rational basis for the inference which brings mind and will under subjection to the passions, when these have outrun knowledge and experience in their intuition of the best. That love is the answer of the soul to the touch of the Infinite —or something more poetical to that effect—has been said so often by poets and philosophers that poets and philosophers in a critical and irreligious age begin to have a scruple about repeating the time-honoured sentiment. But if we suppose the mind to have acquired, in the course of continuously varying contact with things external to itself, the power and even a correlative inclination to receive an indefinite number of heterogeneous impressions, it is evident that the strongest impressions of an infinite external existence to which the mind is likely to rise, would be given by the miscellaneous revival of all past harmonious impressions if it could be effected, rather than by a new concrete impression, however rich or agreeable.

The conditions of the inward impression need not be reproduced, provided some indirect suggestion brings the consciousness round to a state answering to that which it would have left behind if objectively associated with every kind of welcome or exalted influence at once.

But we are much too far from understanding even the ordinary relations between thought and feeling to have a right to be surprised at the discovery that it is often in the form of a human being, an Other-self, that the Not-self acts most compendiously, forcibly, and suggestively upon the consciousness of the self. From the remotest star disclosed by the telescope to the strangest depths of joy or pain in human consciousness, whatever within the universe is, is felt, known, done, or believed, has an influence within the universe that may be gathered together with innumerable others alike and different into the focus of consciousness of a single human brain. And if we suppose a mind, incapable of rising to a direct intuition of the Not-self as a moral force, to come in contact with another more richly endowed, more highly organised than itself, with, in fact, a human superior; since new faculties can scarcely be improvised for the occasion, it is natural to suppose that the influence of the superior mind or character will make itself felt by stimulating and reviving pre-existing faculties and susceptibilities. The self, seeing in the mirror of another consciousness as much of the still larger Not-self as it is capable of being moved towards, comprehends the mirror and the reflection in one act of devout recognition, and thrills, according to its extremely finite capacity, with an *Ahnung* of the Infinite.

Of course this account of the matter is slightly idealised; it has more in common with Plato's inspired friendship or Leopardi's "Son of the Celestial Venus" than with the loves of earthly men and women, but it explains the fact for which an explanation has long been sought, that a restless sense of liberated faculty and unappropriated emotion commonly attends the growth of any strong personal attachment, and that both, failing other channels of expression, exhaust themselves in representing the merits of the beloved in terms of universal perfection. That love and worship are practically indistinguishable when either reaches a given degree of intensity, is a fact which can only be taken as we find it, but the moral tendency of both moods is unmistakable; while the latter normally begins with a recognition of superiority, the former presupposes a community of feeling which is in itself a step towards equality, and as the more complete the community, or sympathy, the more intense the love, it follows that perfect equality between both lovers is the condition of worship which assumes the superiority of one, or, if the relation is absolutely ideal, of each at once to the other. But when the ideal is exalted as well as loved, the lover is drawn after in pursuit[1] of the purity or grandeur he has, it may be, dreamt into the image of the beloved, and analyse the process as cynically as we will, it remains true that character and conduct are gainers by all such visions of "the eternal marriage of love and duty." Of course the fraction of the Not-self which most people, even with this kind of assistance, are capable of apprehending, is humiliatingly small, but it is a further confirmation of our view that imperfectly or unequally developed natures naturally attach themselves to persons whose character is supplementary as well as sympathetic to their own, and

[1] So Petrarch to his love :—

"Sai quel che per seguirti ho già sofferto:
E tu pur via di poggio in poggio sorgi
Di giorno in giorno ; e di me non t' accorgi,
Che son si stanco, e 'l sentir m' e tropp' erto.
Ben vegg'io di lontano il dolce lume
Ove per aspre vie mi sproni, e giri ;
Ma non ho come tu, da volar piume."

In this sonnet aspiration happens to break down into a touch of despair, but more often love, like faith, works the desired miracles—or causes them to be taken as worked.

M

can therefore interpret to them a part of existence that would otherwise escape their vision altogether.

The attempt made in the present century by an eminent mathematician and philosopher to invent a religion without any supernatural assistance, has so much in common with other attempts of the same kind that claim a higher origin, as to confirm the opinion that it is permanently natural to men to have some kind or other of religious faith and worship. Comte was much too positive a thinker to be seduced into pantheism, too rational to confound subject and object in mysticism. With an ardour for intellectual system that in his works makes the organisation of knowledge seem almost more of an end than its possession or use, the only entity superior to himself in the power of assimilating and digesting real knowledge whom he could recognise, was the human race, and for this being his rare powers of abstraction allowed him to feel a genuine sentiment of veneration, which rose to religious affection when the human race became associated in his meditations with the memory of a lady who had enriched his intuition of the Not-self by striking a disused or silent chord in his emotional nature. But there are two reasons why the religion of humanity can hardly be expected to take the place of the other dogmatic religions with which it aims at competing. Positive thinkers would scarcely wish it to be professed with the unintelligent formalism with which the doctrines of older sects are held by the immense majority of their adherents, and it cannot be seriously expected that now, or for centuries to come, any considerable number of men, to say nothing of women, should have either the ideas or the instruction presupposed in a vital, personal conception of humanity as an organic whole, ageless and formless, with a life centred everywhere, a consciousness centred nowhere, and a growth conditioned —the religion does not say by what. Without such a conception the religion becomes an affair of empty phrases, altogether powerless to influence the conduct in the way desired by its founder. With such a conception, no doubt, something of fresh, perhaps religious significance is added to the ordinary consciousness of life, as was done by the early Christian doctrines of communion and membership of the saints in Christ, while they rested upon the intuitions of brotherly charity, not on an ecclesiastical tradition. The Comtist calendar and the metaphysical doctrine of "subjective immortality" are only ways of saying that our affections are independent of time and space, and that spiritual influences are undying in their effects. Most people have had at one time or another some private patron saint, alive or dead, who has been the object, perhaps all unconsciously, of as much fervent adoration as was ever directed towards canonised martyr, idol, or supreme spiritual power. Some have felt as if it were, so to speak, a personal favour to themselves that Socrates was wise, that St. Francis was poor, that Bayard was without fear and without reproach; there is even something religious in the way that the heart of a weary sceptic goes out towards Bruno, with affectionate envy to think that a man could be burnt for anything so certain as the Copernican system. A knowledge of the truth that some heroes, saints, and sages being dead yet speak, does naturally bring about a closer sense of the intellectual solidarity of the race, and does stimulate those who are yet alive in their turn to seek to say such words as they may be content to have survive them. The religion of the future, though it may dispense with a calendar and leave the celebration of centenaries to secular patriotism and enterprise, will always have to acknowledge a debt to Comte for having shown that the men of all times, as well as of all places, are held together by a tie of intellectual brotherhood which it is an element of intellectual strength for them to recognise. But the great Being, Humanity, however great our small powers will allow of our conceiving it to be, is still not supreme, and we do not find in the past that men have been content knowingly to worship "Ein Theil des Theils, der Anfangs alles war "— a single product of evolution, instead of all its absolute, infinite, irresponsible conditions. It was objected to dualism that the strength of the religious sentiment was much impaired by the conception of an internecine division between the powers of the Not-self, and the sentiment would probably disappear altogether if its natural object were that fraction of the Not-self which can scarcely be conceived as most powerful. Even at the present day, the former history of the race, though it may be one of the chief forces, is infinitely far from being the only force that moulds the life of a single man, and the arbitrary preference of one force out of the many upon which the individual consciously depends, is repugnant to the religious instinct which is always feeling its way towards a goal of absolute submission. Modern rationalists, like Strauss, who make religion consist in dependence upon the Universum, modern mystics, like Schleiermacher, who make it consist in the sense of dependence on the Unknown, and orthodox theologians, who place its essence in willing obedience to the Creator's will,—all represent the sentiment as possessing a kind of absolute, inevitable adaptation to its object which is wanting to the religion of humanity, unless it is allowed to borrow cogency from merely moral considerations.

Perhaps truth is in some degree sacrificed to system when we attempt to keep the boundary line between morality and religion clearly marked; but it holds true in general that morality is concerned with the conduct, religion with the emotions; that morality consists in the consciousness of voluntary bondage, religion in the consciousness of a subjective release from all bondage. The moral precepts, which are obeyed by many, are not deduced from the religious sentiments, which are experienced by few; but the connection long assumed to exist between morality and religion is not the less real because the order of it has been inverted, for it is by the acceptance of the most abstract conclusions of morality that the mind is prepared to receive the intuitions of religion. The fruit of religious culture is a disposition to do the good without compulsion, without inducement, by an instinct that does not stop to choose or reason, and on that very account is able to override the force of impeding motives. We act by reason and rational necessity; we feel by instinct; and our feeling will be sane if our habitual conduct is so; and if our feeling is sane, all that we do under the influence of feeling will be right and good, and sometimes better than what could be suggested by any present reasonable motive. But it by no means follows from this estimate of religious feeling that feeling in general is the most trustworthy guide for conduct; it is only the rarefied, disinterested feeling which survives the discipline of moral life, with its lessons of renunciation and detachment, that can—and indeed must—be allowed supreme sway by those who have had grace to become its subjects.

It was seen in the course of the preceding chapter how the disposition of the individual (human) organism to seek its own specific natural good is overruled by the fact that it is placed in a world the natural good of which requires sacrifices, on the part of some of its elements, akin to the partial sacrifices of inclination within the individual enjoined by its own moral nature. The problem of the individual, how to be good of its kind, is modified and complicated, because its kind includes the property of occupying such and such a place in the universe, for its natural good is then, of course, to fill that place in the best possible manner, which is the manner most conducive to the good of the universe, or the human race—after its kind. We must always be the first person in our own action; but as human sensibilities develop, we feel as well as know about things that do not directly concern ourselves. If our personal conduct is sufficiently upright to leave our judgment unbiassed in the appreciation of natural good, all this disinterested feeling and intelligence of the universal good gathers an amount of power which endures even when, for the moment, the universal good demands a special sacrifice; and the habit of making such sacrifices without hesitation or regret is what we chiefly understand by religious perfection.

It may not be very rational that when we find it to be practically impossible to arrange one life, our own, according to our taste, we should turn to the wider, and, as it might seem, more hopeless task of reforming the universe. Yet when the utter impossibility of leading a life of pure personal enjoyment has been empirically demonstrated, what can the disinterested judgment do but direct the will towards the realisation of what it holds to be the best possible world? The irrepressible optimism of humanity comes back, though we drive it forth with the pitchfork of logical dilemma; and many a pious soul, without repining or rebellious intention, seems virtually to say within itself: Since God has not made the best of all possible worlds, *I* will!—and the world is the better, as much the better as material possibility allows, for the resolve. Of course even disinterested zeal may outrun discretion, and the passion for reforming creation, as long as any personal gratification mingles with its indulgence, is liable to be chilled by disappointment and the renewed discovery that, though our actions are in our own power, their consequences are not, so that even the good we would do may miss its aim. The triumph of disinterestedness, which also is moral and necessary, is to labour for the good of the world, even while believing that the labour is in vain, palliative and not remedial, that the world is bad at best, and that all our efforts can but save it from growing worse than it must.

This conception of duty as the active co-operation of the individual will with all the real forces of the universe, in proportion to their reality, may be objected to as visionary and over-abstract, as imposing so vast an obligation that a small human conscience will slip unbound through its meshes—which, indeed, is what generally happens, unless the supreme religious influence of the general tendencies of the Not-self is *felt*, as a clear and present reality, not constraining or controlling the will, but absolutely transforming it, moulding it into acquiescence and conformity with all that exists.

At this point the sceptical reader will probably require all the patience and tolerance of which he may be capable. "Except a man be born again, he cannot enter into the kingdom of God." Jonathan Edwards, and half Christendom with him, repeats, "Without a change of nature, men's practice will not be thoroughly changed;" and the philosophy of the change upon which the New England divine insists, is expounded with great beauty and profundity by a representative of the other half of Christendom, St. John of the Cross, St. Teresa's contemporary and friend, in two treatises of mystical theology, called "The Ascent of Mount Carmel" and "The Obscure Night of the Soul," by the study of which the curious may convince themselves that the disagreement of Christian sects is less radical than they themselves endeavour to believe. Not to multiply examples, the conversion of Tauler by the man Nicholas of Basle, the final awakening of Fräulein von Klettenberg, recorded with Goethe's usual sympathetic realism in "Wilhelm Meister," the new birth of the Calvinists, Mill's reconstruction of his hereditary creed, St. John's "Night of the Soul," are all phases of the same natural and intelligible revolution in the feelings which follows upon the apprehension of a new truth of vital importance, or more commonly, upon some moral crisis which causes an old belief suddenly to acquire fresh force and significance.[1]

---

[1] The suddenness of an illumination of this kind is no argument for its supernatural origin. "Two mathematicians of good repute, both as students and teachers, were referring"—writes Mr. Todhunter in his "Conflict of the Studies"—"to the difficulties which perplex beginners in the Differential Calculus; they agreed in stating that, after groping in the

If we suppose that the thoughts of men do not spring uncaused into lawless activity, but are conditioned by the orderly relations of real existence, it is intelligible that the full effect of a number of connected external influences should remain in abeyance so long as any of them had failed to convey its appropriate impression, but the co-ordination of the impressions follows of itself, too instantaneously to be traced, when the last has been received. A new idea passes the threshold of consciousness at a bound, but the unconscious preparation of the brain for its reception must be reckoned among its premises. And in the same way the sudden revulsion of feeling which may result in a permanent alteration of the character, is itself gradually prepared by successive experiences, not by any means necessarily suggestive, to the judgment of common sense, of their actual emotional *contre-coup*.

All our authorities agree as to the preliminary steps in this spiritual revolution. The certainty that out of all the personal desires entertained by the natural man, an unknown, fixed, and probably large proportion are inevitably doomed to disappointment, does as a fact tend to produce a degree of what Catholics call "detachment" from all, even the most realisable personal aims. Merely morbid asceticism might be compared to the sick distaste for food of a man on the verge of starvation; those to whom healthy pleasures are unknown may set themselves to crush their natural appetites rather than endure the sense of unsatisfied longing, and if they try to make their own privation into a rule for others, the rule is false as well as ungenial. But, taking the world as it is, no character is complete that cannot survive the potential injuries of fortune; and the power of doing without a valued good, if kept alive without enforced exercise, is tribute enough to

dark for some time, light had suddenly appeared, and both regretted that, in spite of many efforts made for the purpose, they could not recollect more than this general outline."

the insecurity of human happiness. A living sense of this insecurity is the first step towards escape from the stupid animal dependence, which is really irreligious, on the natural gifts of fortune. Persons of much moral scrupulousness, whose private desires have proved persistently unrealisable, are tempted to expend the energy thus liberated from the service of appetite in the discharge of all the duties they can discover or invent; but as their powers of doing good are after all finite, and the evil in the world practically infinite, the saint, while still under the law, is oppressed by a deep and painful sense of shortcoming and depravity, as nearly as may be proportionate to the real excellence and purity of his moral disposition. The "conviction of sin," experienced by persons whose moral virtues would stock a regiment of lay philosophers, may be explained as the despair and self-abasement produced by the discovery that even the virtuous impulses of the natural man do not certainly lead their followers to perfect content, or have not force enough to create anew the world which, to natural virtue, seems painfully, intolerably imperfect. Their general disposition was towards what they regarded as good, but particular sacrifices or discrepancies between the possible and the desired were felt as vexatious, and the vexation appeared sinful, as it was accompanied by a general impression that the will of the individual ought to assent to whatever was ordered by the supreme divine will. The attempt to reform the world with the help of radically imperfect, finite, human resources naturally fails, and a very vivid perception of the extent of the failure serves as a Nemesis to chasten the spiritual pride or egotism which could conceive such an ambition.

St. John of the Cross, who treats the subject more intellectually than the Calvinists, represents the obscure night of the soul as a season of complete mental prostration, when all the faculties have been tried and found wanting to effect "a perfect and permanent union in the substance of the soul and its powers." This union or presence of God in the order of nature (we are still paraphrasing the saint) subsists between him and all his creatures, but there is a supernatural union which takes effect when two wills—the will of God and the will of the soul—are conformed together, neither desiring aught repugnant to the other. The soul not being naturally altogether one with God, best attains to this union by being, except for a loving disposition towards assent, altogether blank and colourless. The assent itself (like the illumination of the mathematicians) is seldom or never produced by any one rational consideration; a mass of, as it were, cumulative evidence, of cognate impressions, result at a particular moment in producing the conviction which is complete and effectual as soon as it exists at all. All previously received impressions and beliefs remain the same, but coloured and intensified by the sense of their connection and all-sufficiency. Religious writers insist that there is a fundamental transformation of the will and character, and it seems that the only possible change we can suppose to have occurred, when nothing else is changed in the man, and nothing at all in the perceivable universe, is a change either in his apprehension of the relation subsisting between the two, or a change in the sentiment with which he is affected by the relation as apprehended—in practice the change from a hostile to a friendly disposition towards the real order of the universe. It is the birth of love, the spontaneous opening of the heart to a new affection of loyal devotion, and the affection is as real and irresistible as the personality of its object may be dubious. The change of heart by which the saints felt themselves released at once from the bondage of natural iniquity and of the law of natural morality, may be described as the discovery by a soul that had been out of harmony with its surroundings, that harmony, though not happiness, is possible—at a price; that though the self cannot remodel the universe in conformity to its own best impulses, all its own best impulses can find scope and satisfaction in conformity with true tendencies in the Not-self. Whichever way the change is, the harmony between the soul and its surrounding is preceded, or perhaps rather effected, by a harmonious *consensus* of all the faculties, which, as under the influence of the Platonic love, become the more vigorous and active for their agreement. Such an *Aufklärung* may be gradual, as in the case of Goethe, whose whole life was spent in being savingly converted from the dominion of his strong passions. It is absent altogether from the lives of many even able thinkers who have always been more possessed by the positive aspect of their convictions than by difficulties arising from the relation between them, or from the coexistence of seemingly inconsistent convictions; and to some it is disguised by association with some simple step in their speculative education, with the first apprehension of a pregnant doctrine, or the final adhesion to an impressive system, events that, of course, are only epoch-making in a life chiefly spent in theorising.

Pure science and unreflective action never bring the mind to the religious conviction of its own impotence, which follows from the application of knowledge to conduct, or the attempt to act by reason only, and to give a rational explanation of the impulses followed instinctively. The ascetic discipline which aims at " suppressing desire, even though possession remain," is based upon the experimental discovery that particular attachments impair the general freedom of the soul to follow what it apprehends as divine perfection. The most trustworthy judgments are the most dispassionate and disinterested, and so it is true, as St. John says, that the perfect man first acquires in this detachment from creatures a clear comprehension of them. Rationalists of course will say that the capacity or nature of the soul fixes and limits that which it will apprehend as divine perfection—the Saint himself, for instance, apprehends an All that is merely moral and intellectual, and not so subject to law as to be exactly cognoscible;—but this does not affect the main point, that general perfection and particular appetites are distinct and frequently incompatible. "When thou dwellest upon anything, thou hast ceased to cast thyself upon the All." Even a tyrannical desire to impose upon the Universe conduct which the individual believes to be for its true good is irreligious, unless the ideal has been received from the Not-self as expressive of its real tendencies. Quite in the manner of Spinoza—whom a sound popular instinct has always refused to regard as in any intelligible sense a theist—St. John of the Cross proceeds: "The end of meditation and reflection on the things of God is to elicit the knowledge and love of him. Each time the soul elicits this, it is an act, and as acts, often repeated, produce habits, so may acts of loving knowledge continuously elicited by the soul beget the habit thereof in the course of time." It is remarkable that with a large experience of professed "religious," at a time of religious revival, he repeatedly insists that there are very, very few to whom it is given to reach the last stage of spiritual perfection, in which the truths of religion are conceived as the impression made by the All upon the chastened receptive spirit. Such disinterested cognition, if it were possible, would doubtless impart the highest, most abstract truth, even though we suppose it to be still received by merely human faculties; it is as natural and conceivable for the mind to have a true intuition of the universal as of the particular, for both are in a way external to consciousness, neither its merely arbitrary creation, though reasoning may have to be suspended as well as sense and passion, because the subject is too wide for it until the intuition is complete, when it represents the individual as belonging not to itself to be made the best of for its own sake, but to the world, to be made what use of it can, even though, as the stern realism of the Calvinists saw sometimes befell, it be elected to serve the All by its perdition.

The order of the Universe does not appear to the natural reason of man to be so good that we should co-operate in its "purposes" of our own accord, by choice, unless we must. But of all necessities, this is the most indefeasible, while we live we co-operate, when we die our salts and phosphates go on co-operating, and the influence of our actions is immortal. The human will cannot change the past, but it is one of the natural forces that regulate the future, and it does so according to its apprehension of the present, which is coloured by the sympathies born of a hard experience. The world is the saints', not to possess, but to mend, or at least to alter, and in altering they still co-operate with the "stream of tendency" which has brought to pass that just this generation affirms such and such alterations to be good. The sense of a common misfortune, if life is all calamity, of a common interest in one work, if the race is on the whole not ill-content to go on discharging its natural functions in the scheme of the universe, may no doubt contribute something of religious spontaneity to the life of the social organism by leading men to spare each other and themselves the gratuitous addition to their troubles of destructive rivalry and internecine strife. There were three Christian graces, "and the greatest of these is Charity"—whose existence has the guarantee of necessity, though faith and hope, the pretty parasites of imperfect knowledge, were to vanish in the fuller light of science from a world of realists who would rather see than imagine, and rather be strong to bear what they see than dazzle their eyes with looking into a visionary future. For ourselves certainly, sufficient unto the day is the evil thereof, which makes it probable that all the best energies of most of us will no more than suffice to ensure that the world shall not be the worse for our co-operation, that we have not caused more suffering than we have eased, exacted more service than we have rendered, devoured more of the common patrimony than our labour has replaced. No one would willingly live, die, and leave no sign but a little addition to the mass of human misery, and the danger seems nearer to us than when we believed. The material evil in the world, which men are but little concerned in producing, may be the condition of human progress, and the progress of the kind is its own good, but not Omnipotence itself could cause that good should ever come out of what we call moral evil, except always at the cost of greater good lost. It is because moral evil exists that the Creator of the Universe—if a Universe could have a Creator—could not be esteemed a moral agent.

Piety towards the Universe is the result of a mighty synthesis, towards which moral generalities take us but little way. It is not a moral duty to feel an affection for the solar and the stellar systems, to wax enthusiastic over the properties of space or to admire the circuitous processes in the evolution of life. The emotions are free; but it is certainly a misfortune, and probably an imperfection, to have so little sympathy with the natural order of which we form a part as to take no pleasure in its comparatively successful achievements, and to feel only unhelpful concern when, as but too often happens, evolution halts and limps, law is burdensome, progress imperceptible, and though the poor world may be doing her best, we yet can scarcely persuade ourselves that her best is "very good." But exactly at this point we have a fellow-feeling that must end in charitable indulgence; "the whole creation groaneth and travaileth together," and perhaps the solar system is as near being good after its kind as mortal astronomers and critics after theirs; at least it bears its aberrations in dignified silence, which the puling tribe of pessimists might do well to imitate.

The natural relation of man to the Universe is one of dependence, and the immense majority of men are so simply and unreflectingly a part of the general order in which they live and move and have their being, that it does not occur to them to cavil or rebel against it; their co-operation is spontaneous, but too unemotional to be called religious. It might be argued that such a healthy state of nature was preferable to the state of grace which we have been endeavouring to comprehend. Unintelligent co-operation has its drawbacks, but it may be doubted whether the mind is really strengthened by anything so abstract as considerations concerning the manner in which the sacrifices imposed by the co-operation are made necessary. But when the necessity has once been questioned, since it does not therefore cease to exist, the mind must follow its natural course if the primitive *consensus* is ever to be restored upon a surer foundation. When the attempt of the individual to dominate the world, to make it and its inhabitants the tools of private ends and objects, is given up as impracticable, the antagonism between the self and the Not-self ceases, and the will is reconciled. It becomes conscious of the tendency, not its own, which has made it, and as will, to our knowledge, is only conscious tendency, this is the very identification of the single will with the tendency of the All that is the note of true religion.

The emotion accompanying this acquiescence of the will is one of not untender loyalty. Ancient prophets and modern preachers have tried to enlist the same feeling by calling on a generous congregation to come "to the help of the Lord, to the help of the Lord against the mighty." But the Lord of hosts, we feel, could fight his own battles. The universe really needs our help to make itself as good as it can, and it is to the influence of the universe that we owe whatever power or will we have to co-operate in what we judge to be its true tendencies. We are "a part of its involuntary, palpitating life," and if we are not with it, we are against it. Those in whom these natural influences at times call forth the emotional response which makes the inevitable co-operation seem spontaneous and easy, do not therefore live for ever after in a religious trance. The attempt to reproduce an intense feeling of the solidarity of all existence, when it does not naturally present itself, is a waste of good volitional force. No doubt when the religious emotion fails, the burden of moral duty and the consciousness of moral and natural imperfection becomes again oppressive; but the universe does not exist for the sake of satisfying the religious instincts of mankind, and reason shows that the surest way of preserving the fading sense of harmony between the soul and nature is to make the harmony the more complete, to keep the soul attuned to the tendencies of the Not-self by constant action in obedience to its leadings.

Deus sive Natura—as Spinoza calls the whole of real Being—is not an evil genius; it is a vast system that lives and prospers in proportion as the strength of its various elements can be brought into alliance, and form mutually sustaining relations. There is good enough in the world to stir the affections of those who see it all, and those whose life is spent in active self-identification with all the powers of the universe for good, waste least time in reflecting upon the evil which they are constantly, as it were, leaving behind them. Even if we could persuade ourselves that what is highest and best in man is not his own, not our veritable nature, but a loan, a foreshadowing of something quite outside ourself and our world, the good in this world would still be neither more nor less; and it would in like manner be neither more nor less even though theologians should discover that they had made mistakes about that other world, concerning which they candidly admit themselves to have no direct knowledge. Philosophy can no more make morality easy than surgery can make diseases wholesome, but it certainly does nothing to shake the religious affection of men for that which they naturally believe to be the chief of all earthly goods, the goodness of men and women: tender strength, generous forbearance, disinterested wisdom, and passionate love are good—no true believer in the unknown God, ignorantly worshipped by divers names, will dare to doubt it—and no one who has known and felt for himself that they are good can think that the world in which they are to be found, enjoyed, and increased is quite a howling wilderness, though it be only our world, and not an antechamber to heaven or hell.

One point remains to be considered. Religion is natural, and in the main always the same, that is to say, a spirit of devout and affectionate acquiescence in the will of a superior power; but we may ask, is the existence and strength of this sentiment equally natural and equally necessary to moral and natural perfection in all generations, or is there any natural excuse or justification for the temper of an irreligious age? Is the strength of the religious sentiment an essential part of that natural perfection which we conceive to be the *summum bonum*? Is a Christian, with a strong sense of piety towards the unseen powers of the Not-self, humanly speaking, better than an atheist, who judges the universe to be too imperfect after its kind to call forth feelings of religious devotion or love? In a word, is irreligion a moral defect in man?

This is a practical question, which should offer little difficulty if we were clear both as to our facts and our principles. The natural good of man consists in the abundance of active and perceptive powers; moral good consists in the deliberate and disinterested pursuit of natural good, *quand même* the pursuit is naturally hard; civilised religion is the loving worship of the strongest power known as Not-self, when this power is exerted in behalf of moral good, *i.e.*, of man's pursuit of natural good *quand même*. Now it is a question of fact whether the stream of natural tendency is always equally helpful to the moral struggles of individuals in each generation, and it is a further question of fact, whether men are at all times equally well aware of the real extent of the help thus given to them. In tracing the history of morality, we found that morality was easy when ideals were stationary, and difficult when they were progressive. Of course ease and difficulty are terms relating to human consciousness, and to feel a difficulty more, even if it continues objectively of the same size, is really to be less helped, by things in general, to overcome it, than is the case when the difficulty is less felt. Therefore piety is more natural, and rests on more reasonable grounds, in ages when the powers and desires are pretty accurately balanced, than in periods of transition, when the aspirations have outrun the faculties, or the faculties have fallen off from the standard which contented earlier aspirations. Now it cannot be a part of man's perfection to cherish illusions concerning his relations to the Not-self, and at times when the course of nature does not make high virtue easy to any one, unreserved piety towards the natural order or its author argues a mind contented with less than the highest virtue, *i.e.*, naturally imperfect. The optimism of philosophers and divines in the eighteenth century, when content with low ideals was general, might serve as an illustration.

The religion of a critical, progressive age is more complicated, intellectual, and disinterested, but it is less devout and less personal than that of simpler, more primitive times. We recognise the force of the moral obligations which the whole past of mankind unites in causing us to recognise, we share the ideas and aspirations correlative to our feeling of obligation, and without any unpractical fatalism, we see that the weakness as well as the strength of what we hold to be best in our moral nature is the product of natural causes, before which we were, literally, helpless as the unborn babe, but this consciousness in no way affects the fully developed moral sentiments of our maturity. In dispassionately recognising the responsibility of the past for having lived so indifferently that we, its heirs, are no better than we should be, we do not lose sight of our inherited conviction that it is best to be as good as we can; and as the strength as well as the weakness of our better nature is conditioned by past and present modifications of the Not-self, if on the whole our strength is greater than our weakness, we feel that "the Lord is on our side," that the stream of tendency is with us, that we are with it, a part of it, and that the current of human affairs sets the stronger in the direction of predestined progress for being reinforced by all the power of our intelligent will. Thus to a thoroughly healthy and energetic nature, impiety is an impossibility, a self-contradiction, for if moral good consists in the struggle after an attainable Better, the universe which has imparted strength for the struggle, cannot be felt as bad.

To some minds with an irresistible craving after peace and the mental rest of an absolute attachment, this will seem enough to warrant positive thinkers in transferring to the Universe the affection felt by Theists for the object of their worship, and it is by no means needful to argue away any spontaneous enthusiasm or tenderness with which enthusiastic or tender souls may be affected towards the natural order of the world; if the feeling exists it is because the elements proper to elicit it have a real existence also, and it is not necessary (or possible) for every one to have the feeling appropriate to the fullest knowledge of the conditions of our natural and spiritual being. But, on the other hand, it is neither necessary nor desirable for those who have a clear and adequate idea of these conditions to argue themselves into stronger feelings of devotion than are spontaneous. The complete harmony between all the powers of the mind—which makes religious enthusiasm possible—is a good; and if we were content with a merely subjective standard of good, such as happiness or content, it might seem the supreme good, so that religious teachers might agree with Utilitarians (as indeed they often have) in urging men to restrain those unruly desires and impulses which are not predestined to full present gratification, and therefore perpetuate the irreligious temper of partial rebellion against that which is. But if our standard of perfection is progressive, and includes the maximum of objective relations between the self, society, and nature, the harmony of the moral energies, which gives religious peace, will no more appear to be the supreme end of our being than the harmony of our natural powers, which gives sensible pleasure. The harmony is a good, only attainable by those who are, naturally or morally, good of their kind; but the discord of one generation may be richer than the harmony of another, and the true test of comparison is to judge whether the irreligious age has so much more of other positive good in it as to compensate for the misfortune of irregular, unequal development among its various elements.

This is only one more variation on the familiar theme that the possession of good and the enjoyment of good are not naturally identical. The individual is not always pleasurably conscious of the sympathy which exists between himself and the outer world; he may be most painfully conscious of an imperfect sympathy, which is as different from antipathy as a lovers' quarrel is from dislike. The victim of this unfortunate state is objectively more nearly at one with the external order than if he had narrower sympathies and no wishes or ideas beyond them. Religious blessedness consists in the pleasurable consciousness of the maximum of real sympathy with the moral tendencies of the Not-self, religious perfection in the maximum of such sympathy *quand même* it is not complete enough for enjoyment; and if this be so, it is clear that men may approach to religious excellence without possessing the moral self-satisfaction called religious peace, as they may approach to moral excellence without possessing the physical self-satisfaction known as natural pleasure or happiness.

Of course it is open to any one to say that they do not mean by secular or religious happiness what we have here offered as the definition of those words, but if so we have a right to ask for an alternative definition which shall include a greater number of the marks which we know belong to the things defined. It will be said that the essence of religion is perfect faith and trust in God, that if there is no God, there can be no religion, that there is a God, and that therefore those who wrongly believe that there is none, are by their own wrong-doing left without religion. We do not attempt to argue with persons of strong religious feeling, whose feeling is associated with an equally strong conviction of the truth of some theistic dogma; we address ourselves rather to the many persons of undetermined views, to whom the chief argument for the existence of a deity is that men have generally believed in one or more, and who rather believe themselves to have the same belief as their neighbours than possess any intimate "saving" sense of its truth. To these we submit the following considerations as a ground for transferring their languid adhesion from one body of believers to another.

Men naturally have feelings answering to the sum of impressions made on them by the moral aspects of the Not-self, *i.e.*, by the Not-self in its relations to their moral life; the impression produced by a cause only known through this impression calls forth a feeling about—or towards—the cause, and men do not naturally and at once distinguish between simple and multiple causes of simple and multiple effects. The act of will of a given person may have many consequences, and human feelings towards the agent vary—even more than is strictly reasonable—in accordance with the result of his act; because his act is the *sine qua non* of the event, all the other conditions which helped to determine its character are left out of sight; and conversely, if a variety of acts and accidents contribute equally to produce an effect that affects us as one, we naturally feel as if all the co-operating forces were somehow connected, made one, for its production; they are involuntarily, as it were instinctively, identified in the mind; by a kind of synthesis of the imagination, what is felt as one is supposed to act as one, and is then felt towards as if it acted with a real individuality, and were personally responsible to us for the feelings and the emotions which it calls up in us.

Thus it is that men have come to have strong and intense feelings towards beings that are the creation of their own imagination—as entities, though there are realities to which the feelings are due. But we have to distinguish between the religion which consists mainly in sentiments towards the Not-self, and the religious temper which is wholly subjective, and consciously so. Atheistical religion consists of religious faith, zeal, and love, without an object of worship. We have not deliberately chosen a definition of religion which should include the development of a sentiment without external object; but we cannot justify the existence of the religious sentiment *with* a supposed object, except by reasoning which serves equally well to explain its existence when criticism has shown the supposed object to be a thing of the mind.

Like all other sincere religion, atheistical religion has two parts, the intense inward feeling and the outward yearning or aspiration, both different phases of one mental state, that is, of a state with identical past and indivisible future. The inward feeling, which Spinoza calls acquiescence, is the consciousness of harmony in all the higher powers of the soul, which is only attainable, at least with fully developed consciousness, when the soul is in harmony with its objective surroundings, and this is a state of passive, exalted beatitude; it is a grateful consciousness of what the soul is in relation to the Not-self, *i.e.*, a participator in its best and strongest tendencies; not—if the reader will have patience with such subtleties—a consciousness of the participation, but a general sense of peace and wellbeing, which proves on examination to be the result of this harmonious participation.

The spiritual reward of religious perfection may not always be equally accessible, but the alternative, if it fails, is not impiety, only a different manifestation of the religious spirit, active instead of contemplative. Supposing the maximum of objective sympathy between the individual and the natural tendencies of his age to be positively and comparatively small, he may be painfully conscious of discrepancy between the aspirations and the achievement of himself and his best contemporaries, but the aspirations after perfection are to the full as natural as the imperfect achievement, and either way of approaching to the desired sympathy is good. If circumstances trace a possible and satisfying ideal, the religious duty of the soul will be obedience, but if, on the contrary, the environment appears in consciousness as a check, a hindrance to the perfection of the soul, then obedience is time-serving and not religious; and though it may be said, with truth, that rebellion against some existing realities may be an act of obedience to the highest spiritual influences of the Not-self, which are at least equally real, still it is naturally impossible for acts of an opposite kind to be performed in the same spirit, even though they have the one element of dutifulness in common: and to feeling no two attitudes can be more unlike than that of resisting and yielding to the nearest external tendency.

The distinction which we should be inclined to draw between the religious spirit of a critical or progressive age and one contentedly stationary is only this. In what are called the ages of faith, men live by sight, in sight of realised ideals, satisfying objects of worship exist for them. In what are called ages of unbelief, men must live, if they are to have any spiritual life at all, by faith in unseen ideals, and for them idolatry or the worship of anything that is known or clearly imaginable is a sin against the spirit of perfection. The works of the spirit are always the same, or at least always alike, but man's relation to the spiritual influences of the natural world and his conscious affection towards them may vary. Hence it is that religion takes different forms, and those who look for it in the costume of three or five centuries ago may fail to recognise it in its contemporary garb. Nevertheless religious minds at the present day are as far as ever from being content to think that the truth is only a fiction agreed upon, and that the future may agree upon a lie. Our premises do not compel us to accept as a natural law, a necessity following from the nature of things, the tendency which we observe in human beliefs to oscillate from prejudice to denial, and from the criticism of one error to the construction of another. We may have a just sense of past compulsion and present instigation without disguising our ignorance of what lies in front of us or pretending to limit the future to conformity with our theories; and yet we want a theory of theories to bind together every age and make our faith reasonable. We have not to attain the ideal of a thousand years hence, or of a thousand years ago; we have ideals now, though most of us are ashamed to own it, and it is the ideal of to-day that we have to pursue with religious faith and zeal. The *summum bonum* is the best possible growth, and the perfection to be sought in every age is the best growth of human power and sensibility possible to that age, and we know no formula that serves better than this to justify the perpetual pursuit of a changing goal, which seems to be the condition of healthy life.

But, it will perhaps be said, if there is nothing better *in rerum natura* than the noblest of living men or women, what have they to aspire after? If there is no God holding an ideal in front of them, to which it is their duty to be conformed, what sense is there in the passionate struggle after ideals, which no one will go to hell for not reaching, which no one *can* reach, which no one will go to heaven for endeavouring to reach? In this way the *advocatus diaboli* describes the never-ending circle of objection: what motives have we for acting in accordance with natural causes? what causes us to follow natural motives? Why —meaning for what motive or inducement—are we reasonable, law-keeping creatures? Why—still meaning for what motive—are we moved by other inducements than the promise of reward, temporal or eternal? and again, when reason good has been shown in the natural history of our susceptibilities for the existence of disinterested emotions and aspirations, Why—meaning for what cause—are we led by this or that motive, which we are not *conscious* of any reason for following except that we are spontaneously moved to do so?

In the ordinary transactions of life, the "why" of conduct and feeling admits of being indefinitely put off, one reason after another may be alleged, while leaving us as far as ever from the ultimate root of things. It is only when we have forced ourselves to the highest generalisation of all that it becomes impossible to shirk the question in its most trying form. Do we—do I the thinker—feel at this present moment in my inmost soul that I have sufficient reasons and irresistible motives for doing that which the stream of natural causation, culminating in my will and actual circumstances, has determined me to do? Put in this form the question answers itself, but in many minds at the present day there is latent an uneasy doubt as to whether—not now for themselves, but in general for everybody—natural causes can be trusted to supply efficient motives for the choice of right action. One of the many attractions of theism is that its adherents, when they do not really *feel* as if they had sufficient reasons or motives for being or doing their best, can nevertheless turn the scale in theory by supposing real but inadequate motives to be reinforced at need by contributions from the vaguely imagined infinitudes of supernatural sanction. As Mephistopheles observes: "An Worte lässt sich trefflich glauben;" and the mere name of a deliverer affords spiritual consolation, if not practical help. But it is becoming increasingly hard to believe in false gods, while the moral and spiritual nature of many is craving for a believable truth; and if God is only a name for "the Best we know," the sooner we learn not to trust in names, but to attach ourselves to the Real Best, the better for our spiritual welfare.

The natural history of morality accounts for the sense of obligation in particular cases, for the fact that when men have to choose between right and wrong, they feel more or less bound to prefer the right. But even those who accept this naturalistic explanation of the simple precepts of the moral law, often speak as if some further supernatural power were required to explain why men should prefer an abstract right, so as to go out of their way to imagine duties not sensibly imposed by circumstances; why they should love the right for its own sake, and instead of following the lead of circumstances, seek to remodel circumstances into a form admitting of a better right for themselves and those to come; why the taste becomes the accomplice of the will, and the edifice of obligation is voluntarily extended beyond its necessary foundations. But religion, as we understand it, is a matter of natural feeling; natural feeling is the product of constant natural or necessary sequences, and to feel on all points with the best and strongest tendencies of the Notself *is* to feel the sufficiency, as motive, of those natural facts which are the efficient cause or *sine qua non* of that which is about to happen with the co-operation of the will. In other words, a man who is at once moral and religious does not ask what is the good of morality, or demand a god to praise and recompense him; he acts virtuously under a natural sense of obligation, and his habitual state of feeling is favourable, not adverse, to the existence of such obligations as he owns: he does not wish for a different kind of liberty from that which he possesses by natural grace, the liberty to will nobly and well.

But, it will perhaps be said, this religion of ours is a fair-weather creed: that nature, in the form of the world, the flesh, and the devil, is by no means always on the side of man in his struggles after what is Best. To many it seems hard to believe in a truth which calls no *Deus ex machina* to the rescue of human souls in trouble or temptation. The powers of darkness are as real, albeit as impersonal, as the divine principles of truth, purity, and loving-kindness, and man seems in evil case alone between the conflict of superhuman tendencies, his deliverance hard to believe in. But no Gospels have ever yet been preached according to which it was easy to have a saving faith; and our faith has as much power as another to save human souls in trouble and temptation; the difficulty lies only in attaining to the faith—that man alone, for his own sake and the sake of his fellows, freely desires and necessarily labours to attain the measure of human excellence which has been granted him implicitly by his antecedents. And by his own efforts, and by the help of his fellows, this measure he may and does attain.

This is the simple history of the matter, and it is found increasingly hard to make room for gods or devils at any stage of the whole process. But it is also true that in the recurring times of trouble and temptation which fall to the lot of mortals without distinction of creed, mortal weakness will send out sighs, not unlike a prayer, for the help that will never come for wishing. The mind looks round for succour because it is wanted, not because it is to be had. So in bodily pain, if the will suppresses every sound of complaint and controls every muscular contraction, the eyes still wander restlessly as if to seek some way of escape, though the reason has submitted to the knowledge that there is none. So it has been, and so it will be: there is nothing harder on earth than the agony of a solitary soul in pain or temptation. And there is no God to make the rough ways smooth. But, though the struggle is hard, victory is always possible to the single-minded lover of truth and rectitude; and what more is needed, in the hour of trial, than faith in the possibility of victory? alone or helped by gods or men the struggle is hard, or why this craving for some help? But though it is hard, it is none the more hopeless, although there are no gods to help. A man has but to will, to resolve with an undivided mind, and the past, from a master, becomes a slave; all that has been done or suffered before him, served to enable him to will thus, served to prevent his willing otherwise than as he has chosen. We say the past is our servant when we have done what we thought well to do; it is our tyrant when we have done ill, and life is on the one side a struggle to escape from the tyranny of natural evil which we hate, on the other an aspiration after the possession of natural good, which we love and delight in the more, the more we know and possess of it in ourselves.

To conclude briefly: the sum of objective influences go to make men wish to do and be the best they can. The "Not-ourselves makes for righteousness," not by holding out rewards for good works, but by material incentives to their performance, which in the long run, and as a rule, prevail over carnal wilfulness or seductions. The virtue of men is conditioned by motive forces behind them, not by inducements before; but the strongest passions and desires of men are either an echo or a prophecy of their strongest tendencies, and nothing is more certain, taking the experience of the race or of the individual as a whole, than that the affections will become engaged on the side of whatever conduct is habitual. Faithful, unswerving performance will turn every duty into a labour of love.

And yet it is a common charge against atheistical moralists that their doctrine is sad and comfortless; they show the life that now is with ruthless candour, and they hold out no hope of compensation in a different future. They are dreaded and distrusted as false prophets of evil, because they avow that evil exists, and have no arts of logical legerdemain to prove that its existence is a good in disguise. Perhaps it is true that we have fallen upon evil days, when the sympathy between man and the course of things is exceptionally intermittent and incomplete, but certainly not less sad than ours is the creed of those who believe in a heaven to come for the few, but think and preach that our generation is rushing steadily towards the opposite goal of perdition. What can be more intensely miserable and depressing a creed than to believe that there *is* a right, that there is blessedness to come, and that our fellows are wantonly and wilfully turning their backs upon it? Perhaps we ourselves have fallen upon evil days: it is long since men have felt so severely critical as they do now, not of each other, but of themselves; for ages past there has not been among us so much of that "divine discontent" which lashes the strong to mastery, the weak to despair. We crave after supreme good, we imagine that if we could only see and know what was absolutely best for us to-day, no sacrifice would be too great to buy the salvation of its possession. But, alas! we do not know, at most we guess doubtfully, or if we know, the best for us to-day may be an unlovely compromise, a sacrifice which leaves us ashamed and disgusted with the order that has no nobler, more fruitful duties to impose on us to-day. But, granted all this, is the best that we can do to curse our day and despair of the morrows of our race? Is this the duty to which we are most strongly impelled by our natural, inborn appetite for the very Good? Is the fact that *we* find it hard to meet with duties to our mind a proof that the Right is not adorable? hard or easy, it is our doom to love the best, and seek it where it may be found; and if the search is harder than usual, now or at any other time, in proportion to the difficulty of the quest will be the delight and triumph of success for those who live to reach it.

And we have nothing in common with those prophets of evil who say there can be no success, or that all the roads by which men are seeking now are roads to no result but ruin. In the words of an ancient: "Deus est mortali juvare mortalem et hæc ad æternam gloriam via;" the way is open, and the combined, concerted efforts of mankind may yet make it the thoroughfare of nations. We are not so much in love with the past as to think the victory is won if we live our life no worse, after its kind, than the ancestors gone before us into everlasting peace, lived theirs. But there *is* a victory to win; it is the great mystery which no prophet has power to reveal, the open impenetrable secret of the future whether, man pitted against the powers of darkness, man will triumph, or at last succumb, or must for ever linger on as now, struggling, compromising, bartering old loss for new gain, journeying leagues upon a treadmill that would crush him in its cranks if he ceased to keep up the form of progress which holds him rooted to the spot. People cry out after an Unknown God, and reverence an unnamed Unknowable, and thus much of piety we profess towards the unsounded infinites of real Being; we do not believe, feel, or see them to contain the materials for a law of stable imperfection. Evil there is, change there is, but we see no inherent vitality in the mal-adjustment of things dooming the real changes which shall take place to preserve unbroken just this measure of mal-adjustment which makes life to many of us an evil lot. The success that we should praise, that we desire and sometimes almost believe in, is growth towards a more and more harmonious social life, such an organisation of material interests that it shall not seem to any one as if the imperfection of a fellow could minister to his good, or the suffering of a fellow to his happiness: it is such a general development of scrupulous intelligence that men shall live in religious awe of consequences, and act as those who must give account for their doings, even to the third generation of effects: it is a life so lawful and orderly for the masses that the leaders of thought need not despair of finding a fulcrum in their hearers' feeling when they point to a better that might be done if we willed: it is agreement, outspoken agreement, a friendship as brotherly as in primitive religions, between all those who have one faith, in human nature; one hope, in human effort; one God, in the soul's vision of a perfect right; and alas! one baptism of sin, sorrow, and privation, from which few of us emerge without wounds, stain, or discouragement.

We cannot tell, for the experiment has never yet been tried, what human life might be if all the faculties of living men and women were spent in making it easy to each other to live as human beings should. At present it is difficult, and the few who are born with the power of doing much to make the existence of the many less difficult are hampered in the exercise of their function by our stupidity, and wait with patient compassion, scarcely touched with scorn, for the time when great deeds may be again possible to those who may again have a united multitude to lead on what it shall have learned to be its own way, and who, seeing the natural order ere it yet exists, will once more dare to believe that the record of their vision is prophetical. But if the heroes delay too long, we need not wait their help to build up

> " The Being that we are;
> Thus deeply drinking in the soul of things,
> We shall be wise perforce, and while inspired
> By choice, and conscious that the Will is free,
> Shall move unswerving, even as if impelled
> By strict necessity, along the path
> Of order and of good. Whate'er we see,
> Or feel, shall tend to quicken and refine ;
> Shall fix, in calmer seats of moral strength,
> Earthly desires, and raise to loftier heights
> Of divine love our intellectual soul."

V.
THE NATURAL HISTORY OF ALTRUISM.

"Whoever was to be born at all, was to be born a child, and to do before he could understand, and be bred under laws to which he was always bound, but which could not always be exacted; and he was to choose when he could not reason, and had passions most strong when he had his understanding most weak, and was to ride a wild horse without a bridle, and the more need he had of a curb, the less strength he had to use it; and this being the case of all the world, what was every man's evil became all men's greater evil; and though alone it was very bad, yet when they came together it was made much worse; like ships in a storm, every one alone hath enough to do to outride it; but when they meet, besides the evils of the storm, they find the intolerable calamity of their mutual concussion, and every ship that is ready to be oppressed with the tempest is a worse tempest to every vessel against which it is violently dashed. So it is in mankind; every man hath evil enough of his own, and it is hard for a man to live soberly, temperately, and religiously; but when he hath parents and children, brothers and sisters, friends and enemies, buyers and sellers, lawyers and physicians, a family and a neighbourhood, a king over him or tenants under him, a bishop to rule in matters of government spiritual, and a people to be ruled by him in the affairs of their souls, then it is that every man dashes against another, and one relation requires what another denies; and when one speaks, another will contradict him; and that which is well spoken is sometimes innocently mistaken, and that upon a good cause produces an evil effect. And by these, and ten thousand other concurrent causes, man is made more than most miserable."—JEREMY TAYLOR.

"That which hitherto hath been spoken concerneth natural agents considered in themselves. But we must further remember also (which thing to touch in a word shall suffice), that as in this respect they have their law, which law directeth them in the means whereby they tend to their own perfection, so likewise another law there is, which toucheth them as they are sociable parts united into one body; a law which bindeth them each to serve unto other's good, and all to prefer the good of the whole to whatsoever their own particular; as we plainly see they do, when things natural in that regard forget their ordinary natural wont, that which is heavy mounting sometime upwards of its own accord, and forsaking the centre of the earth, which to itself is most natural, even as if it did hear itself commanded to let go the good it privately wisheth, and to relieve the present distress of nature in common."—HOOKER.

Retrospect—The "sufficient reason" for moral conduct naturally identified with the standard of morality: Conscience, Utility, or Perfection—Action instinctive or rational; instinctive action disinterested—Power of acting (which generates wish to act) increases more rapidly than power of enjoying—Power of acting with or upon other men craves exercise as it develops—When sensible pleasures are too few to supply ends for all the active energies, men borrow enough of their neighbours' consciousness to furnish new ends for rational pursuit—The natural history of altruism—Social discords accidental—Social wisdom and virtue consist mainly in harmonising the tendencies that exist, not in bringing them all into conformity with some outer standard—The general law of social duty enforced by penal sanctions, the force of which upon the human will is due to those same natural tendencies which caused the law to be proclaimed.

V.

THE NATURAL HISTORY OF ALTRUISM.

IN the foregoing argument, the critical reader will perhaps be inclined to object, that we have travelled a long way in search of a starting-point that we might as well have taken for granted at once. We have thrown no new light on the philosophy of legislation, or the nature of human duties, or the propriety of religious observances. We have only vindicated, by somewhat far-fetched processes, our right to speak of law, morality, and religion in the tone of good, common-sensible people, who do take for granted that the law of the land and of conscience are to be obeyed and reverenced, and the Best they know reverenced and loved.

Such a task may well seem unproductive. We have added no stone to the sacred building of human duty and aspiration; our part has been rather that of the idle spectator, who assures a frightened child that the building will not tumble down, though the workmen are busy knocking away the scaffolding that seemed to hold it up, and really did support the builders—whose work is over for a season. When the last defacing plank is carried away, we see the edifice erect, and ask what stone of it is wanting? but we have not yet described the fabric. We have tried to show that moral obligation may be recognised without unreason, and that the natural feeling of man is not hostile to the supreme forces which rule his will, but we have avoided entering in any detail upon the substance of the moral law till we could speak of its precepts as at once supremely authoritative and yet enforced by purely natural sanctions.

If our reasoning has been correct, the dictates of nature, law, morality, and religion substantially coincide; they are different phases of the same general tendency, varying only in the intensity of their self-consciousness and in the number of phenomena presented by each one in orderly relations. The existence of the universe is a physical, to our apprehension, an ultimate fact : but as soon as this fact has been perceived or postulated, everything within the universe is, at least in theory, equally explicable; that is to say, every real process may be observed if the human senses are acute enough, or aided by sufficiently delicate instruments, to record the phenomena as they occur; and every real relation amongst the different series of observed facts may be known and classed with other real relations, if the human intellect is comprehensive enough to take in and co-ordinate all the material furnished to it by perception. The simplest phenomena of life are to us as mysterious as the refinements of the intellect and conscience, and the result which we call "understanding" in the one case is, humanly speaking, equally attainable in all.

To make the existence of law, morality, and religion appear reasonable, we must take account that it is also natural and real. We do not suppose any transcendental or metaphysical necessity at work to make men peaceable, moral, or affectionate; and if habits of order and virtue could be proved to be unreasonable, that is to say, conducive to ends not deliberately desired by sane men, we do not doubt that the human race would very reasonably put an end to its own existence by their disuse. But reason does not operate *in vacuo;* it presupposes some data in nature and fact; and if it is on the whole natural to man to act generally in accordance with the rules of law and justice, this fact gives an element of reasonableness to the sentiment which survives the most rationalistic criticism of moral obligation—the sentiment of acquiescence in the force of those rules.

The difficulty experienced by a candid theist in conceiving how disinterested virtue can survive if religious faith is lost, arises from the fact that all his own disinterested feeling towards the Not-self is associated with his own particular beliefs about the Not-self and its nature. But where those beliefs are entirely wanting, their place is taken, not by the comparatively few natural impulses that, if uncontrolled, might lead to impiety or lawlessness, but by a still disinterested apprehension of the real relations of the self to the Not-self, which could scarcely be expected to contain within it a motive for the—impossible—subversion of that relation. The explanation of such harmony as there is between the will of man and the laws of the world in which he lives is that the evolution of human consciousness took place, historically, under conditions of which those laws are the record. Individual men are numbered amongst the elements of which the whole, the universe, is composed, and their life as parts includes cohesion to the other parts with which their existence is bound up; and since the cohesion is real, the after-reflection which acquiesces in its reality cannot be called unreasonable.

It would be vain indeed to hope to persuade the mass of men to co-operate disinterestedly with the universe in perfecting the human species up to the highest point which the constitution of the universe will allow—if they would really rather not. We only suggest that most of them have a slight natural tendency or inclination to do so already, that is likely to grow stronger rather than weaker by becoming increasingly self-conscious. We have no standard of human perfection outside the suggestions of human attainment, and there is no apparent source, except the practice or aspirations of men, from whence the moral ideal to which they themselves think they "ought" to approximate can have been derived; but science cannot ignore the fact that they *have* an ideal, and, fortunately for our peace of mind, science does nothing to destroy or lower whatever ideal they have. Naturalists at least escape the mental trouble of religious doubts and difficulties, which are so familiar a trial to those who, consciously or otherwise, try to serve two masters, and own two laws, of nature and super-nature.

The subjective aspect of morality, or the feeling of obligation in general, is the product of a certain minimum stability of type in the human species, conjoined with the highly evolved consciousness peculiar to man, which adds a peculiar sense of subjective necessity to the persistence in certain classes of natural actions when they are in any way impeded; this is the physical or natural explanation of conscience, and if correct in fact, would be perfectly satisfactory to reason. The matter of morality, or the nature of the moral ideal which their common humanity, so to speak, sets before the mind and will of individual men, has not the same appearance of a logical or natural necessity as that which ensures and demonstrates the existence of a moral law of some sort. If men had been, by nature or kind, something quite different from what they are, they might still have had a morality, if their consciousness and their relation to the medium of their activity had been of the same order as at present, but its substance or precepts might have been altogether out of relation to the life with which we are familiar. Yet morality, to us, is so essentially a practical matter, that our feeling does not recognise, as a motive for doing what—to us—is right, this general fact of *conditionedness*, which might conceivably have allowed us to become subject to a different moral law from the one we actually own. We do not say that the right is right *because* we have come to feel it so; it is right because we *do* feel it to be so, though we acknowledge, as an intellectual possibility, that a different species in a different medium might be bound by quite different rules of feeling as well as of fact.

The existing difference of opinion as to the sufficient reason for doing right is really a form of the existing uncertainty as to what constitutes the "rightness" of an action. It is agreed that some things are right, and that what is right ought to be done; but we want a satisfactory test, which shall at once guide and verify our judgment and impulses, and itself receive verification from our intuition that in every case the conduct which satisfies the test is really and truly the very right. Moral science can have no existence unless such a test is to be found, for we own no duties except such as are knowable and feasible, we feel no obligation to stumble by guess work in the dark, and the moral antinomies with which some writers are pleased to darken the counsels of perfection are as repugnant to sane feeling as to clear and adequate thought.

This demand for a test or standard of moral right suggested itself at the beginning of the discussion, but in repeating it here, we do not reopen the whole question; we have still, it is true, to choose between the lists of obligations made out in conformity with rival tests, but we are free to accept, without metaphysical scruples, the force of whichever code our choice virtually accepts in its entirety, by its acceptance of the appropriate standard. Our will is—reasonably and necessarily—bound by *some* moral law; we have only to agree upon its substance and proclaim its sanctions.

If we leave out of account theories which include an appeal to divine revelation, the competing standards may, for practical purposes, be reduced to four: the test of conscience, or conformity to the moral feeling of the individual; the test of Hedonism, or selfish Utilitarianism, namely, conduciveness to the greatest happiness of the agent; that of Social Utilitarianism, *i.e.*, conduciveness to the greatest happiness of the greatest number; and lastly, the test of moral and religious idealism, conduciveness to the greatest general perfection. Of course we cannot attempt to decide *a priori* which of these classes of considerations "ought" to be preferred, or assume that one standard is intrinsically more beautiful and exalted than another; our business is only to ascertain, by analysis, comparison, and inference, which class of considerations most men are, or habitually wish to be, guided by, because natural wish is incipient tendency; and though the order of nature is not so adjusted as to provide for the indulgence of every individual human wish, general tendencies, or wishes common to a whole species, cannot, we suppose, have arisen, and become even to some extent hereditary, under conditions habitually adverse to their growth and exercise. Even when the nature of the moral ideal generally accepted had been determined, we should not therefore be entitled to say that each individual "ought" to feel the pursuit of the same ideal binding on his conscience. *My* belief or conviction that *you* ought to do your duty (especially to me) is too much reinforced by my obvious interest to be allowed any serious scientific weight, and not the least among the practical advantages of our theory is that it promises to relieve us from the burdensome and unremunerative task of keeping our neighbours' consciences; for since consciences can honestly disagree, while the moral beliefs of the individuals are an essential condition of the obligations he feels, the subjective rule of right may differ for you and me, even though we both believe that there is only one true objective rule.

In order, then, to find the test of right in conscience, we should either have to assume that most consciences agree, and that the majority are right, which would leave the decision of conscience in each particular case open to debate, or we should have to take *conscientiousness*, a word with a perfectly exact and intelligible meaning, as itself the standard; assuming not only that most consciences are right, but also that most decisions of the same conscience are right too, so that the most conscientious persons, *i.e.*, those who most uniformly act in accordance with their own belief as to what is right, are also the best or most virtuous. The association of merit with the word "conscientious" proves sufficiently that this is the general conclusion, but the double character of the process of inference makes the standard more than usually uncertain as a practical guide. If, as previously maintained, what people honestly believe to be right is the nearest approach possible (to them) to their own natural good or perfection, conscientiousness must be called a good; it is the quality most essential to the individual that aims at being good of its kind. But the species man, we must remember, is divided into many sub-classes, and the same, or nearly the same, degree of conscientiousness may be accompanied by great inequality and divergence of tastes and faculties; to a certain extent even, in matters of morality, each individual may be said to constitute a class apart, for the natural aspiration of the individual is to attain its own good, not a good as like as possible to that which its neighbour thinks good; and if the attempt is successful, since nature is her own standard of perfection, it is not easy to see how we can rationally give the preference over one well-developed nature to another nature, no better developed, of a different kind, unless by reference to some naturally existing objective standard. The naturally conditioned aspirations of different individuals fix the outline of what is good for each of them; but the mere existence of a strong inward bias in favour of one class or another of actions or abstentions gives little presumption in favour of the wisdom or goodness of the acts determined by the bias. The bias of the majority is right in the majority of cases, but such an empirical generalisation as this gives us no help in the only cases where help is needed, *i.e.*, when the doubt arises whether we have to do with an example of the general rule or an exception to it.

The standard of Utilitarianism is open to precisely the same objection as the standard of conscience; in the one case moral, in the other, physical inclination supplies the rule, and the ruling of inclination is not invariable. Constancy in the subjective element is secured by taking spontaneity, in the first or the second degree, as the essential part of lawfulness; but the impulses of conscience and desire do not always and necessarily lead to an objective good, and we are loth to abandon the faith that evil results must spring from some other root than good. We want a rule that can never falter or mislead. The external motives to the pressure of which men are exposed, and the internal susceptibilities which determine the effect of the motives, are in general innocent as well as natural in their tendency, and in general men act as comes natural to them without scrupulous self-questioning. Sometimes the inner rule of conscience narrows the area of natural choice, and forbids the will to choose a demoralising pleasure or to follow a maleficent impulse. But there is a still higher tribunal before which the conscience itself may be arraigned, and found guilty of narrowness, prejudice, and short or oblique vision. Sensible good and moral good are excellent things in their way, but they are each only parts of the supreme natural good of Natural Perfection; and it is to this ultimate standard of natural good that we must appeal before we can find a rule at once recognisable and acceptable to the will, feeling, and intelligence of each man as supreme for other men as well as for himself, and for himself as well as for others. That which is praised as good, *semper, ubique, ab omnibus*, is not man's changing sense of pleasure, not his changing sense of duty, it is the perfect life, made up of pleasure, duty, and energetic impulse, with their unexplained substratum of natural force.

We have before this met the anticipated objection that the standard of natural perfection itself must vary, if growth and evolution are among the facts of nature. Moral obligation is always the same, as regards man, the moral agent, however much the range of dutiful action may be extended; and the perfection of the moment is always the same, as regards the sum of things and persons then naturally existing, though each succeeding age may witness the development of fuller and more varied being than its predecessors. The standard of natural good varies with the multiplication or differentiation of natural existence, but the standards are always alike in the form of their exactingness, and there is only one standard at a time to which conformity is right, while the relation in which the men of each generation stand to their own proper standard is unchanging.

Of course it is an effort to the mind, and still more, perhaps, to the feelings, to recognise the permanence of relations amid the flux of things, and the permanent qualities of things amid their varying relations; but we have no right to expect either the theory or the application of ethical science to be easy, seeing that it deals with the most complex relations of the most complex of natural beings—the relations of men amongst themselves. But it is at all events needless to afflict ourselves with difficulties that neutralise each other, and combine speculative despair over the unintelligible prejudice men feel in favour of right conduct with querulous complaints over the absence of a sufficient reason for practical rectitude. It is impossible to find broad general arguments to support the paradox that it would be better for every one, everywhere and always, to have preferred natural evil or imperfection to good. It may be said with truth that many persons would get more sensible, personal pleasure out of their lives by well-chosen lapses from virtue than by conduct uniformly in accordance with the counsels of perfection; and any one who has the courage of the opinion may add that the reasons available in such cases are not sufficient to make self-sacrifice rational. And we know in practice that they are not, unfortunately, found sufficient—by many persons of dull moral sensibility. But this does not make it any more possible to maintain, on abstract grounds, the paradox that dull moral sensibility is a natural good or condition of good. A law, to revert to our first definition, is a statement of constant relations posited by the nature of things, and no constant relations follow from the nature of things in so far as they are abnormal, *i.e.*, of irregular or imperfect development after their kind.

Moral good has no existence apart from human feelings of obligation, but the law accepted and proclaimed by conscience is not one of its own invention; it formulates necessities which owe at least half their being to external influences, and these outward conditions of all the true provisions of natural law subsist independently of the human sensibilities which they help to keep alive. It is because the broad conditions of life and association are the same for every one, everywhere and always, that we count every one as subject to the same moral law, and blame imperfect sensibility to moral considerations as a flaw in the human character, and it is not a valid objection to the natural generality of the law that it is sometimes broken and sometimes obeyed with difficulty.

The history of morality, for any one capable of dealing with so wide a subject, would consist mainly in an account of the successive development of impulses, feelings, and desires which resulted, under historical conditions, in forming the human character into those habits and capabilities of feeling and action which give their actual force to natural and moral motives; and at each stage we should find, as now, the rival standards of utility, conscience, and idealism (more or less obscurely expressed) used to measure the distance between what was, and what, it was supposed, "ought" to be. The only part of this process that immediately concerns us is the relative share of moral and utilitarian considerations in determining conduct to tend towards the objective best, and the several contributions of disinterested and self-regarding motives to the composite system of needs and wishes out of which a supreme ideal of good is to be selected as the aim of aspiration rather than desire.

Grote, in his criticism of the Utilitarian philosophy, has noticed the fallacy of neglecting the energetic principles of human nature, and treating all action as if it were motived by some form or other of sensibility. In point of fact, the division of human motives into selfish and other-selfish [1] ones, needs to be supplemented by a distinction between moral unselfishness, or disinterested action conducive to the general good, and the objective material altruism of acting for or upon other things, for the sake of acting, not for the sake of any personal end involved in the action; between the moral unselfishness of feeling for and with the pleasures of others and the constitutional expansiveness which makes the individual depend even for selfish pleasures on the acts and feelings of other people. And in examining the normal motives for action, we must not be misled by the *double-entendre* of Utilitarianism, which argues that in all cases alike we do as we please, because if we didn't please, we might do something else, and that therefore our pleasure is the ultimate motive of all our acts. In all cases, no doubt, we do as we choose, or will, but the preference is of a different kind, and has different causes, and it is arbitrary to assume that because the result is the same, *i.e.*, some kind of act or abstention, the motive must be the same, either physically or to consciousness. The assumption begs the very question at issue, whether all human motives *can* be brought under the same head, or have any one common quality besides efficiency.

To ascertain the kind of inducements that determine the will to one action rather than another, we need to know the kind of ends which the mind is naturally qualified, which is nearly the same thing as predisposed, to follow. The sensible good or evil of the organism, that is, pleasure or pain, are motives to action or forbearance when circumstances bring them, directly or indirectly, before the mind, but they are by no means coextensive with the possible field of human action. Pleasure and pain are forms of consciousness, but there are states of consciousness that are indifferent without therefore being incapable of

---

[1] Some purists object to "altruist" as barbarous, but we have no convenient English synonym.

determination to action.[1] Except so far as consciousness is *Ding an sich*, our own existence is phenomenal, a series of phenomenal states of consciousness; if other phenomena than those of our own natural life can find a place in consciousness, it is obvious that such consciousness may suggest fresh ends of action, and if such ends come again to be adopted by the will, they may even take the form of personal sensibility and compete with the primary impulses and desires of sense. The only absolutely undecomposable pleasures the enjoyment of which can be proposed as an end are those connected with the bodily senses, for the satisfaction arising from the consciousness of faculty, the exercise of the power to *do* what belongs to a man, as well as merely to enjoy, is scarcely separated in consciousness from the rational motive or instinctive impulse that has led to the exercise of the faculty.

We are not in a position to explain why the pleasure of different passive states of consciousness is much differentiated (*e.g.*, the enjoyment of the gourmand and of the musical amateur), while the pleasurableness of all activity is generically alike, though the localisation of perception in special organs has probably something to do with the fact. The identity of an action that we think and speak of as one is built up of many elements, the connection between which may be entirely ideal, and as consciousness is certainly localised, there can be no bodily sense of a complicated performance capable of developing into a special pleasurable perception or state of consciousness. All human action that is not determined to the gratification of simple appetites is compounded of the blind disinterested impulse to act as we can, accompanied by a

---

[1] "If action were strictly dependent on sensation and emotion, it would be found to be always proportionate to those stimuli, but such proportion palpably and notoriously fails to hold good. . . . Without this spontaneity of our actions the growth of volition or of activity guided to ends, is all but inexplicable."—BAIN: *Senses and Intellect*, p. 84.

faint general sense of pleasure in the consciousness of action, which becomes stronger as the ideal integration of the action proceeds; to which is added an imaginary foretaste of the pleasure or other good that is to be the final effect of the action considered as a whole.

Passive states of consciousness, if they were equally and indifferently pleasurable, would not furnish motives to one variety of action rather than another, and as all action is in itself indifferent, the coincidence of the inducements of sense with the incitements of instinct appears to have been the original condition of the varied life, which is itself the condition of what we call rational action. Increasingly various action among different sections of the community results in the formation of new relations, which suggest new interests, social as well as self-regarding, and the pursuit of every fresh interest under conditions of growing complexity is pregnant with new possibilities of instigation. But the pleasure found in the fulfilment of simple tendencies becomes less clearly marked in actions which, though still normal, are of so composite a character that the intellectual element in the satisfaction accompanying it swamps the sensible delight. In the contrast between the incessant restless activity of the civilised man and the *dolce far niente* existence of the savage in a favourable climate, nothing is more remarkable than the disproportion between the increase of the power to will and that of the power to enjoy. The senses have not grown more numerous or acute, and though susceptibility to their influences may have been in some cases refined and heightened, their solicitations probably suggest, absolutely as well as comparatively, fewer actions to the Western European than to the South Sea islander. It would be paradoxical to say that as life becomes more complicated and intellectual, it becomes less rational, that is to say, made up of actions where impulse counted proportionately for more and inducements for less than with the savage; but when we find an increase in the number and difficulty of the actions habitually performed, without any corresponding increase in the number or strength of the sensible inducements for their performance, we are led to conclude, not that the action is irrational, but that it is still deliberately directed towards the attainment of an end, only to some other end than sensible enjoyment. We conclude that, consciously or not, the sufficient reason which in practice moves the mass of men to their habitual modicum of innocent and meritorious activity is the force of their own native tendency towards the chief natural good of full specific life, not a narrower preference for the limited number of ends accidentally made desirable for themselves.

We do not have to choose between Nature, Pleasure, and Morality, as three rival masters with incompatible claims; life, joy, and virtue are all equally natural, but every natural good is followed by the shadow of a corresponding evil—natural privation or strife—and hence we come to distinguish as good of a special kind the rarer, hardly-won goal of pleasant or perfect life; we distinguish between natural good and evil; between natural perfection and the want of force or want of harmony which makes life painful or abnormal; between the measure of natural imperfection which ends in sensible pain—the injury of one sufferer, and that which results in vital evil—in the self-perpetuating wrongness of action antagonistic to the common natural good. And after contemplating the phenomena of life from every side, we come to the result that man is more essentially a moral agent than a self-pleasing one; that is to say, the largest part of his existence is actually and potentially determined by the tendencies of healthy life within and around him, and consists in more or less conscious service of and co-operation with those tendencies; while only the lesser part is determined by a craving for the personal *sense* of healthy life which constitutes the good fortune of the happy. The more conscious and complete this service of nature at her best, the more morally excellent the agent; the more objectively efficient the service, and the more easily and gaily it is rendered, the greater his natural perfection. But if objective hindrances quite beyond the agent's control make the service of nature's best from first to last a painful toil, man is left with no natural good but the moral good of self-devotion, and we are not justified in imposing the human standard on nature, and praising the virtue of an order which teaches some few of us to attain what, in a world where it is needed, we think the chief good, the power of self-devotion to the common Best. We are only tempted to exalt morality above nature—as we unhesitatingly exalt it above pleasure, when we find human virtue waging unequal war against natural evil, and more naturally admirable in defeat than the most omnipotent of fiends throned in a subject universe. We are the children of nature, and self-respect, if not filial piety, should warn us not to disparage our descent; but our parent, with reverence be it said, is of hybrid birth, and true piety should make us faithful to the finest strain in our ancestry, and it is on this ground that we venture to claim as truly natural in ourselves all that is most in harmony with what we call best in the works of the great genetrix.

The manifestations of innocent natural force in the ordinary activities of life must be called disinterested; but with the development of intelligence, of which the chief feature is the passing into consciousness of an increasing number of natural tendencies, those forms of natural action which have most nearly established themselves as habits are acquiesced in by the will, and the ends which their exercise tends to effect are proposed by reason as the goal towards which other stray faculties and unoccupied impulses are to be directed. In other words, will is substituted for desire as a motive, and the will is so nearly arbitrary that it may almost be called free as well as disinterested; and it is only by tracing something like an orderly sequence in its resolves that we can prove disinterested volitions to be not necessarily unreasonable, or abnormally arbitrary. Granting that there is something peculiarly rational in action which promises to procure the enjoyment of some sensible good, which, under favourable circumstances, is also the natural good of the active organism, some action must also be taken to employ the faculties which are either unfitted for the quest of sensible pleasure, or for any reason temporarily released from its pursuit. When ideal ends of conduct are substituted for material ones, since the substitution is entirely disinterested, the ends that will be proposed will be—not such as are useful or agreeable, but such as are possible, such as the individual is naturally able to propose, and it does not follow that his ability in this respect will be great, for we do not allow that the imagination can do more than rearrange the data of former experiences.

Experience seems to show that when men are ripe for action, but have no motive of their own to act upon, they borrow enough of their neighbour's consciousness to suggest one; or rather, perhaps, when the habit of acting or feeling in certain ways has become deeply rooted in our nature, sympathetic motives or the mere representation of the circumstances are enough to rouse it into exercise. It would be impossible to form, much less to indulge, the complicated artificial desires of civilised life in a total solitude. The actions in which we learn to take pleasure are actions performed with, by, or upon our fellow-men, and as the purpose which makes the action rational is some ideal end—not the material mechanical steps in its performance, with which alone sensible pleasure could be associated—the elements of which the pleasure is made up will be ideal also. The simplest form in which we see the action of borrowed motives is in the observance of custom, which is always a shade more constant than a mere natural agreement of inclination and circumstances would make it, to which fact, indeed, its incipient legality is owing. But the first new faculty, of a distinctly human kind, which we must suppose to have been developed by the practice of social life, is that of influencing and being influenced by the thoughts and conduct of other individuals of the same species. Besides the faint natural pleasure attendant on the exercise of this, as of any other normal faculty (which favours its development, as children learn to talk by chattering for the pleasure of making themselves heard), the mere power of perceiving the thoughts and feelings of others adds immensely to the number of received impressions, *i.e.*, of possible motives. What other people think or feel about us or about our conduct becomes a motive at a very early stage, and when we have once begun to feel an { egoistic / sympathetic } concern in anything so remote from self as other people's feelings, it is an easy step to extend the concern to their feelings about other topics than the sympathiser.

The power which men have of acting upon, or of entering into each other's feelings, is real, natural, and imperfectly developed; we believe a tendency towards its further development to be also natural and real, and the consciousness of its existence as the most essential characteristic of man as man to be the source of all our moral ideas. A few thousand years are not much in the history of a species, and the power of sympathetic passion and moral action— or action towards a good made such by human feeling— are still, we hold, engaged in evolutionary throes. Men wish to act and feel together, but they have not yet learned how to do so, except imperfectly and with effort. Altruism in some shape or other is so essential a part of civilised social life that it does not occur to us to regard some of its more ordinary manifestations as moral. Tyranny, ambition, emulation, all the passions that are most active in leading to the exploitation of man by man, are rudimentary forms of altruism, expressions of the impulse that drives every one to try to enlarge his own life by appropriating, dominating, or identifying himself with the lives of those around him. The men who built the Pyramids were certainly not egotists; and the submission of their subjects, the consent which is the condition of all dominion, is still more clearly altruistic; the great problem of history, how on the side of the oppressors there was power—to oppress the most mighty many—is to be solved, not by such a contradiction in terms as is involved in the physical coercion of the many by the few, of the strong by the weak, but by the habitual weakness of purely selfish ambitions in the majority, and their willingness to identify themselves with the aims and sympathise with the wishes of any one whose wishes are strong enough to carry with him the minds and wills of his tools; and if men can thus be carried captive by each other's baser cupidities, they may in like manner be subjugated by the power of disinterested aspirations.

The moral progress of society consists in a growing harmony between the feeling of different centres of consciousness, or between the personal feeling of each ego and its representation of external feelings. The tyrannical altruist insists on effecting the harmony by modifying the attitude of the subject mind, or controlling its tendencies; the sympathetic altruist desires the harmony of feeling as the chief end, and rather than prolong the discord, submits to take an uncongenial impression. The stronger will, if not naturally bad, *i.e.*, irreconcilable with the general tendencies of society and nature (in which case resistance to it is moral), compels the more imaginative, emotional, or affectionate nature to follow its lead, rather than inflict the pain of arrested power and impeded tendency on innocent involuntary egotism. The rational altruist, on the other hand, endeavours to give effect to the best will, whether it be his own or another's: if his own, not for that reason, but for the sake of the good result; if another's, not from the blind instinct of sympathy, but from enlightened identity of purpose. The importance of sympathy as a motive lies rather in its power to multiply the range of inducement for acts naturally indifferent by the interchange of borrowed motive, than in the essential morality of other-selfishness; but at the same time, to have presented to the mind a strong wish, of another person, that can be gratified with no other sacrifice than that of a weaker wish of our own, is to be conscious of a share in the moral life of the social organism; and though the happiness of one man is of no more account to nature than that of another, the sum total of natural good is clearly greater if disinterested energy and innocent enjoyment coexist by favour of each other, than if energy is limited to self-chosen ends, and enjoyment limited by self-possessed powers. Just as in personal morality the ambitious impulses may overrule the indolent aversion to labour, as pride or vanity may control intemperance, so tenderness towards the fond desire of a weaker friend, mere compassion for another's pain, the will for a result that some one else can reach if enough self-sacrificing industry is placed at his command, are all motive forces as powerful within the consciousness as if they were merely self-regarding in their results, and they impose an obligation so irresistible when it is felt at all, that we seem to escape a danger as we reflect that such a force cannot, in the nature of things, be brought habitually to bear *against* the common good.

The passion for living is too strong to be satisfied with the actions or enjoyments physically possible to one individual; men do not think of the infinite as a possession to be desired for its own sake, but their desires are infinitely expansive, and, it may be, most vast and comprehensive when least distinct and irresistible. Egotism calls the imagination to its help, and enriches the single life by representing it as existing, magnified, embellished, or at least repeated, in innumerable other consciousnesses. When people cannot add materially to their own powers, pleasures, or possessions, they try to add to them ideally by becoming conscious of other persons' apprehension of their existence, extent, and attractiveness; and it is but a step from taking pleasure in the thought that others share our consciousness of the advantages we really enjoy, to trying to make their belief in our enjoyment, especially of power, a substitute for consciousness of its real possession, should that prove the more difficult of attainment. In emulation, or the desire of "going beyond" other people, the object is not primarily to do more than somebody else, only to do much, but "much" can only be estimated by a standard that seems to include another's "little." There is no object in doing more than other people of the same kind, unless the kind of action is good: "excellence," etymologically a term of comparison, owes its complimentary connotation to the fact that the unit, or standard, in other people's practice is assumed to be positively good. As Proudhon used to say, most social wrongs are based upon an *erreur de compte*, and it is only a miscalculation that leads the ambitious egotist to substitute the shadow for the reality as an object of pursuit, and to be content with less of positive achievement than he might secure himself, while hindering the achievement of others, to maintain a perfectly unprofitable, comparative ascendency. The beginning of egotism is the desire for sympathy, or rather the desire for sympathy is a refinement of egotism: the pleasure of being thought strong, or wise, or beautiful adds something to the pleasure found in being so really; and it is an easy mistake to imagine that the second pleasure may be enjoyed without the first, and at less expense, if we disguise ourselves, and cheat or plagiarise.

The imagination in general is neither more nor less moral than the impulses in its suggestions; the real motive for any action is what the whole mind, or as much of it as is brought to bear upon the matter, feels and judges about it; but this conclusion is affected not only by the real strength of competing inducements, but also by the comparative ease with which their respective force can be brought home to the imagination. Some independent faculty, such as reason, has to be called in to arbitrate when it is necessary to decide between such different inducements as a present pleasure to be set against a future pain, or a present pain to be followed by a future pleasure. The imagination is sluggish even in reproducing past experiences, and when really incommensurable motives are brought before it—as, for example, the pleasures of sin, and the pains of everlasting damnation—the result will be arbitrarily determined by the susceptibility of the subject to one class of images rather than another. The imagination furnishes motives for action when sensible appetites or physical impulses are inadequate, but it is only with culture and education that it becomes so realistic as to make it probable that all the inducements it holds forth may have a real existence; then it serves to give effect to those inducements that are real, only not actually present to sense, and these have a rudimentary or provisional disinterestedness. Prudence, for instance, or the taking thought for the morrow, is almost more truly the beginning of altruism than vanity or affection; our future self is another than our present, and to be willing to make sacrifices for its advantage proves that the representative life of intellect and emotion has begun to encroach upon and control the presentations of sense. The reason that so many of these natural developments of ego-altruism appear at times unamiable, or practically mischievous, is that, as aforesaid, men act as they can, not as they would, and make up their ideas of the intention they seek to realise as they go along, resolving while they act, and not discovering till after the event, nor indeed always then, what the consequences direct and remote of the action may be.

The immense majority of the pleasures indulged in by civilised adults are reducible to the satisfaction found in following normal impulses, or exercising natural faculties in the pursuit of ideal ends. The satisfaction of success as such is the same whatever the end proposed, and all ideal ends are alike unselfish, whether the choice of them is dictated by fancy, convention, or a moral consciousness of the necessity for compromise between different natural impulses. The multiplication of human faculties and the tendencies inciting to their exercise, which accompanies the growing complexity of social life, causes an ever larger proportion of civilised conduct to fall under the direction of disinterested will, instead of immediate personal desire, and we hope may even end by substituting direct personal desires for the good of all for isolated, self-regarding aims.

Most of the troubles of society arise from a miscalculation which is commonly made at this point, owing to the will having outgrown the reason, as well as the passions; or more exactly, as the will is properly the expression of the whole nature, owing to the supremacy within the nature of the active impulses over the intellect and the affections. In the early years or centuries of a progressive society, the ends which are sought by an increasing variety of means, are still only the ends desired by the natural man, namely, ease, enjoyment, and opportunity for pleasurable action. Now, as all action is in itself indifferent, and the actions performable by men practically infinite, while they can learn to take a faint pleasure in whichever they learn to perform successfully, it is evident that had men known beforehand which actions each member of the society would have to perform in order to secure himself and every other member in the peaceable exercise of as many natural faculties as possible, no selfish interest was concerned to prevent the harmonious compact. But they did not know. All began to follow natural innocent tendencies of their own, and the tendencies shortly began to come into collision. When sensible pleasures were concerned, there was a common ground, and simple personal rights were easily established by law or custom. The growth of the everyday virtues of temperance, honesty, industry, and politeness is perfectly intelligible as the result of growing social relations, which could only be made easy and permanent by their exercise; the general interest was not always present as a motive for the good behaviour of the individual, whose susceptibility, in fact, was by no means always so developed as to have made the conception of such interests a practical inducement; but the general set of motive power was in favour of the virtues being exercised, always, everywhere, and by every one, even when personal reasons were wanting to bribe the egotist to their exercise then and there.

Knowledge with its unvarying impartiality extends the narrow range of feeling, and the law which a man wishes to impose on his fellows, the constant formula of their duty to him which he ventures to proclaim, imposes itself on his own will as the natural and binding rule, unless his imagination is of the erratic quality, able to conceive the rest of the world as it really is, and himself as he is not, *i.e.*, independent of its general laws. But tendencies not immediately and visibly injurious to a man's neighbours, may, for that very reason, be followed unimpeded till the power of following them has become pleasurable, and the act of doing so a habit, painful to break. The individual then becomes selfishly attached to the pursuit of an intrinsically indifferent end, so that we may find the habit of a disinterested energy once formed and maintained without reference to rational inducements, simulating the appearance and producing the effects of an inconceivably insatiable egotism. To take a single, most obvious illustration : the pursuit of wealth is the principal and most absorbing occupation in modern societies, and it is a commonplace to observe that the pursuit becomes an end in itself to most of those who engage in it, though the enjoyment of possession is in the main symbolical. Millionaires go on adding automatically to their wealth, because their education has been too imperfect to suggest to them any useful or ornamental ways of diminishing it; and men who are so entirely at a loss for any intelligent employment for their money, that they delegate the task of throwing it away to their wives or sons, would yet resist with fervour any social changes that promised to make their labour less superfluously lucrative.

We should have good reason to despair of the social fabric if it were necessary for its safety that we should succeed in persuading the majority, or even a considerable minority of men, to act habitually in a way opposed to their own nature and desires. Such a task involves a logical contradiction as well as a moral impossibility. But nature can be educated, and desires are eminently variable; it is only when one desire has grown into a monomania, as the love of money with a miser, that reason has no hold upon the mind to suggest limits and conditions to be observed in its gratification. To most men the ruling passion, however strong it may be, still does not stand absolutely alone in the mind, other disinterested impulses coexist with it, and only the mental habit of giving precedence to one class of motives, not their greater natural pleasurableness, is answerable for the blind persistency with which men spend money for that which is not bread, and their labour for that which satisfieth not. As M. Littré observes, the chief use of education is to multiply motives for action; for to have many faculties is to have many impulses, to have many impulses is to be accessible to many motives, and to be accessible to many motives is to be in communication with many of the influences of the Not-self, instead of being bound in unreasoning constancy to one form of mechanical energising.

Most people are imperfect rather than bad, ignorant rather than perverse, their will is not radically depraved, but they do not see, or think, or feel, the whole real world only touches upon stray corners of their minds; they are but fractions of men, and need a providence to protect them, severally and conjointly, against the dangerous energy of fractions, acting blindly as if they were wholes. We are apt to take life too easily, forgetting for how many centuries human hands and brains have been at work to make it fruitfully hard; to rest satisfied with a narrow automatic compliance with the machinery of the society in which we live, forgetting that the machinery is all living and plastic, that the parts have to find their own place, to fit themselves together, to discover their own work, and that the machine has to regulate itself. Something more than disinterestedness is wanted here, for a society in which every one spent his time in seeking the advantage of somebody else might rival modern Europe in anarchy unless it had more intelligence in its service, while with sufficient intelligence it would probably come harmoniously to a dead-lock, since no one would have any interest of his own for the others to serve. As it has been observed, however, selfishness, in the evil sense, consists not "in a man's love to his own happiness, but in placing that happiness in things confined to himself;" and since no one really does, or can place his happiness in things confined to himself, it is evident that what society wants is not so much benevolence as common sense, not so much devotion as right reason, to lead its members to substitute, if necessary, for one set of indifferent actions, or one disinterested end, another set not more indifferent or disinterested, but more conducive to the common good.

The heightened sense of his own individuality which comes with the first widening of his mental horizon, leads the half-civilised man to conceive himself as the centre of the universe, which he thinks is only there to minister to his purposes. But as his knowledge extends and his sympathies become more various, he discovers that he can be affected by much that he cannot use, and act upon much that he cannot enjoy. This glimpse of a wider existence which it seems like a kind of suicide to renounce, co-operates with the other discovery which we have seen to be equally natural, and perhaps still more inevitable, that the universe is by no means chiefly concerned in ministering to the personal convenience or inclination of its inhabitants. The pleasures of passion are found to be uncertain or unattainable, just as the pleasures of faculty are found to be infinitely various and rather more than coextensive with the field for virtuous effort. The only source of pleasure connected with the more complex, artificial faculties is the pleasure of exercise, and all such exercises of faculty imply a multiplied altruism—concern with and subjection to many things and persons beside the self. But at the present stage in the world's history, in this nineteenth century, the free exercise of natural faculties is fraught with so many and distant consequences that to act much and yet to act always reasonably, that is, so as not to defeat the ends of any of the proposed actions by each other, has become so difficult that, since action after all is natural, to guide action by reason has become the supreme, almost the one needful, virtue. Reason has no power to invent motives, and no grounds to go upon in giving effect to one natural tendency rather than another, or to all rather than a few, if the subject of the tendency has no will, that is, if there is no conscious tendency pre-existing for the reason to direct. As a fact, however, men have a natural tendency to exert whatever natural faculties they possess, and reason has quite employment enough in guiding each real faculty into the channel in which its exercise will interfere least with other tendencies of equal strength and authority. And since the will is throughout disinterested, enlightened reason draws no distinction between the tendencies of the self and of other men; for the casual attachment of what we may call *self-will* to an end in no way peculiarly suited to the nature of the whole man is eminently ephemeral, its duration could not be calculated upon even if it were desired. The reason then agrees with the religiously disposed will in proposing to itself as an end the realisation or fulfilment of all the tendencies it discerns in nature in proportion to their strength or reality, and while it has no bias in favour of distinctively altruistic or benevolent impulses over egotistic or self-indulgent ones, the fact that all pleasures, except those of sense (which are inadequate to motive more than the simplest acts of life), have an altruistic element, namely, the desire for sympathy, and that some, as sympathy with the pleasures enjoyed by others, are entirely altruistic, warrants the conclusion that nature is at one with morality in the tendency to merge the particular in the universal good.

One life, our own, is too little for the least of us; we seek to impart our consciousness, our thoughts as well as our feelings, to others, and to receive back the impression of their consciousness as a part of our own, a fresh element in our personality, making us by so much the more alive. But while, on the one hand, we try to enrich our life by expansion and comprehension, by spreading it out in space and making concern for ourselves in the doings of others, of which it was not even necessary for us to know, on the other hand, our consciousness seeks, as it were, to integrate itself in time and maintain the continuity of its perceptions of yesterday and to-morrow. It is this instinctive desire to make life an organic whole that revolts against the glorification of pleasures that perish, as all sensible pleasures do, in the moment of possession, over the complex intellectual, and emotional states that pass, perhaps in a moment of comparative indifference, from anticipation to memory, and are as enjoyable in one as in the other shape. Knowledge by itself adds nothing to our desires, except to our desire for more knowledge; fresh powers ask no gratification except scope for their exercise, and the appetites, which cannot help us in our main aspiration, to make life rich, full, continuous, *one*, even if their strength remains otherwise unimpaired, come to occupy less of us in proportion. The power to enjoy becomes weakened by use and deadened by exercise, which makes enjoyment a habit, and as the habit of enjoyment becomes inveterate, its indulgence becomes increasingly difficult, and even laborious, and, labour for labour, the reason prefers a toil that is not spent in defeating its own ends.

It must not, of course, be supposed that a rationalised

account of existing practices has any but the faintest tendency to make practice more rational than it was before. To know what we are doing, and why we began to do it, is not a reason for ceasing from the deed, but neither is it a reason for persisting in it with more ardour than the original motive had inspired. The confusion between the speculative and the hortatory elements in most moral treatises is due, as before observed, to the fact that every one is really agreed in thinking morality good, and that, therefore, theories of the nature of morality expect to seem convincing in proportion to the success with which they represent its excellence to the imagination. The correctness of a theory of virtue is not unreasonably thought to be shown and proved by its practical influence in making its adherents virtuous. But though virtuous conduct is substantially the same with every one, the motives that prevail with each individual in his moral resolves will be as various as his opinions respecting the comparative desirability of different ends. If nobody could be good except the adherents of a sound ethical system, virtue would perhaps not exist at all, or else it would be the monopoly of a single sect. The manifest absurdity of claiming such a monopoly for the small school of scientific atheists obliges the theory to be content with tracing the virtue of atheists and theists to a common root, without pretending to furnish either class, much less both, with one motive of universal application and unfailing effect.

We only claim to have given a ground of common sense and plain reason to a few ethical commonplaces, which without such ground are open to suspicion as edifying prejudices. Such brief and trite results had need to be self-evident. The whole duty of man, we say, is to live a sane and ample life in harmony with his fellows. He does no wrong who lives sanely and innocently; he does right who not only lives well himself but furthers the efforts of others to live well likewise. It is not well to live unhappily, but it is not wrong to prefer the happiness of others to our own, and it is supremely right to prefer the good of others, as well as our own good, to our own happiness or enjoyment. This is the sum and substance of the moral law, which suffers neither change nor diminution from the particular facts included in our moral experiences.

Those men who are all incoherent impulse and ignorant desire—and every theory of morality must recognise the existence of individuals possessing little moral strength or stability—are habitually overborne by the current of more methodical energy, and leave few heirs to their infirmity of will. Those who have coherent, if not altogether intellectual desires, pursue in the main persistently the course that promises to secure their gratification, and adapt themselves almost unconsciously to the conditions which their place in society imposes on the pursuit; each class, like each individual, works out a morality of its own from some fixed starting-point of impulse growing into use, and none of the impulses capable of being followed with disinterested moral resolution are in themselves bad, only, as was observed of the legalisation of class custom, no one impulse is a safe guide in its own cause, and classes with a ruling impulse not much controlled by intelligence are apt to act in a way that their present sympathies would lead them to call immoral if they realised more clearly what it was. Moral remonstrances cannot make humane impulses or sympathetic emotions where they do not exist, and where they do exist, morality exists implicitly, in premises that may be appealed to and built upon with confidence. Ignorance, not disinterested malice, is the arch-foe to the wellbeing of society, and without any addition to the purely social virtues or to the conscientiousness of individuals, the effect upon the will of fresh knowledge or a clearer perception of facts before but dimly apprehended, may be entirely moral in result, though no other sanctions than the natural consequences of the action are present to enforce its performance or omission.

But—if we have succeeded in showing the origin of human ideas respecting the just, the obligatory, and the good to be entirely natural and their existence necessary—critics, who are not quite satisfied with the premises that allow of such a conclusion being reached, will perhaps retort, as sceptics are wont to do to the orthodox upholders of established truth, by asking for an explanation, no longer of the origin of good, but for that of evil, not how virtue is possible, but why imperfection is real.

The human intellect is incapable of formulating or understanding any other reason *why* a thing is thus or thus, than a full, true, and particular account of *how* it is, in itself and in relation to all the other things that are. The origin of evil is the existence of things imperfect after their kind, and each separate concrete case of imperfection has a long history which accounts to the reason for the precise degree of imperfection observed to be a fact; but concerning anything antecedent to the beginning of the history—that is to say, any process or state generically alien to whatever may be apprehended or represented by sense, thought, or imagination—rational thought and sane imagination observe an absolute and unbroken silence; not that science has come to the end of the knowable, or that existing forms of thought are final and inexpansive, but that whatever we know and think has at least the one quality in common, that it is known and thought by men, and is therefore *not* antecedent to the real, historical conditions of human knowledge and thought.

It is a fact that things of various degrees of perfection exist, and the consciousness of his own existence, which is most strongly marked in man, takes in him the form of an affirmation by the will of the precise degree of perfection actually attained at any moment. The will is not a lawgiver imposing a constant course of action on something different from itself; an act of will is the declaration by the individual of that which it is natural to him to do under the circumstances actually existing, and this declaration is determined or conditioned by the nature of the individual and the circumstances conjointly; it states the relation existing between them in a single case, such as, if constantly recurring, would form a law. The most general statement that we can easily make about the effect on the human will and human affections of the objective pressure of social motives is, to say that they determine a moral liking or preference for those actions and feelings which are best *at the same time* for the ego concerned and for other human beings, best for the two parties in their real relation, or in other words, those which establish between them the best of possible constant relations; while there is an incalculably stronger presumption in favour of the best for both being realised if the immediate object of pursuit is the good of others than if it is the personal good of the agent. Duty speaks with the lawful authority of many voices; pleasure has no strength except in the longing desire of the hungry unit, who, in the immense majority of cases, is capable of attaining to a direct perception of the comparative weakness of the force embodied in himself, when that force is not in harmony with the external demands of surrounding facts; and in all these cases the rational and moral nature of the man puts itself, sometimes deliberately, sometimes automatically, on the side which in a superficial sense is certainly "other" than its own.

The truly lawful conduct is motived, in the double sense which that word will bear, by inducement as well as instigation, because there is an affirmation by the feelings of the effect produced, answering to the affirmation by the will of the action taken, when both are in all respects normal, *i.e.*, when the natural tendencies of the agent and of the environment coincide. And Nemesis, the only god who indeed bears a hand, heavy and hard, in appointing the lives of men—Nemesis orders things so that, by acts which are contrary to the natural law of virtuous effort, the doer of them is brought into painful collision with the work of the saner tendencies around. Nemesis, indeed, is but the name under which we personify these recurring experiences of collision, whereby there forces itself upon the transgressor, either as a timely warning or a late judgment, the direct consciousness of real, constant, irresistible power in nature—a power of life and of death for men, but most especially of life to those who have the will to live lawfully, and of death, temporal and spiritual, to all who set their hearts on disobedience. And every fragmentary glimpse we get of this supreme tendency of nature towards self-assertion serves to sanction some special law of human conduct or feeling.

VI.

THE NATURAL SANCTIONS OF MORALITY.

"Even the wise and good have a fear in them which is an instrument of justice and religion; . . . it is a fear that is natural, a fear produced from the congenite notices of things, and the fear of doing a base thing; a fear to be a fool and an evil person."—JEREMY TAYLOR.

"Every hour," answered the princess, "confirms my prejudice in favour of the position so often uttered by the mouth of Imlac: 'That nature sets her gifts on the right hand and on the left.'"—JOHNSON.

Causes and effects inseparable; so the dislike felt for the natural consequences of an immoral act, which in itself is pleasant or temptingly easy, acts as a sanction to enforce the law against it—The natural law against murder, theft, inconstancy, and suicide—Waste of moral force in the exercises of false religions—Doctrine of remission of sins an immoral evasion of the painful stringency of the natural sanction, that a wrong cannot be undone, though atoned and amended—Remorse the consciousness of having acted against the true nature—That human nature is thus and thus is the efficient, not the final cause of the conscious tendency or moral will to live according to nature.

VI.

THE NATURAL SANCTIONS OF MORALITY.

THE penal sanctions by which the injunctions of natural morality are enforced are the objective counterpart to the influence of natural motives or inducements, in strengthening the conscious tendency of will by the half-imaginative, half-intellectual consciousness of desire. The causal antecedents of a voluntary act are also the conditions of the general mental disposition which makes the end or natural effect of the action appear desirable, if it is reflected upon at all; but the reflection, if it occurs, is a new condition, which confirms to some extent the previous tendency towards efficient action. There is a double assurance for the performance of any given rational action (or act implying the adjustment of means to an end) when the individual is resolved upon the end as well as the means, and there is a similar security against the performance of actions naturally uncongenial to the will, in the power of reason to foresee that the consequences of such actions will be even more distasteful to the whole nature of the subject than the action itself. The effects of any action follow certainly and necessarily upon it, and human desire or wish is not a force by which the nature of things or their property of producing given results under given conditions can be modified or controlled. There is a natural necessity upon men, if they will the attainment of any particular end, to will the steps by which it is naturally possible to reach it, and to refrain from willing the means that lead naturally to results that they are seriously resolved or desirous *not* to produce.

The subjection of man, as a conscious and rational agent, no less than as a material organism, to the laws of nature, consists in the fact that he is habitually bound by other powers than his own will to certain classes of actions; the sanctions which conspire with the regular action of natural causes to make the actions of men more constant than their desires are not themselves the most important element in the law, because they only take effect when a rule has been broken, or when—as in most cases contemplated by moralists—it is supposed that the will would break the rule it normally follows, but for a rational expectation that the breach of the rule would entail consequences which the will is not prepared to face. The sanctions have a practical, occasional value, but their existence is not the cause, even in the latter class of cases, of the obedience habitually paid to the moral law, since the compulsion they exercise is only alternative, and it is the disposition of the will, or the whole nature of the individual, that determines which motives will have an attractive, and what sanctions an efficiently deterrent influence upon his mind and conduct.

The natural sanction of the natural law against murder is the impossibility of bringing the dead to life. A momentary act of angry violence may cause the brother who was only hated for a moment to be lost for ever; hence the necessity for controlling violent impulses becomes apparent to the will, which has no abstract delight in violence, and, other things being equal, from the first dawn of society, slightly prefer the life of other members of the community to their death. The natural sanction of the natural law against theft is the impossibility of two people enjoying exclusive possession of the same object at the same time, while some degree of security in the possession of needful instruments is essential to any long course of rational action towards ends, such as civilised life is principally made up of. The natural sanction of the natural law in favour of veracity is the impossibility of sustained intercourse without reciprocal trust. The natural sanctions enforcing personal sobriety are self-evident. The natural sanction of the obligation of parents to provide for their children is the simple fact that infants perish if not supplied with food and shelter; and when the instinctive tendency of animals to nourish their young (without which no brute species would live through two generations) has been so far weakened amongst men that the alternative of deliberately destroying children that it is inconvenient to rear, can be entertained and adopted, the sanction operates with respect to the children whom it is determined to preserve.[1]

It has been doubted by some secular moralists whether there is any natural sanction enforcing the law by which monogamy is prescribed, as we find, historically, that it has been in most states possessing an advanced and balanced civilisation. Godwin, whose "Political Justice" contains, under the head of "Inferences from the doctrine of necessity," much admirably humane and rational morality, proposed to abolish marriage altogether, and as society is almost unanimous in thinking Godwin ill-advised on this point, one of the strongest of the *argumenta ad hominem* commonly used against free-thinking refers to a supposed connection between theological and conjugal infidelity. If—as writers like Godwin were half inclined to believe—priests invented gods in order to make the birth, death, and burial of their dupes the occasion for elaborate ceremonies profitable to themselves, they might be supposed to have invented marriage as well as divers other sacraments, in order to make their influence felt at every important juncture of life. But if

---

[1] It is found in India that even female children, if not exposed at birth, are never afterwards destroyed, being sufficiently protected, we may presume, by the ordinary reluctance of men to sacrifice a life that has become to some extent, through habit, if not affection, a part of their own.

we take a less extreme view of the fertility of the human imagination and its power of baseless invention, we may suppose, as has been done in the preceding pages, that the crudest religious belief has something answering to it in nature and fact, and shall infer that a contract of marriage must have been an event of considerable natural and secular importance before it could occur to religious functionaries to treat it as sacramental.

When the legal, moral, and religious aspects of customary ordinances were confused and interchangeable, only those ordinances were conceived as mainly and primarily religious which were of such general application as to rank almost with the real influences of the Not-self upon the natural life of every member of the community. If we do not allow religion to be of supernatural origin or power, it cannot have lent a supernatural sanctity to the marriage tie; and if respect for that tie is almost as universal as religion, its existence must be almost as universally natural. The rationalists, who ignore this inference, do so, no doubt, because early habit and the constant assertions of the orthodox lead them to accept as logical and inevitable the connection which has prevailed historically between the established religion of all countries and their marriage laws, so that if the one is subverted the other is supposed to share in its condemnation. But it does not follow that, because monogamy ceases to be regarded as a religious duty, some form of polygamy will certainly be adopted in any society where naturalistic views of morality and religion come to prevail. There are reasons of general validity that would lead many persons, whatever their theological views, to prefer—if they could secure it—a freehold in the affections of their nearest friend to a mere tenancy at will; and though the passions are not sufficiently rational to be directly affected by the knowledge of the consequences that follow naturally from their unrestrained indulgence, any real emotion, while it is real, is *ipso facto* a force tending to exclude from the consciousness any fresh passion incompatible with itself. The emotions are natural, and their real strength necessary and irresistible; but since life is not providentially adjusted so as to make the indulgence of every natural tendency easy, or all coexisting tendencies harmonious, it is impossible but that the necessity of sacrificing one natural feeling to another should sometimes arise. It is because such sacrifices cannot be effected by a single deliberate act of will that, in spite of their occasional necessity, they are felt to stand on a different footing from ordinary moral acts or efforts.

To love or hate unwisely is a moral imperfection of the same innocent, incorrigible sort as to have and act upon ideas of moral duty such as the mass of mankind agree to think erroneous; while the passion is felt, and the conscientious belief entertained, it cannot, strictly speaking, be called right for the individual to become false to either,[1] in act or thought. Only as human perfection does not consist in the supremacy of any one faculty or class of impulses, but in the balanced and harmonious development of all, it is not open to consistent rationalists to proclaim the natural autocracy of any one passion, however universal or potent in its influence. If we consent, as rationalists must, to judge humanity only by itself, we must allow that it is an imperfection to fail in intelligence or moral strength of character, as well as to fail in that sensitiveness to moral impressions which is the source of emotional affections. Neither defect can be remedied by a simple act of will;. but supposing the individual to have become conscious of the defect, and desirous for its removal, there is a reaction of the whole nature upon the single faculty that is deficient, which stimulates its development, and indirectly favours its exercise. Nothing can make the affections in themselves rational—though, on the average, people are loved for amiable traits—just

[1] A thesis dramatically illustrated in Mr. Browning's poem, "The Statue and the Bust."

as nothing can turn abstract reasoning into a motive force —though efficient motives are, on the average, active in the direction of deliberately chosen ends; but the affections are the stronger for having their natural movements confirmed by reason, just as thought is the more varied, and impulse the more energetic, when the two unite to supply one the matter, the other the form, of rational action. Each single tendency is weak and short-lived by itself; it requires preserving, propping, continuing, and reinforcing by finding itself at one with other harmoniously parallel tendencies. The will or reason cannot argue away a real affection by practical or prudential considerations, but they can and do show it to be, in the natural and secular sense of the words, both wise and right to take care, so to speak, of certain affections, to protect and cherish them, to let their indulgence borrow strength from habit, and guarantee their durability by a foregone conclusion that they *ought* to be permanent.

The natural sanction that visits all inconstancy, and especially inconstancy in the most serious passion of life, derives its deterrent force from the craving men have to give continuity, organic completeness to their life, to affiliate their sentiments, to make their best emotions fruitful of hopes and memories. If the natural emotions of men who look before and after could only repeat at stated intervals the same short, absorbing, and monotonous story of passion, satiety, and weary indifference, which after each repetition is shorter, less absorbing, and more monotonous than before, the rational will would perhaps adopt the ascetic view, which treats all the natural passions as intrinsically evil. But if no natural tendencies are in themselves evil or naturally self-destructive, it must be possible for the exclusive and passionate attachment consecrated in the ideal marriage to fit itself in amongst all the other interests, engagements, and relations of life, as one element amongst many, making up a coherent and complete whole; and if this has once been accomplished, and the accomplishment recorded in consciousness, no after-incident of natural infirmity or external seduction can make it appear altogether good to the individual will to sacrifice a part of itself and its history to instincts that have neither past nor future.

It will perhaps be objected that such general considerations as these are too remote to influence the will to any practical sacrifice of inclination, and in fact their effect would naturally be felt rather in controlling inclination than action, which is a further confirmation of the view that the emotions have more in common with religion than with morality. But the general belief referred to is the source of the natural cogency in this case of what may be called the social sanction, or the expression of opinion by the community, which in all moral dilemmas gives weight and additional efficacy to the promptings of the individual conscience. It is scarcely reasonable to expect that any legislation, however liberal, or any society, however tolerant, should have power to efface the natural difference observable between persons who have and those who have not made a serious mistake in one of the most important affairs of life. Of course nearly all human mistakes may be repaired, or made the best of, but the natural sanction by which men are reminded to exercise all the moral forethought that they can, is the fact from which there is no escaping, that, though it is better to repair a mistake than to persist in it, it is, humanly speaking, still better not to make mistakes that need to be repaired. Positive law has nothing to do with the natural, almost logical impossibility that a couple married after ten or twenty divorces by mutual consent should seem to themselves or to society to be as indissolubly united at last as Philemon and Baucis or John Anderson and his goodwife. Positive law has nothing to do with the general belief that the perfection of the marriage union is to be complete and absolute—while it lasts—and it has nothing to do with the necessity by which a complete and absolute union appears naturally indissoluble; or rather, it has as much to do with these as with any other natural practices and opinions; its function is to declare their regularity and necessity.

Any propensity, if indulged to excess, tends to cut off its own springs of enjoyment in the healthy power of the whole organism; and the natural sanction which warns every normal appetite to respect the demands of the rest, is the experience that only the healthy, or evenly developed nature has life and freshness enough to return again and again to its familiar pleasures, and find them always the same, that is, always newly pleasant; while the man of one passion, or of one idea, needs to make that one ever more intense or more fantastical to compensate for the growing dulness of his sensibilities, arising from the atrophy of every faculty but the one. And what is true of appetites applies, *mutatis mutandis*, to impulses, which can only survive if followed, with conscious or instinctive prudence, in such wise as not to land their subject at a point beyond which further action in the same direction is made physically impossible.

There is one act to which it is scarcely possible to speak of applying purely natural sanctions, while at the same time its condemnation has generally been regarded as a crucial test of the stringency of moral theories—we mean the practical slight upon the natural order of things involved in the offence of suicide; an offence which natural morality is as well able as any other theory to gratify popular feeling by condemning. The popular illustration which attempts to discredit suicide by the analogy of a soldier deserting his post obviously requires a theological background to give it aptness, for if the doctrine of the conservation of force is applied, as it presumably may be, to thought and sense as well as to unconscious motion, the suicide does not defraud the universe of any profit it had or might have had out of his being, he simply restores to it the force it lent him, which has proved to be inadequate to the maintenance of a human life. Suicide is a confession of defective vitality, abnormal weakness, or exceptional ill-luck, and no man is in a position to say of another that he "ought not" to have made away with himself, because, when the act is done, it is evident that the impulse to do it was irresistible, and natural morality does not exactly condemn or blame the individual who is merely proved to have suffered from extreme natural debility or imperfection. But though the man who can do no good by living may have a right to die, he should look on his own death as the execution of a good-for-nothing unit rather than as the excision of a good-for-nothing world from a too fastidious consciousness. For those, however, who have sufficient strength of will, that is, a sufficiently distinct consciousness of vital force in their organisation, to last as long as their natural, automatic, bodily life, there may be room, when external circumstances are unpropitious, for strictly moral considerations which forbid suicide in the same way as any positive disservice to humanity. Desertion is not a crime in a conscript pressed into the service of a usurper and called to march, perhaps, against his own countrymen; but as we do not believe the universe to be governed by an assailable evil spirit, any more than by an adorable good one, we cannot make a duty of insurrection, or see any magnanimity in the suicide's futile protest against things in general. As George Eliot has it:—

> " Noble rebellion lifts a common load;
> But what is he who flings his own load off
> And leaves his fellows toiling ?"

Though human existence were a losing battle against the Not-man, it might still be worth fighting out for charity; for those combatants who have fewest illusions about an impossible triumph are most at leisure for possible precautions against unnecessary disaster, and can do something, if they will, to save the discomfiture of the doomed host from turning into a disorderly rout, and to assure the panic-stricken troops that they will not reach their last halting-place the sooner, or the later—and which were best ?— for treading on each other's heels by the way.

But such statements of the case are morbid and overstrained. In point of fact, the natural, realistic way of looking at the world and human affairs is as far removed from pessimism as from uncritical adoration; and if criticism of the universal order is carried beyond a certain point, satire becomes as meaningless as panegyric, for in an absolutely bad world, if such a thing could be, we should not have, what we could no more use than in a perfect universe, the ideas of good and evil, or language wherewithal to criticise.

As to the most general of moral duties, the one which includes all the rest, the duty of Christian charity—as we may still call it, on the principle of rendering to all their due, and keeping our diction historical—the natural sanction by which this duty is enforced is the impossibility of excluding from a consciousness of even ordinary intellectual and emotional sensibility the knowledge, or rather the feeling, of the moral as well as the material effects following from causes lying within the determination of the will. Habits of united or concerted action have become so integral a part of our life that the sympathetic feeling which has sprung from them passes now for an essential, primitive quality of our nature, and indeed is so essential that an entirely consistent egotist might be reckoned as one of the "perfect monsters that the world ne'er saw." It is become impossible for us to be altogether indifferent to the feelings we know to be entertained by those with whom we are in relation. What we do or say takes effect, not merely by direct action of its own, or by the action which it suggests or provokes; but the effects are such as can be *felt* by some, whose feeling, if it is such as we cannot deliberately will to cause, is the efficient motive for forbearing from the act. It is not exactly from an overflowing charity that we first entangle our life with other lives, and sacrifice a portion of our natural liberty to act alone and unembarrassed; but the moral life of man is, as he labours to make it, continuous, and his consciousness, at any given moment, is as much controlled by the historical engagements contracted by his former self as by his natural disposition or acquired moral development. The life that we borrowed, meaning it to enrich and embellish our own, may serve that purpose or not, but it grows into a part of ourselves, and cannot be torn off without leaving a moral scar, or wounded without causing an entirely personal pain, which cannot be got rid of by wishing, even though the rise of some fresh personal desire, irreconcilable with older ties, may make it natural for a man to wish sometimes, for the moment, that no one had any feelings but himself.

The physical force, as it may be called, of sympathy, is not to be confounded either with the moral development of sympathetic feeling which makes the good of others as much an end as our own good, or with the weight of the social sanction properly so called, the naturally selected feeling of the mass of men, for or against various actions —a feeling which we share more or less completely ourselves, but which acts upon us, by the mere force of its existence, even when we deliberately defy it. Morality is not only the rule which I think good for myself and others; it is the rule which others agree in thinking good for me. In the immense majority of cases the feeling of the majority is right, and the fear of its disapproval tends to enforce a wholesome conformity; but the inner and the outer conscience are independent, so that if the one is biassed by partial considerations, the other is ready to check its verdict; and just because they are independent, their decision, when they agree, has even more than double authority; each speaks for the other in speaking for itself, and when the two voices coincide, it is not in virtue of a mere coincidence of opinion, it is because, as a matter of fact, the particular and the universal good are naturally concordant. The natural good of each individual is bound up with the good of those of his kind, and thus it is that the natural impulse of each individual organism to escape, if it can, from the pain of natural imperfection, co-operates with the complicated, purely moral and deliberately disinterested tendency of the cultivated conscience to find its good in the wellbeing of the whole, in the rational co-operation of sympathetic desires and resolute, compliant wills, working in conscious harmony towards the multiform realisation of natural human perfection.

Supposing all the good and evil in the actual world to be the result of a long natural process of evolution, which has become conscious in its latest stages, the consciousness of such stages is conditioned, not only by the preceding steps in the process, but also by the various other real surviving effects or consequences of them. Moral action is therefore in no sense arbitrary or accidental, and the practical bearings of a naturalistic theory of morality will therefore depend, not upon the nature of the theory, but on the way in which, we are led to conclude, the objective constitution of the universe compels a reasonable man habitually to will. We do not hold a brief for creation, and it would sound like an edifying paradox to maintain that the natural order of things compels men to the practice of all the moral virtues. There is vice as well as misery more than enough under the sun; we only contend that the *quantum* of virtue, such as it is, actually to be met with upon earth, is not greater than can be accounted for by purely natural causes, still in operation and perhaps not incapable of by-and-by producing more extensive results. The constitution of the universe is the cause, the one real antecedent condition of the existence of virtue in man, but the motive for any single virtuous action is supplied by the virtuous disposition of the man who proposes to perform it, not by the fact—or by his knowledge of the fact—that his disposition is conditioned by the orderly existences around him. Indeed if the virtuous disposition is incomplete, reflections concerning its origin are not by themselves likely to strengthen it, for duties towards the universe as a whole are the least and weakest of the obligations spontaneously recognised by contemporary consciences.

It is possible that as the intellectual horizon widens with "the long result of time," men may become more clearly conscious of the most general laws according to which they lead their life, and to know the laws of life is at least to have learned not to hope for happiness from an impossible escape out of their control. But visions of the future are veiled in a dim religious light, and for the present the only motives that take effect with men, women, and children, who are in doubt whether to do as they think right or not, are reflections concerning other points of principle or practice, concerning which they are not then in doubt at all. All that we call "good" is linked together in man, as the circumstances calling it forth are in nature; and if our theory is sound, it is as impossible for any one at a given moment to be a worse specimen of his kind than he is, as it is for him at the same moment to be a better. But amongst the natural sanctions enforcing the necessity of which men are conscious as binding them to the exercise of all the specific virtue that is in them, not the least efficacious is the natural incapacity under which they labour, of wishing, at any given moment, to be worse, of their kind, than they actually are. People always wish to remain themselves, even when they wish to do something tending certainly to make them worse than they have been. They wish to be able to do what they think agreeable and wrong as often as their present self wishes, and they may be restrained from the vain attempt to gratify that wish by the discovery that a given amount of wrongdoing will make them unable to refrain, on a future occasion, from doing more wrong than they *now* wish to do.

Men of the world, who take it on faith from the clergy (of all denominations) that religion helps to keep the *canaille* in order, and pious persons, who take it on faith from the worldly that the pleasures of vice have a quite peculiar zest and intensity, will probably agree in objecting to all the applications we can suggest for a theory of natural morality that they are unpractical; that the theory is not disedifying—in theory—but that it will not work; that it may do no harm to the few bloodless philosophers, worn-out worldlings, and hybrid pedants who may incline to adopt it, but that it will be powerless against the strong passions and weak brains of the generality of mankind. La Rochefoucauld has said it: "Si nous resistons à nos passions, c'est plus par leur faiblesse que par notre force;" and it may be conceded to the motley army of provisional pessimists, who will not easily improve upon this sarcasm, that the theory we have propounded will have no effect upon the mind or morals of persons who do not sincerely think it true, while it as certainly cannot hope for the fate, which has never yet fallen to the lot of a theory, of being thought true by everybody. Criticism on this point, to be really damaging, would have to establish that the practical inferences which we have drawn from the theory would not follow from it, if it can be rationally held.

By a curious reversal of the Utilitarian mistake, religious moralists seem to assume that happiness is to be found in this world if we only have the courage to be wicked enough: were this indeed so, with the strongest desire to think well of human nature—should we not all turn wicked to-morrow? But those who lay most stress on the assumption have so evidently never tried the experiment they speak of, that to them, at any rate, it is clearly natural to be good. If the world were exactly as we may suppose Saint Anthony believed it to be, if theft, murder, adultery, and evil-speaking were the natural pleasures of the human race, if our best joys came through the senses, without any reference to our knowledge of their causes or the effects of their indulgence, morality would be impossible instead of hard, unnatural instead of necessary; but the balance of inducement leans really to the other side, though not so overwhelmingly as to preclude the possibility of misleading oscillations. There is no prince of darkness baiting cunning snares for our souls, and the charm of forbidden fruit disappears when we see beyond the prohibition to the reasons which dictated it. The clown whose happiest moments are when he is a quarter drunk, may wish to spend his life in drinking. A youth of untaught mind and untrained character, turned loose upon the *Quartier Latin* of a metropolis, may go to the dogs in all innocence and good faith, believing with the fervour of inexperience in absinthe, dice, and courtesans, and the irreconcilability of marriage or professional industry with the higher life of the *genialisch* soul. But the educated naturalist, with whose morality we are concerned, must be supposed to have got beyond such naïve illusions as these. Regard for his health and his purse will keep him sober and moderately decorous in life, as regard for his neck and his personal liberty will prevent his murdering or stealing, the latter, indeed, as Clough observes—

"An empty feat
When 'tis so lucrative to cheat."

Without running such risks, it is open to him to lie and swindle, to hate his neighbour and love his neighbour's wife, to thrive upon the follies, the vices, the sufferings of his fellow-men, to trade upon their superstitions, to draw his profit from their virtues. It is in his power to indulge his appetites as long as he has any, to neglect his duties till he has forgotten they existed, to check his sympathies till they cease to interfere with his most mischievous pleasures. Neither God nor man can hinder: we have assumed that there is no God to punish, and as to the opinion of his equals, if such a plan of life as this really seems the most eligible to one sane man, who has studied the order of the world and learned to view its facts in their true proportions, doubtless the others, being of like passions with himself, will in their secret hearts think him a clever fellow for leading it successfully. If such a prospect does not attract us—and candidly, does it?—the reason must be that this also is vanity and vexation of spirit; that the pleasures of vice, like those of virtue, are an agreed-upon fiction.

The chief advantage to practical morality from the abandonment of the theistic hypothesis would consist in the economy of moral force effected by substituting in all cases the main purpose and immediate consequence proposed for the side-issues and indirect motives, with their attendants, the widening waste and misunderstanding produced by over-symbolical reasoning. The amount of force in the world at a given moment is the same, whatever may be thought about its origin or the possible effects to be produced by it; but the direction given to the force determines its real productive efficacy. As motion can pass into heat and back again into so much mechanical work, conscious force may be suspended or arrested as passion or pain, and when liberated, discharge itself in fresh intellectual or moral action. Theistical morality regards the real world as of secondary importance to the relations between the individual and an unknowable spiritual power; and it is only the fragments of energy remaining, after all the best strength of the individual nature has been expended in an intensity of religious emotion, that is available for purely human ends and interests. It is a remarkable evidence of the general solidarity of existence and the substantial justice of the popular conceptions respecting the tendencies of the moral influence of the Not-self, that an extraneous motive, regard for an ideal third power outside man and nature, should so often and generally have acted as the natural, direct, and present motive of regard for the beings to be affected by our action would do; but the parallelism may be accidentally disturbed, and then, in place of the innocently circuitous argument of Jonathan Edwards—that since men cannot reward the Deity for his virtues, they should do good to their "indigent brethren" for his sake—people may learn to burn, or at least conscientiously to dislike each other, still for the love of God. If, as will probably be admitted, it would conduce to the natural good of society for men's sympathy with each other's pains and pleasures, and their readiness to relieve or promote the same, to be more lively and active than is the case, it is evidently a misfortune to risk the loss of such help or sympathy as may be had, by conducting it to its natural object along an unnecessarily winding channel.

Another way in which theism is unfavourable to morality, or at least less favourable than simple realism, is that it diminishes the sense of responsibility which accompanies actions performed in accordance with fully intelligible laws. Men with a finer sense of natural justice than the ancient Hebrews, believe in a God too just to visit the sins of the fathers upon the children, too just not, sooner or later, somehow or other, to right whatever moral wrongs men in ignorance or wilfulness may have done to one another. In this way the most powerful of all the natural sanctions of morality, the knowledge of the inevitable sequence of effects and causes, is robbed of half its proper influence on the imagination. Many men who would not scruple to sin against themselves or a Creator, would hesitate to sin irreparably against a fellow-mortal, if they did not half believe in a power Not-themselves, able and willing to undo the natural effects of their work. To understand that the will of every man is a moral power, second to nothing except the united or compounded will of many men, does not make men less, but rather more disposed to value the type of human perfection which they have no choice but to conceive as the supreme good; and to understand that, if they wish this type to be realised, they must realise it themselves, does not make them less, but rather more disposed than before to take the practical action which they suppose to be favourable to their desire. If we want anything done, do not like doing it, and are quite assured that if we do not do it ourselves, no one else can or will do it for us, to say in pique at this ungenerous behaviour of nature—It shall go undone—is perfectly possible, but nature has the last word in the quarrel, whether the object we had in view was happiness or virtue. We may take or leave the small quantum of pleasure offered to us by the natural order, but if we take it, we take it on the prescribed terms, if we leave it, it is at the price of our own natural loss. Similarly if the desired end of undesirably difficult attainment is moral, *i.e.*, such as the judgment finds it impossible not to approve, the approbation is not affected by the difficulty, and continues to be a motive in its despite. A person of ordinary moral sensibility would feel it to be unjust to visit the cross-grained arrangements of creation upon an otherwise deserving object, already, probably, a victim to some severe natural ordinance; and it is scarcely conceivable that a person bent on doing a good action from the disinterested love of good, should be deterred from doing it by the discovery that he will have no supernatural assistance in the process. It may be a misfortune to mankind that there are no gods, but the weak, wicked, and ignorant of the present generation, who are the natural objects of humane solicitude, are obviously not to blame for a misfortune which, it may be thought, falls most severely on themselves. Certainly it does not prove that there are gods, that the maxim, "Every man for himself, and God for us all," may prove extremely comfortable to those who do not doubt their own ability to take care of themselves without divine assistance, and feel at liberty to exercise their natural powers of self-protection the less scrupulously and considerately for supposing such assistance to be at the service of their weaker brethren, who—to translate the secret thoughts of some robust liberals—are such fools as to want it.

In ascribing an empirical relational necessity to morality, instead of a transcendental force or fitness of which the working cannot be followed either by sense or reason, we certainly do not weaken the practical efficacy of its precepts. If there is a specific type or standard of human excellence, varying almost imperceptibly, and not seeming to the members of the species in whom the tendency to approximate to the type is conscious, to vary for the worse, the natural tendency towards such approximation, which exists more or less strongly in every sane human being, exists equally whether we suppose a power to exist outside consciousness that approves of the subjects of the strongest tendency or not. To follow the tendency in order to secure this approbation is a course that would occur to no one who had not previously discovered, or imagined, points of intellectual agreement and moral sympathy with the power by whom it is supposed to be bestowed; such a sense of harmony between the individual and the Not-self regarded as a legislator is religious, and a sincere and enlightened religious faith enforces the moral instincts by sanctions which are undoubtedly binding upon the few with whom religious faith is a reality. But these sanctions, which are efficient, though not universal in their operation, are immaterial, emotional, and subjective. Religion generalises the tendencies of the universal order, and represents them collectively as binding upon those who acquiesce in their isolated reality, in the same way that morality generalises the impulses of the individual, and represents his habitual disposition or will as a force controlling partial and ephemeral inclinations. And as, out of all the real tendencies of the universe, there is no one more constantly influential on human life than the self-assertion of human nature which we call morality, none is more influential in determining the religious generalisation, which, being wider than the moral generalisation, seems to include, and even in a measure to explain it, by standing between it and the irrational finality of an ultimate fact.

It is a remnant of superstitious optimism to assume that if morality is natural, moral imperfection must be impossible, and the objection that our theory takes no account of the moral struggles of a divided will, cannot on reflection be maintained. The fact that a person may know and believe that an act is certainly right, and yet not do it, proves nothing for or against one system of morality rather than another. We do not maintain that any man, much less that all men, are absolutely perfect after their kind; kinds are always making, never made, and the consensus of all the powers of the soul which makes knowledge or belief practically effective, is rare and seldom complete. Were it otherwise, the consciousness of voluntary effort in men towards the realisation of their own perfection, and the perfecting of all the other modifiable elements of the natural world after their kind, in which we have seen morality to consist, would not need the stimulus of religion, or of any other natural sanction, to give it persistence. But when moral action has been made difficult in proportion to the strength of the tendency towards perfection of which the individual is conscious, or when the consciousness of the real tendency is imperfectly articulate, the secondary representative influence of the natural sanction is neither superfluous nor ineffectual. The immediate motive for the performance of any virtuous action is the judgment of the individual that the act is good and *ought* to be done: the sanction by which the doing of it is enforced is the knowledge of the natural effects of the omission; the consciousness that every single failure to act as human justice and charity demand is irremediable in time or eternity; that by the act which we call wrong, we contribute in our measure to make the world other than, seriously and deliberately, we would have it to be—to mar creation out of wantonness and imbecility. This is the most general form of moral necessity. The world suffers—is the worse—for every laches of every individual, for every sin of omission and commission, in the present ill, in the chance of unforeseeable consequences, and in the future deterioration of the sinner. Of course there are degrees, but this is the sufficient reason and real explanation of the general *rule* that the best possible ought always to be done; and while we tax any other moral standard than this with incompleteness, it cannot be said that this is itself preternaturally high. We recognise no impossible ought, and the duty of each individual is really limited by his powers—as well as coextensive with them. No one has done his duty who has done less than he could, *i.e.*, produced less than the good effect which his particular gifts conscientiously employed to the best advantage might have wrought. The responsibility of the man as a whole is coextensive with his consciousness of definite powers, and duties of imperfect obligation are only so styled in reference to an imperfect susceptibility to the force of a real claim. If from constitutional feebleness these powers are not exerted, we call the man, not indeed wicked, but weak, distinguishing, among various forms of imperfection, simple defect of energy from its pernicious malapplication.

Remorse or repentance, the state of consciousness which follows action done in opposition to the sense of duty or moral obligation—is the pain of discovering that an act done with a divided will remains and binds our future life; to have done wrong is to have bound ourselves by a will that was not truly our own, and not ourselves only, but all those who may become sensible of the consequences of our action. Devout theologians have questioned whether it was within the power of God himself to cause that what was should not have been; certainly man has no such power, and by his knowledge of this fact, his will is bound to justice and consistency. The will is seldom or never directly self-contradictory, and the explanation of most wrong-doing is only that people fail to imagine all the consequences of what they do, and reject or resist the indirect results of what they would otherwise have willed. But there are two offences which the canons of natural morality might pronounce to be unpardonable, if it were possible for them to be committed with a clear and adequate apprehension of their tendency—the direct infliction of unprofitable pain, and the forcing a fellow-mortal into crime—the ranking oneself among the brute obstacles to the natural efforts of a human soul towards its own proper perfection. To do less than the good we physically might ourselves is imperfection, the other is sin; for though of course it may be said that the root of all, even the deadliest evil, is only imperfection, yet in the present state of our moral ideas, the duty of being perfect ourselves is generally felt to be of imperfect obligation; on the other hand, deliberately to interfere with the possible perfection of another, is felt by every one in the court of conscience to be wrong, and what every one agrees in feeling as well as thinking to be wrong, may as well be called sin for distinction, since the word is in our language and practices answering to it in our lives. Indeed we should have little faith in the power of any religion which should banish from its liturgy the cry thrown up in all ages from the depths of human hearts for " mercy upon us, miserable sinners!" Side by side with an irrepressible aspiration after the perfect good which we shall never see, or know, or possess, there is also an ineffaceable conviction that our life is nothing worth except in so far as it grants us glimpses of the unattainable divine; and because these glimpses are so few and dim, we cry out upon ourselves for miserable sinners, perishing for need of mercy and spiritual help. But for most sinners there is a place of repentance, if they seek it earnestly and with tears: the unpardonable sin is to know what is permanently good and to say deliberately: " I can get more pleasure for myself by other conduct than the right—I can overreach creation; I and my desires can get the better of the natural law of virtue, of the rule that is good for all; I will sin and some one else may suffer." There is, we say it advisedly, no power in nature to prevent this calculation being sometimes made and acted on with impunity. The ungodly *do* flourish, even to their death full of years and honours— not always, but quite often enough to make Utilitarians of little faith ask themselves in alarm, Where is now their god? and truly their god is nowhere, but the spirit of goodness is in the souls of men teaching them to despise the wages of iniquity. These men are rebels, successful thieves and usurpers, but not for that do theft and disloyalty become the law of life; these men are the enemies of each generation, and the end to which our labours point is such an adjustment of social sanctions as shall strengthen the hands of natural justice, and bring the ungodly even to temporal judgment.

The Christian doctrine of the remission of sins is an attempt to disguise what a growing acuteness of moral sensibility caused to be felt as intolerable—the appalling stringency of the natural sanctions of morality: a morality based upon religion is always liable to relapse into antinomian quietism, for it is felt that the supreme being cannot be injured by our frailty; and though a genuine regard for the powers of the Not-self is normally associated with at least average strength of moral purpose or virtue, there are no natural sanctions confirming or perpetuating merely emotional states, and it is easier to weak, impressionable characters to profess a general submission to they do not clearly know what, than to co-ordinate their impressions and harmonise them with a course of energetic action. If the practical sense of moral obligation is superseded by devotional sentiments recognising no worse sin than their own cessation, repentance is limited to ideal, so to speak conventional wrongs, which may be excused at the option of the person offended, but—by the hypothesis—not substantially injured by them. But there is no such way of escape from the consciousness of real material wrong done to living sentient beings; Gods or men may forgive the sinner if they please, and men at least, we argue, have no call to resent each other's imperfections; but of what avail is it that others should acquiesce with religious resignation in an act in which we cannot and will not acquiesce ourselves? Those who believe in an external tribunal competent to call the guilty to account for what they have done, thought, or neglected, may think it pertinent to plead in excuse or justification that they did not know, or did not mean, or could not help what they have done; but of what avail is any formal justification in the face of a real regret that we could not help, that we did not know, that we have done what we did not mean? What consolation is it to us to consider that the universe is neither angry nor vindictive, if the act done with the will that was not truly ours lives and glares at us in the consequences that we hate? Prayers and penances may distract attention from the lamentable reality, we may forget our own natural, righteous self-reproach by dreaming of imaginary consequences for which imaginary remedies are real enough, but there is only one true remedy for human error, a remedy that cannot be applied from without—to undo the evil deed and bury its memory by the acts of an atoning energy; and here we may observe the restorative powers of nature, or rather the simple fact that not all imperfection is mortal, and that the natural tendencies of real beings, though they may be arrested or impeded, are still the source or manifestation of whatever good or perfection is attainable in nature. For an intense regret, like any other strong emotion, is a potential force, painful while suspended as passion, but convertible into active energy, and then serving to heighten and animate the natural faculties, so that the sinner that repenteth may so much more than undo his original ill-work as to give the world more occasion for joy than ninety-nine just persons who need no repentance.

But the evil is evil all the same, and though it is well

for sin to be atoned for, it is better for it not to be committed; no unimaginable eventualities hatching under the brooding wings of the Unknowable can turn its commission into a good in disguise.

There are no natural sanctions that can permanently and habitually affect, in favour of morality, the will of beings with no moral impulses or sensibilities. If there are men without a conscience, or with a conscience that allows them habitually and contentedly to act in a manner called immoral by general consent, they form a type of being that it is perhaps a mistake to call imperfect, or morally bad, for it may be perfect after its kind—a kind materially mischievous, like rattlesnakes, cancers, or volcanoes, bad in relation to the rest of the world. We may look upon it as a fresh proof of the imperfection of the universe that it includes some kinds of beings the existence of which is naturally injurious to the perfection of other kinds, but sound morality and rational religion alike protest against the admixture of any personal animosity with our apprehension of the nature of things. With the spread of intelligence, for which tolerance is another name, it becomes possible to controvert an opinion or to resist a policy without arrogating to ourselves the right of passing exactly *moral* condemnation on its supporters. If they act, as we think, wrongly, their mistake may be pitiable as well as mischievous, for they may perhaps discover, and, as we have seen, regret it; while if they are acting against their conscience, against the tendencies of a nature that is the same as ours, they are still more certainly to be pitied, since failure or success must be alike uneasy to them.

If there is no prospect of the wrongs of earth being righted in heaven, the secular judgment, which really, of the two, prefers the right, becomes convinced of the idleness of procrastination, and compelled by the irresistible pressure of natural facts to efforts of rational beneficence. Human carelessness, not divine providence or infernal craft, is to blame for half the evils that surround us, and since it is evident that no miracles will be wrought for our deliverance, we must either bow our necks to the yoke or use what natural means of throwing off the same are offered to us by the unconscious, unimpassioned order of the world. But, in any case, it is impossible to trace a logical connection between the abandonment of erroneous theological or religious opinions and the adoption of anti-social principles of morality. The negative opinion known as atheism is not a chief, much less the only article of faith with modern rationalists, realists, positivists, naturalists, or however else they may finally agree to call themselves. Atheism is not a creed, only a passing protest against those portions of existing creeds which consist in affirming the existence either of arbitrary and naturally incalculable influences acting upon the minds or bodies of men, or of a tract of human knowledge and experience which is naturally and permanently confused and disconnected from our ordinary perceptions of fact and relation. The reasons for this protest are not all self-evident, and accordingly, "*n'est pas athée qui veut :*" a little science may convert men from Christianity to "spiritualism," or to the dogmas of agnosticism, or to an undogmatic reliance on the existence somewhere of mysteries explanatory of the essences of things; but this is only the substitution of one confused belief for another, and certainly does nothing to make morality more intelligible, rational, and consistent. But men who *wish* to disbelieve in the existence of a Personal, more or less righteous Deity, because they imagine that such an existence is the only obstacle to their finding happiness in unprincipled self-indulgence, have not even taken the first step towards embracing the doctrines of scientific atheism; they conceive the Not-self as a fetish, and the self as another, and if they were to develop their conceptions, would be more likely to arrive at some form or other of theistic superstition than at the recognition of the universe as a system of phenomena bound together by laws, or existing in constant intersecting relations.

The connection which we observe to be constant between certain causes and effects is not a sign of any *animus* in the connected phenomena either severally or collectively ; the moral action of natural influences upon moral agents demands consciousness in the subject of the influence, but by no means necessarily in its source, and the sanctions by which the voluntary submission of men to the influences of which they are conscious is enforced, do not take the form of rewards or punishments, bestowed or inflicted by some third Essence, distinct alike from the conscious agent and the medium or conditions of his activity. There is no watchful Providence or natural equity at work to apportion human success to desert, to make the pleasurableness of normal action proportionate to the moral effort expended in its execution, and the crowd of disconnected antecedents to any single composite state or volition is too great for all their results to be spontaneously harmonious. Merely to do habitually what is right is not enough to secure habitual happiness, and we think, as long as we think confusedly, that it is immoral of nature to insist, for instance, on our being prudent and far-sighted, and of sound bodily organisation, as well as honestly good-intentioned, if we wish to enjoy more than the minimum of natural pleasure which attends the consciousness of normal action. The reward of a virtuous action is its successful efficiency, as the reward of self-indulgence is pleasurable passion of uncertain duration and intensity. The reward of virtue is not happiness, though the happiness of the virtuous man lies in virtue as the happiness of the profligate in vice. To ordinary men, in so far as they are virtuous, happiness lies in following their disinterested impulses towards good; in so far as they are vicious, in indulging propensities which do not conduce to the greatest happiness or the greatest perfection of mankind.

The choice of Herakles may be a choice of evils; the way of transgressors is hard, and the paths of virtue lead less surely to pleasantness than peace: but for ages the common sense of mankind has been agreed as to how the son of Zeus will choose. The problem is still the same, though reduced to the unheroic proportions of modern daily life, and we find small men and women choosing, equally with the hero, virtues on a scale with their strength and their temptations. The old serpent of Eternity, Time, has kept the promise of that other mythological snake, and man, as a god, knowing good and evil, chooses the good at his will.

VII.

SOCIAL AND INDIVIDUAL PERFECTION.

"Da ist's denn wieder, wie die Sterne wollten:
Bedingung und Gesetz und aller Wille
Ist nur ein Wollen, weil wir eben sollten,
Und vor dem Willen schweigt die Willkür stille;
Das Liebste wird vom Herzen weggescholten,
Dem harten Muss bequemt sich Will' und Grille,
So sind wir scheinfrei denn, nach manchen Jahren,
Nur enger dann, als wir am Anfang waren."

GOETHE.

"How were Friendship possible? In mutual devotedness to the Good and True: otherwise impossible; except as Armed Neutrality, or hollow Commercial League. A man, be the Heavens ever praised, is sufficient for himself; yet were ten men, united in Love, capable of being and of doing what ten thousand singly would fail in. Infinite is the help man can yield to man!"—CARLYLE.

"Look straight to this, to what nature leads thee, both the universal nature through the things which happen to thee, and thy own nature through the acts which must be done by thee."—MARCUS AURELIUS.

The best possible attainment, at any given period, a question of fact—Various types of specific excellence only comparable when tried by the standard of social serviceableness—Mutual dependence of the ruling few and the subservient many—Alternative vocations: Politics, Industrialism, Art, Science, Philanthropy—Political ideals: postulates; that progress is normal and privilege unjust: definition of social progress—Danger of social disorganisation comes not from the fact of social development, but from its partial and unequal extent—Popular and providential theories of the function of government—Differentiation of social functions; self-willed service honourable and compulsory obedience base—Natural ability privileged to render the most honourable services—But beneficial services must be accepted as well as proffered, and so far the leaders of society are at the mercy of their followers—Growing complexity of the social ideal which makes the obligations of individuals less clear and notorious—The ideal in legislation neither more nor less attainable than the ideal in government—Legal rights of property subject to the common interest—Effect on proprietary rights of an absolute physical limitation of supply in the case of any commodity in demand: *e.g.*, land—The waiving of anti-social rights a step towards the formation of improved social custom which may in time rank as law—Organisation of public services—Theory of the production and distribution of wealth—Natural *versus* competitive value: cost and utility the essential elements—Third element in the price of labour: the *Wille zum Leben* of the vendor—Personal motives not always forthcoming to urge every one to the end generally most desirable—Inexpedient to interfere with the accidental consequences of unequal natural ability—Desirable to substitute a rational estimate of value for the fluctuating competitive price—Partition of the "unearned increment" of social wealth—Natural value not diminished by increased production, nor real purchasing power—Honorary services the natural price of unearned wealth—The ideal state on all points practically unattainable—Query, whether the best possible be an approach to the unattainable—Demand that ethical theories shall carry with them their application to the practical emergencies which concern us—The duty of individuals traced out by the social and the personal ideal conjointly—Temporary reluctant and conditional exaltation of the philanthropic reformer—Æsthetic emotion—Positive truth—Moral diffidence of a critical introspective age—The asceticism of secular fastidiousness—No real antagonism possible between the claims of social duty and individual perfection—Specialisation of function among individuals usually a gain, but increasing differentiation of classes a loss, if it extends beyond an external division of labour to a radical contrast of nature—Personal completeness a condition of the best action however highly specialised.

VII.

SOCIAL AND INDIVIDUAL PERFECTION.

THE natural, necessary, and real standard of moral good has been described as consisting in the greatest possible perfection of individuals and society. While we give our statements a degree of generality that allows them to apply with equal truth to all times and places, we also condemn ourselves to a rather empty formal accuracy. For the question that interests the minds and passions of every age is a practical one: What is the greatest perfection possible to this present generation of ours, and by what means may we attain it? And in answering this question we have no longer to depend on reasoning, but on direct insight or appreciation at once of the powers and the desires actually and potentially dominant in contemporary society, for these are the factors of the sought-for result; and an abstract formula of perfection rather chills than encourages the healthy working of enthusiasm for present possibilities by the calm impartiality with which it surveys possibilities in general and allows the praise of moral excellence to the realisation of all alike.

And yet we also have our own special ideal, and a quite special ambition to make our ideal the most complete and attractive among its kind, as well as a special sensitiveness to the chance of inadequacy in our conception and failure in our attempt, which seems great in proportion to the growing height and breadth—I will not say of our ideal—but of our conception of what an ideal ought to be. He, indeed, would be a bold man who should attempt to trace for us all the sublime ideal possibly to be attained by the sum of personal aspirations, duly harmonised and disciplined in practical co-operation; an ideal in which every man's best should be included, while yet their zeal remained uncrushed by the discovery that this best was not the absolute good, because—best as our good is to us—it will become better still when seen with its light shining undimmed in the full blaze of universal perfection, a perfect part of a perfect whole.

And scarcely less hopeless would be the attempt to catalogue all the special ideals lawfully and naturally cherished by men and women of varied gifts and antecedents. The votary of one ideal can hardly do justice to his neighbour's worship, and the writer, whose own ideal is to do justice to that of every one else, is somehow a degree further from the spontaneous sympathies of a pure fanatic, than another fanatic, whose range of vision offers no arrogant appearance of superior breadth. Still, a beginning must be made, and while the ideal sages and inspired prophets of the future still linger in the womb of time, we blunder on after a statement, a hair's-breadth truer, fuller, juster, more livingly sympathetic than we have yet attained, of what is common in all idealism and of the relation of each man's good to the universal perfection which crowns it Best.

The problem is necessarily two-fold. We ask ourselves not only what is the best life possible for this or that man, with such and such passions and capabilities, but also which lives is it best for society to see multiplied, or what is the best proportion for the divers elements that do and must co-exist to bear to each other? How much of each ideal may modest men dream of making their own, and what considerations may have weight with them at the period which comes to many, when an aim and an ideal have to be chosen with more or less conscious determination, or the doom of aimlessness deliberately accepted. We say that individual perfection consists in the union of the

SOCIAL AND INDIVIDUAL PERFECTION. 277

greatest possible number and variety of energies and susceptibilities, all reconcilable with, or conducive to, the objective good of other human agents and patients. To be a perfect instrument and to work perfectly is the sum of the best possible human achievement; but so broad a statement is insignificant unless we have a distinct image of the various functions which men have the choice of discharging, and the various qualifications which extend or limit their range of choice.

The great mass of mankind live, and perhaps always will live, mainly by routine, occupied by the tastes, sol aed by the pleasures provided ready-made by their circumstances; for them, therefore, the social question includes the personal, and their best development is conditional on the ideal organisation of the community to which they belong. They follow uncritically (but not, therefore, without some moral sense of faithfulness to their surroundings) one or other of the more or less mechanical industries which produce together what we call our civilisation; and it is for their sakes, and mainly by the help of their native docility, or leadableness, that substantial social progress appears at once as supremely desirable and even possible. There can be nothing—good or bad—in the whole except what is in the parts, and we cannot alter the essential nature of any element of society by direct action or persuasion; but an infinitesimal improvement in the mass of men, too slight to be of much account as an end for individuals, will, if common enough, amount to an appreciable change *in the medium of life for individuals*, which involuntarily and unconsciously modifies the whole future of every unit in the mass, by making a better average of existence easy and possible for all, including the minority whose choice and resolves are more consciously deliberate, if not more really independent of determining conditions.

The uncle in Goethe's *Bekenntnisse einer schönen Seele* expresses the conclusions of human morality when he says that man's chief merit is to determine his circumstances as much as he can, and to be determined by them as little as he can; that the world lies before us as a quarry before the architect, out of which we have to carve our own ideal self, and that it rests with ourselves whether the resulting edifice be a fine work of art or a helpless failure. But though it is certainly a weakness to be at the mercy of every accidental motive and external impression as it arises, though morality may consist mainly in the reaction of the character against the dominion of isolated events that interfere with its normal development, if that which is now the normal development and proper nature of the character has previously been determined or conditioned by the collective action of forces in the Not-self, it can scarcely be regarded as a weakness, it may even be the truest strength to allow the nature and the conduct together to be determined, not indeed by chance collisions with fragments of the Not-self, but by the sum of its coherent, harmonious influences. Still, if the best action of the natural forces of the universe on the self depends on the nature of the self, there cannot be one and the same universal ideal for all the world, without reference to their special natural aptitudes; and it is not strictly speaking reasonable to express anything resembling a *moral* preference for one kind of nature over another, except so far as one kind is supposed to be more useful, or to contribute more to the natural good of the species than another. Questions respecting the comparative dignity or excellence of the active and the speculative life, for instance, or of the industry of the artist, the student, or the merchant, are altogether idle for want of a common measure by which they could be gauged. There may be shopkeepers, artisans, or maid-servants more nearly perfect of their respective kinds than any contemporary poet or statesman, and it is a vain conceit to say that one variety of human kind is intrinsically better than another, except in reference to a common (social) standard.

A strong bias in favour of one class of actions or another

gives little presumption in favour of the wisdom or goodness of acts determined by the bias; but *some* bias is a condition of natural force and efficiency, since without it the will must remain the tool or plaything of circumstances. A disinterested preference or admiration may be felt for human beings in whom all the most important and characteristic of human faculties, intellect, imagination, energy, and benevolence, are developed in the highest perfection and most just proportions; but this natural appreciation of specific excellence does not take the form of moral praise or admiration so long as the faculties in question are misapplied, or—which is seldom altogether the case—applied in merely self-contained, self-regarding accomplishment. To praise great men for the help they give humanity to be its best self—both by the direct addition of so much human faculty and by the assistance its exercise affords to the development of other organisms—is as reasonable as any other natural tendency, for humanity cannot well fail to think its own best good. As Dr. Newman remarks in speaking of the intellect as a moral influence: " Individuals will occur to all of us who deservedly attract our love and admiration, and whom the world almost worships as the work of its hands. Religious principle, indeed— that is faith—is to all appearance simply away; the work is as certainly not supernatural as it is certainly noble and beautiful." And we fail altogether to appreciate the criticism that such words as noble and beautiful have no meaning when used in an exclusively natural sense in connection with the characters or actions of men. With the utmost desire for impartiality we cannot promise to sever the natural associations of those words from their appropriate use; nature, not the faint trace of half-forgotten religious prejudices, is to blame if we can never quite get rid of the notion that we are praising a thing when we call it good.

We cannot draw a hard and fast line between the nature of the many and that of the few, but the aristocracy of nature distinguishes itself mainly by the proportion of self-originating, self-determining power possessed by its members. The social action of this aristocracy is dependent on the power and will of the masses to be led this way or that, but their individual development is in their own hands just in so far as they can turn their surroundings into its instrument; while the social ideal, which must be the same for all, depends for its wealth upon the free initiative of those who have received—as an unexplained natural inheritance—the power of giving more than they receive in the course of their natural life. These aristocrats differ from their humbler fellows in degree only, not in kind, and the comparative strength of personal and altruistic impulses and feelings is much the same among them as among the masses, so that from this point of view again we do not find moral inequalities always corresponding to the inequality of natural power.

Now, if we attempt to classify the courses open to these weightier personalities, each of whom is, in a manner, representative of the tendencies of a sequent class, we find some pursuits primarily consisting in the action of the self upon other men, some in action which is primarily self-regarding, and even so far as in relation with the outer world, not mainly in relation with its human denizens; while among actions or pursuits that are objectively altruistic, there is still the distinction between classes of motives, or the purpose, personal or disinterested, of the altruistic course.

Practically the ambitions of educated intelligence take one or other of the lines which we indicate vaguely by the words, Politics, Industrialism, Art, Science, Philanthropy, Self-culture. Men aspire to rule the many sometimes for the pleasure of ruling, sometimes for the benefit of the ruled: they seek to produce, to multiply articles of material utility or luxury, sometimes merely to gratify the impulse of production, sometimes for the sake of material reward, more rarely with the intention of ministering to the material wants or convenience of the community; men devote themselves to art, the worship and creation of the beautiful, partly from inward impulse, partly for the delight of the worship, partly from a disinterested, almost religious reverence for those mysterious qualities whereby the sounds and sights of nature stir the feelings of men—a piety not the less real because wholly free from *arrière pensée*, an involuntary, uncalculating, and most profound sympathy between man and the natural harmonies of the world to which he owes his birth. Men devote themselves, again, to the acquisition of knowledge and the discovery of natural facts, partly from natural curiosity, partly in view of the use that the knowledge may be, and partly from a purely intellectual sympathy with the real relations of things, an affection for intelligible statement not less strong and constant if less enthusiastic than the passion of the artist for the beautiful. And besides all these pursuits, in which concern for the common good may have a secondary place, there are some who make the common good their end, and use and value the methods of art, science, government and industry as themselves means of secondary importance compared with the all-embracing ideal.

It is not enough to enumerate the various goals of human ambition considered from the point of view of individual aspiration; we have also to consider the impersonal best, the result which is naturally good for all, provided the needful functionaries can be met with for its development; because the realities of the common life limit and condition the possibilities of individual attainment, as well as, more remotely, of individual desire. And we must therefore endeavour to give some precision to our ideas of the best social state possibly attainable in the approaching future, before trying to define the outlines of individual duty which follow by implication as binding on all those who own the ideal.

We speak of "politics" as a sphere offering interesting and absorbing occupation to rational men, and the question then presents itself: What is the most acceptable political ideal? Is a paternal or democratic government best for modern civilised communities? and when the form of government is settled, should its spirit be liberal or conservative, and what is the precise significance of those contrasted terms? The only foregone conclusions to which the course of the argument has committed us on this subject are two, that progress is normal and privilege unjust; in other words, that the ideal government must be prepared to recognise and direct the progressive development of its subjects, while it will reject the claim of any class or individuals to be officially secured in the possession of more enjoyments than their neighbours, at the expense of the latter. The good of society, at any given moment, as distinguished from the interest of individuals, may be held to consist in the attainment by the greatest possible number of its members of the greatest possible amount of satisfaction of all their conscious desires and impulses. Social progress consists in the multiplication, among the greatest possible number of the community, of impulses, faculties and desires with their attendant possibilities of gratification. The doubts of those who question whether progress is in all cases necessarily a good, rest upon the practical experience that the multiplication of powers and sensibilities in some members of society may outstrip the development of general customs favourable to their habitually receiving the appropriate satisfaction. In an ideal state of things the function of Conservatism would be to protect, as far as possible, every extant source of public good, while the function of Liberalism would be to introduce as many new sources as possible of future good. The antagonism between the two tempers is due to the fact that, in a state of things which is far from ideal, the pursuit of new problematical good often entails the sacrifice of old sources of certain satisfaction, while on the other hand, an obstinate attachment to the latter may be powerless to arrest the growth of tendencies which can only be satisfied by innovation.

According to this definition of social and progressive good, the ideal of society will be conceived as a continual approach, not towards any definite state, but towards the general diffusion among its members of increasingly various active powers, and increasingly intense and refined sensibility, such increase being further attended by a growing harmony between the indulgence of individual impulses and desires and the common good, present and to come. The opponents of any special, local progress, the purpose of which is to multiply the faculties and develop the sensibilities of a backward race, class, or sex, are committed to the pessimistic theory that permanent defect in some members of the species is the condition of the utmost attainable perfection in the residuum. The opinion is supported by the high authority of Aristotle who makes it the ground of his defence of slavery. But modern history and reason incline us to the more cheerful view that the true cause, or *sine qua non*, of such modest progress as has hitherto resulted from human effort, has always been the possession of some positive ability by the superior portion of the species, not the inferior ability of another portion.

The danger of cultivating additional ability in a class of *ci devant* inferiors is not chimerical, because the ability of existing superiors may not be equal spontaneously to the additional strain of supporting, directing, or assisting the new development towards ends of general social advantage. At the same time it may be remembered that even Aristotle, while arguing that it is a means of perfection to the inferior to obey superior authority, does not question the advantage to a superior of having as excellent subordinates as possible; and we have no reason to suppose that those sections of society now supposed to be the seat of natural authority and superior merit are in any way naturally less progressive, less capable of improving upon their present condition, than those of their actual inferiors whose emancipation from injurious disabilities is recommended in the interests of the general progress of society as a whole. In our own country the political emancipation of the masses has already gone so far that the importance of such remaining steps as the enfranchisement of women and agricultural labourers is mainly social, and is debated on corresponding grounds rather than on the strict base of political equity and expediency; but it will perhaps conduce to clear and coherent thinking on these questions, which seem the more difficult from their mixed character, if each measure, as it becomes practically urgent, were to be dispassionately referred to some intelligible standard of desirability apart from the momentary inclinations or prejudices of disputants. And many will admit that the progressive good of society, as above defined, affords such a standard, who are by no means yet convinced that *e.g.*, universal suffrage or compulsory education would appear desirable when tried by this standard.

Even when the progress of society has been accepted as the final goal, there remain two rival schools of opinion as to what is or should be the precise aim and function of political government. This function may be either that of ordaining what is to be done, at the choice of its own plenary wisdom, or that of regulating in the most convenient manner the doing of those things on which the will of the community is bent. An omniscient and benevolent dictator is the ideal of one party; a competent delegacy appointed to harmonise conflicting and enforce wholesome customs is the ideal of the other. A sovereign assembly is virtually an elected monarch, who governs less than the ideal dictator, because the knowledge and good-will diffused through the many-organed body does not readily come to a head in practical commands, and, accordingly, enthusiasts for the principle of authority are dissatisfied with governments in which the popular element is as strong as in our own. One of the latest exponents of this view seems to think that adequate powers of direction might be developed in a few members of the community if the remainder of the mass were predisposed to yield obedience to all beneficial commands, and that the accidental seizure of administrative power by persons disposed to use it for interested purposes might be remedied by a quasi-royal right of veto, or the power of changing its ministers, reserved to the community at large.[1] But whatever might be most intrinsically desirable, it does not seem to be the fact that the lapse of time tends to widen the gulf between the wisdom and vigour of the many and the few. The task of government conceived as wholly initiative grows more difficult every day from the greater variety and complication of the forces which have to be directed, and no proportionate development of mental grasp appears in the actual body of contemporary rulers. What does appear is a growing diffusion of political intelligence, and an increasing interest in the objects of good government among all classes, down to those most remote from any wish to direct the fortunes of the state as a whole. And it is for this reason that the party which chooses liberty rather than authority for its watchword, seems to represent the strongest objective tendencies of the day. The ideal of this school is the self-government of the community, the legislative assembly and its ministers having for their function to discern and record and give effect to the will of their constituents. Its justification lies, not in any optimistic faith in the all-wisdom of majorities, but in the conviction that no administrative manipulation can extract out of a nation more effective virtue than is in it; and that no artificial machinery for extracting the efficient virtue can be permanently relied upon to serve its primary purpose, while no community will refuse its consent to the best laws which its then state of virtue will allow it to observe. The complaints of modern anarchy appear to proceed from statesmen, amateur

[1] " Order and Progress." By Frederick Harrison.

and professional, who feel their own powers to be equal to the task of forming plans for the good of the community, but not to the more difficult task of persuading the voluntary co-operation of those who are to be benefited by the execution of the plans. The heaven-born ruler knows better than his subjects what is best for them to do; and rulers who are not heaven-born think that they might do quite as well as the missing great one, if the community would submit to the effort of seeing—without the compulsion of revelation—what is really for their own good. The liberal creed, on the contrary, is that those classes of the community which are capable of seeing what is for the general good, with the very moderate assistance afforded by contemporary politicians, are capable of knowing better than such politicians what is for their own good, except in cases where an obvious bias of egotistic inclination calls for correction by the enlightened self-interest of the whole community. The function of government, or the official organ of the public will, is to find out which are the strongest tendencies of the social body, and especially which can be made so by discreet administration.

The use of a civilised government is to execute the people's will, whether the people knows its own mind or not, and certainly without looking to it for instructions, which it is rarely or never able to give, as to the way in which its will shall be carried out. For example, the people clamour for education before they have education enough to know what it is they are asking for; but the demand gives a golden opportunity for any administration that has wit to offer the best education with a free hand, and strengthen itself by turning the excited clamours outside into denunciation of any less adequate provision. We hold that a well-educated people is easier to govern—to the ends of civilisation—than one possessing all the qualities of rustic ignorance; but there are rulers who think differently, because in effect it *is* harder to govern the growth of a civilised nation than to keep the peace among a passively servile mass; only for rulers who accept the more ambitious task there can be no *via media*, because when the work of education is begun it must either be directed towards an enlightened completion, or the masses will be left to all the dangers of partial instruction—self-taught as to their inclinations and claimable rights, but ignorant of the logical consequences of co-existent and reciprocal social obligations. One chief characteristic of a democratic age is the tendency to minimise the original distinction between government and legislation;[1] the administration of public affairs comes to be carried on on the same principles and with the same self-effacement of the rulers as are desirable in the case of civil legislation. The administration of the public services takes up an increasing part of the rulers' care, and tends increasingly to outweigh the importance of government in the primitive political sense, the commanding of the behaviour of different classes towards each other, or the determination of the external relations of the community. And a corresponding change appears to be taking place in the popular estimate of the rights and immunities of office-holders. The function of government used to be coveted as the post of highest dignity and power, but, until recently, it was assumed that the ruler would give effect to his own will, and though he was always praised if his will was beneficent or judicious, the specific excellence of a ruler was supposed to consist more in the greatness of his power than in the wisdom or benevolence of its exercise; in fact, virtue of a kind was recommended to rulers because certain forms of vice threatened the stability of their power rather than from any sense of moral responsibility on the part of the sovereign to the subject.

The beginning of social organisation is made with the discovery that human beings can be of use to each other; but this relation of service has two sides, and it is a curious psychological question why some services are held

[1] *Vide supra*, p. 36.

to be honourable to the person by whom they are received and others to the person by whom they are rendered. Practically, the test applied seems to have been the action of free choice, will, or liking in the agent: it is a mark of inferiority to be compelled by force to do something distasteful, and admiration or gratitude are not spontaneously felt, even for needful services, when these are not freely rendered. But again, in primitive society, as well as now, what is done voluntarily is assumed to have been done for the agent's own satisfaction, and in this way the intrinsically admirable element of ability—to do as one chooses—becomes associated with the strength of desires or passions which it would be harsh to call antisocial, though their indulgence may become so as soon as the struggle for existence has advanced a step, and there is competition between many, who are able to enjoy, for the means and ministers of enjoyment. The idea of rendering, voluntarily, services to others for their good is of tardy growth, and though there are always some qualities more useful and edifying to society than others, it is not always the same quality that bears away the palm of natural excellence or entitles its possessors to the strictly moral admiration which is reserved for voluntary serviceableness.

Social organisation, or the multiplication of functions and exchangeable offices of service, begins, historically, with the want or wish of the strongest natures to be served, not with a magnanimous desire to serve, and indeed it would be a psychological impossibility for those who had had no experience of the convenience of service received to enter with sympathy into the natural desire of others to obtain the same advantage. By one of those pregnant coincidences which lend a false air of rationality to the course of history, it was also historically true that the natural aristocrats who were best able in the first instance to serve themselves (and incidentally their inferiors, since indifferent rule may be better than anarchy), were also best able to imagine means of exacting the less honourable kind of service in return. Considered in the abstract, the aptitude to issue commands and the aptitude to yield compliance are morally void and intellectually worthless; everything depends upon the character of the commands issued, and the purpose and character of the compliance yielded. The improvident wilfulness of an oriental despot is as unreasoning as the canine submissiveness of modern low-life Griseldas. The exercise of the former quality makes most immediate and undisguised addition to the suffering of sentient beings; at the same time it is the caricature of a power, the *reductio ad absurdum* of a principle which may be thought to have contributed more to the general progress and benefit of humanity than the opposite habit of non-resistance. But again, the habit of commanding *à tort et à travers* can only be kept up by the help of a proportionate readiness to obey uncritically, and if social advance must in all cases be purchased by the juxtaposition of the two dispositions, it is impossible to localise the merit and responsibility for the joint result in either one of the contracting parties. Authority has no moral weight, as such, only we find, on the whole, that persons able to command obedience are, as a rule, able to invent services which are both agreeable to themselves, and also remotely serviceable to social growth and civilisation. And this observation serves retrospectively to justify the natural tendency of mankind to admire ability for its own sake.

There is always some element of natural reason in a widespread, instinctive feeling, and we do feel that loyalty, like the best forms of religion, implies reverence for that which is above, not compassion for that which is below. To serve a superior may be a proud privilege, it is anyway an honourable obligation, but to serve the many-headed, the leather-sellers and sausage-makers of our modern demos—is that, we ask, the highest function of our best men? or are our best men to leave their natural trade of shepherding to hirelings? Are our heaven-born guardians to content themselves with dilletante criticism while

T

"politics" become a paid trade like cotton-spinning? The latent disposition to acquiesce in such a result forms one of our nearest social difficulties and dangers; and yet it seems as if only a slight change of mental attitude were needed to set our feeling free to follow its natural bent,— to honour power most in its most efficient and influential manifestations.

After all said and done, where is the great glory of having wants that inferiors can be made to supply? True greatness consists in having better, larger wants than other men, and the ideal ruler at any rate, according to our present ideas, is the man whose strongest *personal* desire is for the righteous and felicitous organisation of the subject-classes. We despise equally the demagogue who makes himself the slave of the lower passions of the many, and the despot who makes the many slaves to the lower passions of the one. The truest service that man can render to man is to make human life the better, and this is a service which the greater renders to the less; but we associate the idea of service with subjection, and the subjection of the better to the worse is a moral contradiction. In times past this difficulty has been evaded by a phrase; the Redeemer of men made Himself their servant, to teach them to serve each other for His sake. But we may ask, for whose sake did Christ serve? And if the Christian model is divine, why should it be denaturalised by giving every Christian a different motive from that which moved his Lord? Men have imagined and believed in a God ready to endure all things for the salvation of men; leaving all legendary incongruities on one side, is it not thereby apparent that men are willing to give their best reverence when the higher consents to serve the lower, if thereby the service of the immaterial highest is to be advanced? There is no touch of metaphysical mystery or sentimental asceticism in such a faith. The choice of the many may be determined or confirmed by the urgency of the few; and in this God-forsaken world it is well for human voices to ring divinely. There is nothing unreasonable or unintelligible in our craving for a hero whose transcendent power shall be serviceable, and the would-be heroes of the day only miss the glories they would aim at for want of courage or discernment—or, perhaps, native heroism—enough to render the services on a sublimely ample scale. The right line is the shortest way between the two points of useful action and solid fame, and there is no abnormal severance of the natural connection between the two ends. It is true that we see signs of a growing indifference, not to say contempt, among the intellectual classes for what are called "politics," or the practical exercise of the power of ruling, which extends nearly indifferently to all shades of opinion, except advanced and militant radicalism. But this may be explained by the bent of aristocratic prejudice, which, having been brought to waive its claim to anti-social privileges, still resists the democratic pressure of social obligation. The formula "to every one according to his wants" has been applied in complete disregard of the aristocrats' hereditary want—to dominate; and the aristocrats accordingly feel little inclination to accept the remaining clause, "from every one according to his powers," which would have re-established their superiority on a fresh basis. At the same time, disinterested ambition naturally proposes to itself attainable ends, and whatever kind of superiority a community is ready to recognise will be cultivated by those whose most selfish desire is for recognition— of their own merit, such as it may be. And the more reasonable popular demands can be made, the more prospect there is of inducing the natural leaders of society to accept the conditions on which their old ascendancy may be enjoyed.

Here, however, we are met with another difficulty which hampers the development of political ideals with a commanding charm. We concede that in the perfect life, action, feeling, and intelligence must go the same way, and not only personal but also sympathetic feelings and impulses have to be brought into harmony with each other and with the objective medium before the whole man can hope to accomplish the best destiny physically within his reach. But a reformer, by the nature of the case, lives and moves among the abuses he is labouring to remove, and unless he buries himself in the ranks of a small reforming sect, seeing no prospect beyond the destruction of their own pet grievance, the reformer is indeed a kind of outcaste, a parasite of social ill, in whom the normal self-assertion of the *Wille zum Leben* would be an inconsistency. We protest on behalf of our leaders against their being called on to serve stupidity, and then, as a crowning compliment, we expect them to serve vice, and both services are a war of extermination. The practical difficulty is that an energetic and sensitive nature needs to feel the stream of tendency to be with it in its best efforts, or else lives a life of martyrdom, or rather, the half life of a mutilated soul. Hundreds of thousands among us are ready and willing to take their part in the orderly discharge of social duties, but they cannot feel it to be a duty to scramble for a function and vindicate their right to it in debate, and so they stand on one side; and some say, What is the use of living when there is nothing useful to do? and others, What is the use of doing anything useful if people would as soon have it left undone? and others roundly, that life is tiresome, and we might as well be dead because there is "nothing to do," and no sufficient reason for doing that. Saints and sinners are agreed upon the one need of living *some*how, and those who are embarrassed about the "how," find their difficulty increased by the very fact that society seems to have no fixed principles and intelligible rules, by respecting which a man can certainly put himself *en rapport* with the feeling of his neighbours. Society takes its members at their own valuation, and is slow to find fault with those who find no fault either with themselves or with their place in the world; and yet society is too far from perfection to be able to afford itself the luxury of unbroken self-satisfaction, and it is neither right nor reasonable for us to be permanently discontented with a necessity which we, on the whole, feel bound to accept.

At the same time, the needful reforms would be already accomplished, and, therefore, no longer needed, if every one had a sufficiently lively sense of the need to take part in supplying it; and we might seem to be entangled in a vicious circle of conservatism, if it were not for the disinterested way in which the spiritual nature even of the unspiritual masses shoots ahead of their grosser propensities. Long before we have either the knowledge or the resolution needed for living an ideal life ourselves, we may feel the attraction of a high ideal and be ready to applaud and follow leaders of the highest ambition. The many must always depend upon the few for their best gifts and instruction, but the few depend upon the good-will of the many for the crowning perfection as well as for the efficiency of their work, just because it is a part of the highest ability to be sensitive to external stimulus and external discouragement. It depends upon the many whether the best energy of the few shall spend itself in unavailing protests, in stern endurance, or in fortunate and fruitful action. We depend on ourselves (or on our antecedents) for our possibilities; we depend on our contemporaries and our surroundings for their realisation; and, humiliating as from some points of view the confession may seem, it does not rest altogether in our own hands to make the best of ourselves; morally, a man is free from blame, nay, is deserving of the highest praise and admiration, if he has done his best under difficulties, but if we are to judge with the dispassionateness of science we may have to recognize the natural imperfection of the result that we are thus bound to praise; and the martyr of circumstances shares our feeling to an extent which is a part of the martyrdom, for there is no more bitter grief, short of remorse, to be known by men, than regret for the better things they might have done under a happier fate. But this discord between the verdict of spontaneous feeling and deliberate judgment is not naturally or necessarily permanent. It is not reasonable for us to judge our chiefs by a standard which we do not allow them to reach, and it is not reasonable to withhold our sympathy from those who make it their business to pursue the very objects that our judgment approves.

In point of fact, the mass of public feeling and opinion only wants concentrating, clarifying, and pouring forth, to prove itself, as it should be, at one with the best and strongest individual aspirations, which are now half-starved for want of such support. There have been times before now when the whole community accepted the same ideal, and had but one feeling towards those who spent their lives in its pursuit; and though our ideal cannot well revert to mediæval simplicity, there is no reason why the reformers of the future should not be sustained by the same speculative appreciation of their work as that which made the miracles of monasticism possible in ages of even less moral culture than the present. Creeds may be believed in with personal fervour of conviction, or taken for granted as incuriously as most of us take for granted the revolution of the earth on its axis; but the path of social progress would be cleared of half its stumbling-blocks if we all either believed fervently, or else took for granted as an unassailable axiom of social faith

> That man's perfection is the crowning flower
> Toward which the urgent sap in life's great tree
> Is pressing—seen in puny blossoms now,
> But in the world's great morrows to expand
> With broadest petal and with deepest glow.

Now, as always, each new step in advance must be taken with effort through opposition, but there is no reason why all those to whose share the burden of the effort falls should not find help in their need from the sense of a common faith giving promise of agreement, soon or late, between all who own it. And the promise will be kept when the creed is so deeply rooted in the hearts and minds of the majority that they only need to be assured of what it really commands in order to sacrifice their own interests or prejudices at its bidding. This is the true religion of humanity—so to honour and love the manifestations of human strength, wisdom, and loving-kindness as to feel that in them the best is realised, and that for them the utmost of pain and labour may be dared and done. But living religions are congregational, and we want it to be a household word amongst the many, as well as a speculative conviction among the few, that the sufficient reason of human life is to be found in the lives of men and nowhere else, and that our collective stupidity is to blame if we do not feel, and let each other feel, that the forces which stir our souls have a right to stir them, and that not we, but those who remain callous to influences whose rightful power we confess, are the heretics and infidels.

The elements of harmony or natural human good are in our reach, if we could only agree to seek them; it is partly because we are not agreed upon a formula for the desired end that so many moderns dispense themselves from effort, saying that there is no end in view. We contend that social opinion is more nearly agreed upon an end than upon a formula, and that the true stumbling-block in our way is not the want of worthy and adequate employment, but the objective difficulty of the task before us. In fact, the end which we desire most, an ideal organisation of civilised society, is so difficult that single efforts can go little way towards it; and the difficulty of the task placed before individuals is increased by the fact that each reformer has not only to see what he himself can do, but must include in his plan the fitting in of his efforts to this or that work of others. It is more reasonable to complain of such a mission being oppressively or impracticably hard than of an absolute "nothing to do," and we have no right to criticise the natural order for leaving us without a function if we decline the work naturally traced out for us, on the ground that it is too hard.

The reason that the educated and leisurely classes suffer more from *ennui* than the hard-working poor, is that the habitual actions are done from weaker motives, and the problem of the day is to find and bring home to the will sufficiently strong motives for performing, if not the actions now habitual, some others in their stead. The shopkeeper or the manual labourer is entangled in a petty round of duties, not one of which can be omitted with impunity, and an equally irresistible pressure would be brought to bear upon every intelligent conscience if the workings of the social mechanism could be so vividly realised as to supply motives for larger doings and forbearances, since the correspondingly large needs are an objective fact. At present it is given to very few to find mental rest and moral stay in a routine congenial to their mental tastes and moral cravings, but if we take a general survey of the whole field of human life and action, it can scarcely be said that, apart from the common human temptation to prefer the pleasant to the good, there is a general discrepancy between the tendency of existing motive forces and the latent willingness of men to move in this or that direction; there is only an accidental and temporary divorce between the two conditions of contented and efficient action, which it is the object of an improved social organisation to terminate.

There is one real objective good which we can never go wrong in taking as the goal of effort, the development of faculty and the arrangement of facilities for its exercise, and it may be urged that the good which is built up side by side with other goods — even though the latter may impose sacrifices—is still better, richer than an isolated final unprogressive attainment. But the chances of friction are increased with every addition to the complexity of the social machine, and to minimise such friction we want every member of the community to be ready, not only to work well in his own place but to help his neighbours into the place or function for which they are naturally most fit; not because they are most useful or least troublesome in such a place, but disinterestedly, because it is best for themselves, and when they have been got into the place that is objectively best for them, they should be helped with praise, sympathy, or compassion, to feel themselves at least comparatively well off in it.

In the highest moral and religious sense, each member of a community depends upon the virtues of his neighbour to develop his own, so that the best good of all is bound up with that of each one, with a closeness that can never be attained by purely utilitarian calculations. The showiest virtues are perhaps those which stand out in relief against a dark background of opposing crime, as the veriest schoolboy is tempted by the fame of a martyred sage or patriot; but perfect virtue must be able to dispense with either foils or victims, and we must either renounce our faith in the perfectibility of mankind or find our way towards the acceptance of an altogether positive ideal.

But if this way of looking at the common problem were generally accepted—as generally as the main dogmas of Catholicism five centuries ago—we should only have the intellectual and the practical difficulties of the position left to contend with. Strength and knowledge would not be left idle for want of good-will on the part of their owner, nor expended in vain for want of good-will amongst those interested in their exercise. Our wishes would be guides instead of tempters, an aid instead of a distraction in the serious work of life, and human action would again have a chance of approaching to the æsthetic perfection, which, in this case as in that of all other natural phenomena, belongs only to work done with an undivided soul, or by virtue of some natural harmony, recognisable after the event, though not perhaps to be analysed or deliberately invented beforehand.

The value of a political formula and the significance of a political programme varies so widely with the change of circumstances, that it is hardly useful to dwell in detail on the purely political measures which seem now to be demanded as corollaries of our ethical creed. We agree with Utilitarian liberals in deprecating legal interference with the self-regarding action of individuals, but we look upon it as the duty of the community—as the natural function of its collective wisdom—to provide the individual members of the social body with every possible facility for complete and healthy self-development. All are interested in the well-being of each, and even on Utilitarian grounds it may be argued that they have therefore a right to legislate for the personal advantage of individuals, but there is a vast difference between the claim of individuals to legislate all at once for their own good, and the resolution of the authorised government to promote the well-being of every fraction of the subject group—all the difference, indeed, which we associate with the contrasted terms of blind instinct and enlightened reason. We should not get an exhaustive account of the phenomena of human life by merely adding together the vital motions of all the bodily organs; and, in like manner, it is only natural for the intelligent action of the social body to have a degree of organic unity and coherence, which would be wanting to a mere aggregation of individual wills.

The matters of common interest which the state may be expected to care for with increasing efficiency with the increase of intelligence and unity of purpose among its members may be briefly summed up as the provision of good laws, good administration of the public services, a sound system of social and industrial economy, and a sound system of national education. The machinery of government is a point of secondary consideration, and the international relations of the model state must inevitably be modified by the temper of the other civilised communities with which it is in relation. The duty, however, of such a state towards barbarous but improveable populations is more clearly uniform, and we should perhaps include among the functions of the state the direction of independent colonists in their dealings with aboriginal inhabitants, and perhaps even the organisation of some secular counterpart to Christian "missions" in those districts where the spontaneous relations of two races of unequal development are not likely to be altogether conducive to the best interests of both.

With regard to laws, it will be remembered that we have not been able to lay down any absolute rule or standard of equity; now, as always, the best laws for a community are the best that it can be induced to obey faithfully and intelligently, and in the case of any special reform, it is a practical question how near an approach to the best possible rule the actual state of the community will admit. Mr. Herbert Spencer has almost exalted into the dignity of a natural law the observation that men in guarding against one evil are apt to find that their remedy itself has made room for another perhaps as bad. But there is no metaphysical necessity at work to perpetuate this simple result of human short-sight. Very often the reform carried out is not exactly the one proposed on the merits of the case, and the practically successful à peu près has undesired consequences; but very often also the exact remedy, if proposed in time, might succeed as well and have no ill result at all, while in any case it is quite within the competence of human reason to foresee and guard against new opportunities for abuse incidentally provided by a measure in the main beneficial.

It is faithlessness, verging on impiety, for one man to profess himself possessed of a remedy for social evil and to proclaim in the same breath that his wisdom is of no use because none of his fellows have the wit to see with him. What one man has seen all men may come to see or believe in, and we may even go so far as to question the value of a vision which can find no second seer. It is a self-destructive caution which attempts nothing because it may not be able to accomplish all it would attempt, and we have not much tolerance for the weakness which lets "we cannot" wait upon "I would" in cases where power is optional and will contagious. We have a right to assume in theory that whatever is desirable is possible, and to act as if it were so, even though we know that our approach to the most desirable of all results—whatever that may be—will be infinitely gradual, and the date of its completion, therefore, practically out of reach. But the pursuit of perfection is independent of time and the continuous life of nations or sects exists only in the continuity of effort towards one purpose, and thus to every generation the sufficient reason for present effort is always the next step practically possible towards the supreme result, always present to the eye of faith, though never brought within the grasp of material possession.

At any rate there can be no excuse for adjourning needful legislative reform based on the best contemporary practice carried out to all its logically consistent developments. What men can do, men can certainly describe systematically, and a code is simply a systematic description of the different doings of men in their constant relations to each other. It is not necessary for any one to know by heart the innumerable varieties of fact upon which litigious issues may be raised, but it is eminently necessary for a civilised community to be in possession of a coherent set of principles, in accordance with which any possible number of cases may be uniformly decided, and it would be well if lawyers as well as moralists and politicians could gather together enough faith in human reason and courageous reliance on human energy not to despair of the heroically difficult task of ascertaining what is now, and for the next few centuries likely to be, the best practical rule for every kind of leading case. There always *is* a practical best, one course which appears more perfectly and unexceptionally suitable than any other, and with candour and diligence this course can be defined beforehand in outline fully precise enough for popular needs.

Thus we want a consistent and intelligible criminal law, which shall apportion the penalty for every offence to the heinousness of the offence estimated in view at once of the present injury actually inflicted on society by the crime, and the chronic injury, so to speak, inflicted on it by the moral perversity of the criminal. If the criminal is incorrigible, the sole aim of legislation will be to protect society against his misdeeds, otherwise reform rather than retribution will be the aim of judicial sentences, and in a perfectly ideal scheme, the old system of fines and the modern system of damages will probably be blent into an equitable method of compensation for wrongs as an alternative for the merely personal expiation of a penal sentence. All offences, old and new, from obsolete crimes of violence to the most recent developments of fraud, should be classed afresh upon an uniform plan, and the mere act of impartial enumeration would give rise spontaneously to a beginning of re-arrangement. Each act would be judged according to its actual character, and the anomalies arising from historical survivals—of penalties which have changed their significance for acts which have changed theirs—would be at once removed from cumbering the path of justice. The theory of legal wrong is, we know, much simpler than the theory of rights, but even this is not essentially unknowable or inexplicable. Some laws we must have, bad laws we have had, good laws we might have, by virtue of the self-same facilities which enable us to have laws at all, only we are too idle to make them.

The reasonable rights of persons over and against each other are perfectly assignable: sane adults are free to pledge themselves by contract to each other, and those contracts, which are customary in the community, and which the community is interested in having faithfully observed, may be reasonably enforced by law upon either of the parties who had voluntarily entered upon the same. Contracts of marriage, of partnership, of hired service, are binding as the provisions of a positive law are binding, if the contract fulfils the conditions laid down for normal agreements of that particular kind; but we want to be rid of all the archaic curiosities of legislation, which make one agreement involve another, that it has nothing to do with now, because six or seven centuries ago the two were customarily associated; and we want still more urgently to be relieved from the incubus of archaic forms of contract which bind, perhaps to their mutual amazement, parties who omit to contract themselves out of the obligation. In relations that are assumed to be permanent the legislature should provide a typical form of contract, available for all those who do not deliberately modify it, or who modify it in a direction which the law refuses to sanction (as if a servant sells himself for a slave), and this typical form should embody the last word of contemporary practical reason, which many of our present laws, concerning marriage, bankruptcy, legal procedure, and a variety of other topics, are far enough from doing as yet.

The proprietary rights of persons offer a wider field for discussion, because there is not an absolute consensus of opinion as to their normal extent. All rights of permanent property in things are the creation of positive law, which makes itself the guardian of every man's possessions during the time when he is not in actual occupation. The metaphysical jurisprudence of the seventeenth century, finding proprietary rights established, assumed that they had an abstract and eternal right to State recognition, in virtue of some native inherent sanctity of their own; and the early Utilitarians were equally peremptory in vindicating them to their fullest extent, in the name of the unmistakable personal interest of owners. Of late years, however, the wilder forms of socialism have shown a tendency to settle down into sober criticism of the history of special rights, with a view to the abrogation of those demonstrably injurious to the public welfare. It is argued that what the law gave the law may take away, and the appeal is virtually from law to morality when the opponents of change in the proprietary rights of individuals cry out about the injustice of a policy of confiscation, while the advocates of change are equally vehement about the iniquity of the existing partition. The best way of bringing the controversy to a manageable issue is to insist upon the distinction between the justice of rules and the expedience of facts, for Government, in those wider functions which include legislation, has to take account of both, and is legally, as well as morally, within the sphere of its competence in decreeing the gradual extinction of an obnoxious class of facts.

The title of a Russian noble to the possession of his serfs was legally good, but it was the creation of historical enactment; and in England, at any rate, we should find few theorists prepared to characterise the emancipation as illegal. We should, however, find a good many who would justify that interference with the rights of ownership on the ground that one man has "no right" to own another, and that, in fact, positive law cannot give an indefeasible right to any power or privilege which is morally wrong. And this is the very contention of the qualified socialism of writers like Mill or Laveleye. It becomes then a question of fact, not of principle, whether any rights, of persons over things, now consecrated by law are morally unjust, *i.e.*, generically mischievous to society, with its various coequal and counterbalancing claims; and if this be the case, of two things one, either the legal rights must be allowed to lapse into desuetude—as English landlords escaped the tax of compulsory emancipation by allowing their villeins to drift gradually into prescriptive liberty— or they must be authoritatively limited to the measure of general practical expediency. The question whether it is just for the law to sanction every possible development of proprietary rights only arises in practice when the actual development of those rights has resulted in an extremely unequal distribution of the national wealth. Such inequality is a social evil, and we deny the perfect equity of law which sanctions the development of social evils. A right conferred by the community should be regarded as a trust, for which the holder is responsible to the sovereign power by whom it was conferred; but if the exercise of legal rights and liberties is to be avowedly independent of moral restrictions, the law, which is never bound to sanction immorality, may at any time withdraw the liberty which has been abused in practice.

Let us suppose that at the date of the emancipation of the serfs, all Russia had been the property of the nobles, and that the traditional hold of the villagers on the soil had been ignored; suppose further that the nobles had been bribed to consent to the emancipation by the promise of salaried offices under the Government, and that the whole class had with one consent begun to live upon its salaries in St. Petersburg and Moscow, leaving the rural districts waste for shooting-grounds. In a few years from such a beginning, the condition of the peasantry would have become such that the country would have had to choose between civil war and an agrarian law. We deny that there can be wrongs without an equitable remedy, and we assert the right of the State in such a case to ordain a redistribution of proprietary rights in a manner more conducive to the common good or the interest of the nation as a whole. This is an extreme, or rather an imaginary case, but minor grievances may be rectified in accordance with the same principle, subject only to the general consideration which is at the bottom of all reasonable dread of revolutionary reform. The foundation of social stability and well-being is the security of life and property afforded by association. The assurance of this stability lies, we hold, in the natural regularity of men's desires and impulses taken in the mass, but those who look upon mankind as by nature lawless and only kept in order with difficulty

SOCIAL AND INDIVIDUAL PERFECTION. 305

by heaven-sent pastors and masters, are naturally staggered by the proposal to make the self-estimated good of the community the standard of justice and the rule of law. We contend that all laws and contracts may be safely submitted for revision if they are found to work unsatisfactorily in practice, provided the test applied is taken from the general interest, in its most liberal sense, not from the personal interest of either party to the quarrel; and we cannot doubt that this test of general utility will enforce the needful degree of stability and discourage any tendency to apply larger remedies than are desirable to small and temporary inconvenience.

The only kind of proprietary rights that have been seriously called in question in this country are those touching the possession of land; and though we are far from saying that the present state of things is so bad as to call for exceptional legislation, we unhesitatingly assert in principle the right of the community to dispossess the whole body of landowners of any part of their present privileges which they may be found on investigation to abuse habitually. Practically, it would be most unfortunate for the need of exercising such a right to arise, and it is more desirable, and even more probable, that landowners should become increasingly scrupulous in exercising their present legal rights than that the rights should be forcibly curtailed. The danger, however, of provoking exceptional legislation to deal with special inconveniences that would be better dealt with by voluntary self-denial, is increased by the maintenance of special legislation surviving from the times when exceptional privileges were fearlessly and openly secured to certain sections of the community. If land circulated as easily and descended as equitably as personal property, there would be less need and less desire to insist on the natural difference which there is between a kind of property of which the supply is limited by natural causes and kinds that can be indefinitely multiplied by human industry. It is one of the results of civilisation to make the personal possession of land less and less of a necessary of life; but certain uses of the land, as to dwell on it, to cross it, to be provided with its perishable fruits, and to be able to rest at intervals in sight of its uncontaminated verdure, are necessary to so rapidly increasing a population as to menace the theoretical right of dukes and millionaires to appropriate whole counties to serve as sites for picturesque private hermitages, or as happy hunting-grounds for a select group of well-born barbarians.

Suppose—as seemed not improbable in the first half of the century—that the wealth acquired by commerce and manufactures were to get habitually concentrated in as few hands in proportion as the landed estates of the country, while the labouring millions continued on the verge of pauperism: we should then apply to existing methods of production and distribution the same standard of criticism as is invoked in the case of land laws. There is something wrong either in the laws or manners of a people in which such extremes of wealth and poverty are the rule; and though the corruption of manners cannot be directly remedied by law, the law is at no time bound to sanction consequences adverse to its own spirit.

Suppose an industrial population so ignorant and inert as to be incapable of making reasonably equitable terms with the employers of labour, while the latter were deterred by no scruples of prudence or humanity from driving the hardest bargain they could get; it would be then within the competence of the legislature to fix a minimum rate of wages, and maximum hours for work, in order to give the servile population a chance of developing the power of self-protection—as in times past a maximum price has been fixed for commodities, in the hope of protecting consumers against the arts of monopoly. This is practically how a civilised government acts towards two classes, of oppressors and oppressed, both belonging to an inferior subject race; but the case is imaginary, because the government in modern states is naturally recruited from the propertied classes, and it is scarcely likely that a class whose members were individually so unscrupulous as to need a government check on their exactions should be willing, collectively, to impose such a check on themselves. We only give the extreme case, in order to assert the general principle in regard to all kinds of property, that the claim to State protection for extant legal rights is conditional upon their being exercised in conformity with civic duty, as recognised by the official conscience of the community. And if law may in this way interfere to rectify the tendencies of bad customs and low morality, much more may it hereafter come to sanction and enforce the observance of better customs than those now prevailing, as soon as they have spontaneously established themselves. When the majority of rich men look upon themselves as functionaries charged with a special debt towards society, and hold it a part of their privilege to discharge the debt, many rights which are now unquestioned will then be classed with such antiquarian curiosities of semi-civilisation as the *droit de seigneur*, or the sale of feudal wards.

We must not venture to pursue in detail the discussion which invites us, of special measures of legal reform, as tried by the test of universal practical expediency and morality. Nor need we dwell in detail on the development of various branches of the public service, when governments apply themselves undividedly to the task of ministering to the common good. In spite of manifold practical imperfections, it would be dishonest and ungrateful to deny that within the last quarter of a century real and permanent advances have been made in this direction. We have seen with our own eyes the beginnings of an application of science to the regulation of matters of common interest, which must inevitably expand until the whole physical police of the country is brought methodically under the control of its organised common sense,— not of a scientific hierarchy, entrenched behind a veil of esoteric mysteries, or a parasitic army of Chinese functionaries and salaried examinees, but a body of public servants, whose business it should be to keep the country healthily habitable, and to facilitate the maximum development of its material resources. Even now we have functionaries to whom a place in the public service means an opportunity for productive work, and not either a sinecure or a share in the mechanical routine of administrative circumlocution. This is the sane and living side of our civilisation, most easily undervalued by those who shut their eyes to its existence. The demand for such intelligent and conscientious service will go on increasing with growing intelligence of the needs of the community; and as in all cases a want is more easily felt than supplied, no conceivable improvement in the standard of popular and academical instruction is likely to keep pace with the demand for thorough and versatile ability in the Civil Service; and if the State is thus exacting, private undertakings, we may be sure, will not put up with inferior administration. And as half the force and knowledge that are wanted to reach ends which we already see to be desirable would suffice to disclose fresh ends, vast and remote enough to provide arduous work for generations of our grandchildren, it is clear that local accidents and personal ill-luck are more in fault than the natural order of things in general, if so many of us find wholesome action impossible for want of a clear and cogent end.

Meanwhile the obvious function, for those who have no other, is to criticise their more fortunate neighbours; and it must be admitted that the different grades of our industrial population, who are probably on the whole better satisfied with themselves and with the harmony of their own mode of life with the "spirit of the times," than any other equally considerable section of the community, are still far from having attained to an ideal organisation of their own pursuits. In touching on the law of property, we were reminded of the social and economical difficulties attendant on the acquisition and distribution of wealth; but we have no wish to disallow the claims of political economy to rank as a separate science with laws of its own quite independent of positive institution, and facts which fall into special relations among themselves. Many definitions of the subject-matter of the science have been offered, but for our present purpose, as we consider the phenomena of production and distribution in relation to the nett social result, not to the several motives which lead individuals to contribute to it, we may describe the science as dealing with the remuneration of services and the exchange of commodities. Most professional writers on this subject are anxious to exclude any importation of ethical considerations, and to describe only the *natural*, not the *right* way of paying for services and estimating values; or the way in which people do, rather than that in which they ideally should transact their bargains. And in this they are certainly right: commerce may be moral, just as science, art, or religion may be moral, but morality is not a part of its essence; only, as all normal pursuits alike tend to constitute themselves in the only way in which they can permanently survive as parts of our natural life, commerce as well as all the rest tends slowly and painfully towards an organisation which shall be altogether acceptable to the whole of our nature, or, in other words, to a state of natural morality in its methods and processes.

We do not ourselves believe in the existence of any such antagonism as some economists accept, between the natural and the right, and it is in the interests of speculative truth rather than of practical morality that we should wish the foundations of economical theories to be widened. Political economy, as at present understood, affirms the natural value of everything to be just what it will fetch, *i.e.*, what somebody is willing to give for it. The unknown is to be measured by the uncertain, and the only possible inference is that nothing has any natural value at all, only an always varying competition price. But supposing this chronic uncertainty as to the normal rule of exchange for services or commodities to be a source of economical inconvenience, we cannot think that there is any such metaphysical sanctity in the principle of competition as to preclude tradesmen from making use of some other test. In practice, indeed, a certain mean value for most common articles of commerce is, in fact, established by the help of all naturally relevant considerations, and the fluctuations of the market are in the main conditioned by accidents, which really do for the moment alter the proportion of supply and demand, and so cause a natural rivalry of competition on one or other side. But it is misleading to speak of competition as *par excellence* the economical motive, to the exclusion of still more indispensable elements in the estimation of price or value. The two primary elements in the value of services or commodities are, on the one hand, cost, on the other utility: scarcity or abundance in proportion to demand may modify the natural value fixed by those two considerations, but it cannot fix a value by itself. What costs nothing or is of no use (real or conventional) can have no market value, whether it be as common as moonshine or as rare as the transit of Venus. The competition price of things, in fact, varies between limits which are fixed by their natural value. An article of absolute necessity, such as food, may be worth—to the man who wants it—the whole of his other possessions which are of less use to him than the life they might buy; but men cannot give more than they have got, and even the competition price of bread in a famine is limited, first by the total sum of wealth available for its purchase, and secondly, by the depreciation of all other kinds of wealth except food, when all the community is ready to give everything it has for that alone.

Similarly with regard to the price of services, a man will pay for labour which is necessary to his life as for any other commodity, but he will not buy work that he is able to do for himself if the price is more than his personal ease and leisure are worth to him; and on the other hand, men who live by the sale of their labour will rather fight or starve than labour continuously without prospect of earning what they regard as the necessaries of life in return. Just as there is a natural limit—namely, the extent of our possessions, to the highest possible price of necessaries, there is also a natural limit—namely, the extent of our wants, to the lowest possible price of the labour by which necessaries are produced. A slave can be made to work himself to death in an average period of five or ten years; free labourers can be brought—have been brought—to labour under conditions which give a scarcely higher average length for the term of able-bodied industry. But slaves and labourers rise in insurrection at the point—whenever it may come—at which the image of their own death comes so near to them as to overshadow the prospect of living miserably for a few days more if they don't risk instant death in a struggle for liberty and life. The love of life is the most elementary of economical facts, for our first conception of utilities is derived from what we call its necessaries, and the wish to procure these necessaries is the first motive that urges men to industrial production and commercial exchange.

The double fallacy of economical writers is to lose sight of this starting-point; ignoring the elements of cost and utility, they take the proportion of supply and demand as the sole guide to the price of commodities, and then proceed to treat human labour as an inanimate commodity, subject to the same unlimited depreciation of price under variations of demand as air and water. No scarcity of demand—natural or artificial—will cause a commodity to be continuously brought to market at less than its cost, and the strict cost of labour is the maintenance of the labouring population. If the maintenance is murderously inadequate, we have peasant wars and bread riots—unless indeed the latter are claimed by economical enthusiasts as only an extreme form of the "higgling of the market," which fixes the price of bread as well as the rate of wages. There is, however, this difference between labour and other commodities. If the labourer can live as he pleases without selling his labour, no urgency of demand will bring him into the market, but if he can only live by the proceeds of his labour, no slackness of demand can modify his desire to sell. The demand may fall so much short of the supply that the natural competition price of the labour—if it were not alive—might be brought down below the minimum cost or what is known as a subsistence wage. But even when this minimum has been reached, the supply of labour may still be in excess of the demand, and as it is not possible to stimulate demand by yet further reduction of price, we may have a minimum of absolutely unsaleable labour.

Economists of the strictest school, *i.e.*, the Malthusian, will say—unsaleable commodities lie on hand till they rot, and when some of them have rotted away and others are worn out by use, the demand revives for a season. What the economists do not see is that this decomposition of a live portion of the community is not a simple economical process, but on the contrary a grave political act, charged with political risks and entailing serious responsibility on the timocracy which may—the police force aiding—cause it to be peaceably accomplished. "Unsaleable" is not a simple epithet describing some quality of the labour; it refers to the accidental proportion existing between the desire of the propertied classes to be worked for in this or that way, and the need of the class without property to dispose of its labour, somehow to somebody, for a maintenance. If we imagine an immense accumulation of manufactures, and a sudden arrest of enterprise and imaginative cupidity, the capitalist class might, for a generation, dispense with nearly all labour but that of personal servants; in this case all the labour of the operative class would become unsaleable at once; and the principles of utilitarian morality would be invoked in vain to prove it to be the duty of the majority to prefer the alternative of collective suicide to civil war. There is no such sanctity about the commercial gospel as to give it a right to State protection when it has landed its professors in a political dilemma. There is no reason why all classes should not buy in the cheapest and sell in the dearest market if it suits their convenience, but if the cheapest market is a pest-house, and the dearest a hell, the care for life, of body and soul, may take precedence of zeal for a per-centage. And because buyers and sellers alike have to live a human life as members of the same human community, we deny that it is in any peculiar or permanent sense "natural" for the master of the situation —whether he be buyer or seller—to push his economical advantages to the limits beyond which civil war begins. It is economically possible for him to do so, just as Manchester merchants may shut themselves out from the markets of China by the immoderate adulteration of their goods; but though both courses may be forms of competition, and, therefore, of an economical nature, they may be ill-judged economically as well as socially and politically; and in the interests of economical science we must protest against the notion that miscalculations are "economical" if they are made by persons desirous of driving a good bargain, while sound estimates of price and value are not economical unless direct personal interest has served as a guide for their formation.

Already, even within the commercial camp itself, voices are beginning to raise themselves in honest practical uncertainty as to the lawful extension of this idea of cheapness in the market. It is not lawful to buy stolen goods however cheap, but is it lawful to buy the goods of an insolvent debtor when he offers them as cheap as if his object were—and is it our business to know whether it is—to steal away as much of his assets as he can before going into liquidation? Political economists of the old school would say it is no affair of one tradesman whether his neighbour is honest or no; the thing is to make a profitable bargain while there is a chance. But how if a form of enterprise grows up which consists in buying up the stock-in-trade of bankrupts just before they fail, and selling them at prices with which honest tradesmen can in no way compete? We have here goods sold a miracle of cheapness, but does political economy forbid our discerning that by such transactions the rogues and the receivers derive a profit, earned in no sense by their own industry, but purloined by their astuteness from the honest creditors of one rogue and the honest competitors of the other? It will be said, perhaps, that sales with intent to defraud are already illegal, but if we once admit that a purchaser is bound to satisfy himself that the other party to the contract has a right to sell—and is only the more bound to do so if the proffered goods are suspiciously cheap, the thin end of the wedge of moral responsibility is inserted, and every kind of fraudulent cheapness may be condemned alike, whether it be the fruit of stolen or half-paid labour, or of stolen or half-withheld workmanship, or of sharp practice in the actual market.

It is practically impossible that every one, in making a special bargain for immediate profit should look forward to all the consequences of his own decisions and the consequent actions of others. An average mind would give way under the strain, and political economists generally sanction the disposition of the average trader to leave deliberately out of account everything but the clearly visible personal advantage. But the pursuit of a clear, present, personal advantage, if uncontrolled by general considerations, may entail unnecessary loss to other persons or classes; that is to say, the individual might be able to do as well by himself, and better by other people, if he recognised positive duties to the latter, instead of seeking the shortest road to doing well by himself alone. Experience fails to bear out the optimistic assumption of utilitarianism, which has its stronghold in political economy; that the whole sum of lawful motives will certainly and always press in the way of personal inducement upon each individual agent, so that each several centre of consciousness will always feel, by direct experience, the force of all those manifold converging lines of tendency which in the long run, by their joint action, certainly do lead the majority of men to act in conformity with the general good. If the calculations of self-interest were always so providentially inspired, we do not see why economists should need to distinguish as they do between economical and moral propriety. But if the economical as well as the moral interest of the whole community is liable to demand sometimes, from some individuals, conduct not exactly coincident with the promptings of personal inclination, then it seems certain that economical science, instead of contenting itself with the empirical *à peu près* of competitors bargaining, will lay down some general principles or rules in accordance with which the general welfare may be most economically secured.

The destruction of forests by the first settlers in a new country is a typical example of discrepancy between the counsels of private and public prudence. Such settlers may not, perhaps, live to see the price of timber rise to a remunerative point, but the settlement, if it survives them, will infallibly before long regret the idle waste of a long inheritance of natural growth, which, as often as not, is of no real service, even for the moment, to its perpetrator. The history of the American oil-wells,[1] gives a still more compendious illustration of the inadequacy of selfish calculations to protect a most obvious public interest. When the oil-springs were first tapped, the oil was so accessible and so incredibly abundant, that its commercial value fell almost to zero on the spot; hence reckless waste and the actual destruction of large quantities of a valuable natural commodity. The means of lighting cheaply some millions of houses were squandered because the first owners were con-

[1] Professor Owen on "Petroleum and Oil Wells," in *Fraser*, for Oct. 1875.

scious of no personal inducement not—if the trite proverb may be allowed—to kill the goose with the golden eggs if the contents of her ovary at death were sufficient to provide themselves with a fortune on which to retire luxuriously. The oil was first depreciated by its abundance, and then had its commercial value increased by the waste, which made it again, by comparison, prematurely scarce. The common interest suffered by the needless destruction of an article of natural utility, and out of the crowd of speculators making haste to be rich, the success of some entailed the failure of others, so that unless we think gamblers prudent, because every gambler hopes he will be the one to break the bank, it cannot even be said that the individual speculators understood their own interest better than if they had sought to make the best of the natural store for all concerned. In commerce, as in personal morality, forethought is the beginning of altruism, and if the individual were but immortal, he would live to expiate every disregard for the interest of his neighbour or posterity; but as one age is as near to science as another, the general rule which is to provide a check for the anti-social vagaries of speculation, and alleviate the natural calamities of dearth, must fix the standard for the normal value of services and commodities in reference to their permanent utility to the many, not their occasional saleableness by the owners.

In the often-quoted case of a shipwrecked crew, the scanty stores of food are not put up at auction to the highest bidder, but dealt round by common consent as far as they will go; the demand for food is far in excess of the supply, and every member of the group would be glad to diminish the supply of hungry mouths, but no one dares to say to the other, as a Malthusian millowner to the mob at his gates—Get a few of you starved or hung, and then come back and bargain. And the true nature of social problems is not altered, only disguised, by their additional magnitude and complexity. The poorest country of modern times has never been so poor that its whole wealth would fail to find its population in bread and cheese and fustian, and yet capitalists once and again have told the swarming millions to make themselves scarce, because there is not wherewithal to pay their labour, meaning that there is not enough to pay their labour out of the surplus left after the supply of every other want of those in whose hands the wealth of the country is accumulated.

The fact is that we find it best, as a rule, "that they should take who have the power, and they should keep who can," because there is no sufficiently independent and capable human tribunal to revise the spontaneous adjustment of natural recompense for natural ability. But when the organisation of society has advanced so far that many social prizes are awarded by a concatenation of chances, in which ability plays no part at all, society has a right to revise deliberately the result of its involuntary awards, and to lay down the conditions under which individuals shall be allowed to enjoy the "unearned increment" of natural advantages which the social compact bestows on the favourites of fortune. We do not assert the right of the many to confiscate periodically the accumulated heritage of the few. The momentary benefit derived by the less wealthy from such a redistribution of existing property would be much more than compensated by the discouragement of industry in all classes, and the substitution, at best, of one kind of anti-social exploitation of man by man for another, privileging, in fact, the improvidence of Esau instead of the wiliness of Jacob. But as the one indefeasible natural right (and duty) of society is to consult the greatest possible advantage of all its members, it is clear that we are justified in regulating the distribution of those gifts of fortune which are not the reward of personal merit, so far as can be done without discouraging the development of such merit. Merit is discouraged by legislation which robs it of its comparatively near and natural, though incidental, advantages; but it is also discouraged by legislation, or legislative inertia, which allows the incidental rewards of merit to be paid, like prize-money, to the heirs-at-law of long-departed valour, instead of to those still engaged in the battle of life; and if too large a share of the good things of life, available for the living generation, is reserved for the descendants of those who lived well or wisely before it, society is pauperised and left without wages to recompense the living services rendered to itself.

It would not be possible, even if it were desirable, to induce any class or classes to acquiesce permanently in a rate of exchange for services or commodities which was deliberately unjust to one party to the contract, that is to say, deliberately out of relation to their natural equivalence as spontaneously estimated by our present feelings and judgment. But it is eminently desirable, if it can be shown to be possible, for all sections of the community to agree upon a common measure of social value, and to be guided in their particular bargains by a general opinion as to the comparative merit or use of proffered services; and supposing the common conscience and common sense to be intent on promoting the common welfare, the community might, as it were, insure itself against the risk of those local disturbances of the natural equity of exchange which distress society when the ordinary course of peaceful competition is embittered by positive scarcity or unsatisfied want. The natural value—using the words in their highest sense—of any service or commodity is commensurate with its fitness to contribute to the natural good or perfection of the community making use of it. Supposing such a—by no means inconceivable—degree of enlightenment to be reached by an industrial community as that both the giver and the receiver of any customary service should be aware of its social importance or insignificance, and accept, as a matter of course, the remuneration proportioned to the estimation in which it was held on both sides, the accidental scarcity or abundance of one commodity as compared with another would be accepted as a common loss or a common gain, instead of the whole profit or loss being allowed to lie where it falls, at the unguarded cast of hazard.

One of the most pressing and difficult questions of the day is this concerning the natural rights and natural duties—if we allow both to have a rationally recognisable existence—of the labouring classes. Is it, we are compelled to ask, is it their duty, *i.e.*, is it for the common good, that they should acquiesce voluntarily in the working of a system of competition which may end by pointing out to them the last resource of self-destruction? Are they, in fact, bound to make their work as much like a brute "commodity," and as little like a reasonable service, as they can? The way in which the question presents itself to the different sections of a commercial and industrial community like our own is practically this: When, from a variety of circumstances, which no one has planned, and of which no one clearly understands the history, there is a present discrepancy between the demand for labour on the part of those who have the means of paying for it, and the supply of labour seeking to be paid for, is it the capital or the labour that should suffer diminution in its share of the gross profits of the national industry, or is the loss to be divided between them? and if so, who is to determine in what proportions?

Trade unions, the great instrument for fixing wages by other considerations than simple competition, do not in practice accept the theory of a "wages fund" of fixed amount; they take the whole wealth of the country as the source from which the remuneration of labour and capital must be derived, and they do not see why the division of the national inheritance should take place—to borrow a significant technicality—*per stirpes* rather than *per capita;* *i.e.*, by proportioned division between two stocks (whether of different race or different class) without regard to their numerical strength. Of course, it is not to be expected that men of scanty education, and opinions formed under the immediate pressure of personal feeling, should be able to correct the plausible generalisations of the class above their own, in which opinions are formed in accordance with fixed *habits* of feeling, themselves formed at leisure by the general tendency of interested motives. At the same time, it is clear that unless these habits of feeling have been formed under healthy conditions, the ideas answering to them will be no better guides than the passion or inclination of the moment, though they may have an impressive air of calm fixity which, unluckily, is attainable by prejudice as well as reason.

The crude notion of the trade unionist is, that a combination of workmen to limit the quantity of work turned out by the vendors of labour will result in raising the price by diminishing the supply of the article on sale, so that, while less work is being done, the mechanical action of supply and demand will make the workman's share of the gross wealth of the country larger. Malthus proposed, as an economy, that men should die, or never see the light; these too docile followers propose, as an economy less jarring to some of our prejudices, that those who live should copy the unproductiveness of the dead, as a means to the same happy result of causing the fruits or wages of industry to circulate more freely. The crude notion of the economists, on the other hand, is that society can somehow make a good thing out of the necessities of its members, and get more work out of them for the same or less equivalent the more urgent their need to receive the equivalent. Most economists regard the unionist's view as rank heresy—an uneconomical limitation of supply—but we fail to see why it is more of an economical heresy for the labourers to hold back their superfluous industry from an overstocked market than for a manufacturer to do the same with his goods for as long as he can afford. There is a short-lived profit to the consumer if the manufacturer sells his stock at a loss rather than not sell at all; and there is a profit to the manufacturer if the labourer, rather than not sell his labour, sells it for starvation wages. But social science would be another name for pessimism if men were debarred from the calculation of any but immediate consequences, and labourer and manufacturer alike have a right to consider the social tendencies of bargains that they both have to spend a lifetime in carrying out.

The real difficulty lies elsewhere, for the restricted employment of labour certainly diminishes the capital fund out of which labour, as well as everything else, has to be paid; and if the will of the labourer is once allowed to count as an economical force, it is as much within his option to refuse to give his work for less share than he thinks equitable in the capital fund, as it is to aim indirectly at compelling the employers of labour to offer better terms by limiting the number of available labourers. The way the case practically presents itself is this: in a particular trade, or for a special season, the number of labourers is slightly in excess of the demand, *i.e.*, there is more work wanted than is to be had. Economists expect the labourers to bid against each other for the first chance of earning wages; while trade societies look upon the competition of workmen against each other for the coveted work as an evil to the class, and a doubtful gain even to the individual. If the wages fund were for the moment rigorously limited, say to the equivalent of 1s. a day for every adult labourer throughout the country, trade unions would urge each man to take his 1s. a day in peace, instead of bidding against his neighbours for the privilege of selling 2s. worth of work for 1s. 6d.; and they believe that the result of unregulated competition among labourers, who treat their industry as a commodity subject to unlimited depreciation, will be to tempt those who are deprived of their chance of 1s. a day, by the competitor who does a day's work for 9d., to undersell the first bidder and take 7½d. In such cases as we are supposing, the hypothetical

x

7s. a week need not represent any reduction in the current scale of wages; it may be only the result of "slackness" of demand, or such a scarcity of work as will only keep the labourers employed for half or a quarter of their time. If this is the fact, it may often suit the employer's interest to keep a few hands in full employ, and turn off the rest; and then the union again interferes with the course of individual competition by causing those workmen who are in full employment to subscribe to secure a bare maintenance for their possible rivals, lest the latter be driven to the kind of competition already referred to, the beginning of the operative's race to ruin; and this is regarded as being nearly as grave an economical heresy as the modified Malthusianism above noticed, for the ideal theory of bargaining imagines all members of the same class to be rivals, whose hostility lays them open to *exploitation* by the members of other classes, to the greater glory of the principle of self-interest.

To put these rival views in their true proportions, we have to take a position outside the natural feeling of both buyers and sellers. The interest of society at large is to have as much efficient and serviceable work done as possible, and to have the fruit or reward of the work enjoyed by as many members of society as possible. The final cause of work is to be of use, not to fetch a price, and though, now-a-days, people live mainly by bartering services and commodities, we need not confuse the act with the end, or exalt the transactions of commerce above the results of civilised life. There must be some confusion about the premises of a theory that lands us in antinomies, such as the popular bugbear of over-production, as if a country could be impoverished or its wealth diminished by its producing too much wealth. A country may produce more, in the way of food or manufactures, than it can find a lucrative market for outside its own borders; but whatever may be the condition of its foreign trade, a country is materially the better off the more abundant all useful and agreeable commodities are within it, and the more general and equitable their distribution. Bales of calico unsold in the warehouses and barns of grain reserved by the farmer are not elements of national wealth while the cotton-spinner is half clad and the farm-labourer half fed, and yet the more of their respective manufactures the industrial population hurls into the market in its distress, the less and less their means of acquiring any portion for themselves, for the lower the money value or competition price set by commerce on the work.

The mental bewilderment into which we are thrown by this apparently suicidal fate of industry disappears if we remember that in practice what is called "over-production," or production in excess of the demands of an external market, usually extends to all branches of production alike, so that if the employers of labour made themselves the channel of communication between the different classes of producers, the home trade of an industrious population might maintain itself without any very elaborate methods of exchange. Any increased economy of production that enables a commodity to be supplied more abundantly than before may lower the price of that commodity as compared with others, but the positive value of these others, or of the circulating medium, is increased when this purchasing power, in that one direction, is enlarged; for while the positive value of things is not increased by making them scarce, the positive value of life is raised by whatever tends to make the goods of life plentiful and accessible to all.

The real difficulty is concerned not with production, but with distribution. As wealth multiplies, society has to determine whether the increase is to go to him that hath that he shall have more abundantly, whatever the present value of his services, or whether the "unearned increment" of social inheritance is to be enjoyed under conditions. Our civilisation rests upon an inheritance of accumulated materials, tools, traditions, and commodities, the fruit of past industry and saving; but it is not quite certain that the self-denial now involved in a rich man's living on his income instead of on his capital can be regarded exactly as an act of merit for which society owes him material reward. Wealth increased through the able direction of labour by the great "captains of industry" belongs to them by the same title as to their employees as the fruit of work; but we do not accept as normal or permanent the current practice which limits the share of each individual in the inheritance of preceding generations to the particular lot —of lands, debts, or halfpence—which he receives as his portion from the next of kin. The wages fund is limited after all to that which the skill and industry of each generation can produce out of its capital, and if we are to encourage the most useful forms of industry, we must be prepared to distribute the rewards of labour in proportion to its usefulness. Given a perfectly free circulation of natural ability, the incapables of all classes would sink gradually and gently to the lowest level, the social "residuum" would deserve its name, and the problem to make existence tolerable for even the residuum would receive more careful attention from rulers who felt that their own flesh and blood were likely to swell the numbers of the class.

The *raison d'être* of the capitalist in a moral and intelligent community lies in his use, not in his merits, for wealth will be piled up in an industrial age, even though no father dreams of enriching his children's children. The privilege of dispensing unearned wealth is not a reward given to the son for the father's economy, for unless the wealth is to be well or wisely dispensed, society owes the father no thanks for the hoard withdrawn into private hands out of the common fund. The service by which the rich man earns the wealth entrusted to him is exactly that of distribution. Those engaged in the details of production who have no surplus wealth of their own cannot afford to render unsaleable services, or services which, by their very generality, fail to command a price from individuals.

Services rendered to no one in particular, but to all who need or accept them, are the best acknowledgment of rewards earned by no one in particular and paid no one exactly knows how or whence; the rewards are concentrated by chance, and though they might almost as well be scattered by chance, so far as any personal desert is concerned, yet if society is ever to attain to an orderly distribution of functions among men, seeing and owning a supreme duty to each other severally and collectively, it will certainly have no need to abolish the class of unpaid servants of the commonwealth whose mission it is to give freely what they have freely received, in accordance with other canons of fitness than the quotations of the Stock Exchange. Sumptuary laws to prevent the accumulation of riches in the hands of a minority will lose their charm even for the most doctrinaire socialist if the accumulation is only a step towards more orderly and intelligent distribution; and though it may seem utopian to look forward to such a result, it is not really contrary to nature, reason, or possibility, for the habitual exchange of services and commodities to be organised as a means of providing all classes with the necessaries of life, those who wish for them enough to work for them with the material luxuries of life, and those who are able to use and value them with its spiritual luxuries and graces; in a word—to furnish wholesome life for all, pleasant life for the energetic or the amiable, and life the most varied and intense for those whose varied powers and intense resolves spend themselves in perfected subservience to the common good.

We do not undervalue competition as a spur to industry and inventive enterprise; but the community as a whole would be better served if traders, producers, and consumers agreed to seek their common interest with one consent, instead of trusting with a queerly-placed piety, in the beneficent result of the uncompromising commercial struggle for existence. If we get on so fast and so harmoniously when every man spends, say, three-fourths of his energies on his proper work, and one-fourth in shoving his work to the fore at his neighbour's expense, how much further and faster should we go if the results of the struggle were taken for granted, and services were amicably grouped in order of merit without the friction of a preliminary trial of strength? Economists will not question the prudence of buying social order and felicity in the cheapest market, but no true economy in the social service can be effected by merely nominal reductions in price affecting all services at once, still less by a real partial reduction serving only to intensify existing inequalities. If we measure services against each other, not by their competition price in some common standard, social progress and profit will consist in the multiplication of exchangeable equivalents, so as to make a day's work more valuable because it produces more, and a day's wages more valuable likewise because it will buy more services in return. This, and not the pauperisation of an overproductive race, seems to be the natural goal of industrial aspiration; and though it may seem utopian to dream of a land where wealth shall not exclude cheapness, the dream seems more in keeping with the logic of common sense than the waking realities with which we are familiar.

The general aim of political action and social reforms is, we assume, to assure to every one every possible facility for living the best life they can, and to continue developing the possibilities of every one, so that the realised best may be progressive; and under this short name of "best" we include the healthy discharge of every natural function—efficient action, competent understanding, and satisfied affection for each individual. But it is as certain as the divinity of truth and holiness, that none of us will live to see this perfect state—except in the momentary glimpses of some twilight revelation; and some may regard it as an open question whether, in the face of this knowledge, the present practical best for living men can be the cultus of the unattainable. We contend that the best attainable is a step on the road towards the absolutely good, but this is one of the cases in which judgments are formed, neither by reasoning nor conscious choice, but by the intuition of feeling and pre-established affinities of taste.

The main interest of ethical science lies in its bearing on the most intimate personal concerns of individuals. We may call it egotism if we please, but this question: How am *I*, I myself, and not another, to live my own life, now, to-morrow, and through the fated years to come? is, and inevitably always will be, the most urgent of questions to men and women whose first need is to live, and whose first desire is to live pleasantly or well. The inexhaustible fascination possessed by the problems of morality comes from the fact that in them alone man sees his own needs in relation to the general facts of existence, and imagines it possible to derive from them instruction and direction for his own personal course. The cravings after help and guidance to which religious systems owe their power can find no more rational satisfaction than in the apprehension of eternal truth as it affects the life of every man. The truth is the same for all, but its practical application is as various as individual circumstances; each individual has impulses and aspirations which it is his wish to rationalise and bring into harmony with the general rules that he is prepared to accept, provided always that the rules can be made to apply to his own case. Men may be honestly unable to discern what their duty is, but the obscurity comes from their defective insight, not from any objective uncertainty, and we acknowledge our grasp of a supposed truth to be incomplete and feeble, unless we are able to verify its power, in the case of any concrete problem, by pointing to the postulate or proposition in which the desired solution is implicitly contained; and we feel that when once a clear and adequate apprehension of the natural end and the reasonable means had been attained, the present outlines of our moral convictions might be filled in—

at the indefinite leisure of the race—as minutely as the most scrupulous conscience could desire.

But the outline is not filled in yet, and consequently the intellectual problem, what is best for things in general, is complicated by, and helps to complicate, the moral problem, what is the best possible for the agent. The best for each individual to aim at is the best of which he—and not another—has a clear and adequate vision, giving birth to desire. It is idle to urge one man towards a vocation that he has not the gift to follow, though for a better man the choice might be good. The crowning reason for devotion to the general rather than the particular good is, that each man's best possible self can only live in the best possible world; and we have a right to keep hold of this abstract certainty, even when we are unable to trace the connection between the two, or even when, as may sometimes occur, there is *no* present personal motive for the conduct that we see to be abstractedly best. At rare intervals we are overtaken by a ghastly sense that the strength of right motives is not irresistible, and we feel for the godless world in which our lot is cast something of the horror that has been felt for the atheist's creed; but though the painful impression is not to be forgotten, rational faith can survive this momentary shock in the strength of two considerations: first, that the pain of the shock comes from its rarity, whence it follows that, *as a rule*, the powers of light are in the ascendant; and, secondly, that the divine is not lost, even in the darkest moments, when there is a human soul ready to revile the world for having nothing more divine to show it than its own unbought appetite after the truly right. And though it is not possible to determine *à priori* what contribution each individual is to make to the general wellbeing of the social group, we have generally an image of the most admirable character existing parallel to our conception of the general best, and the nature of the character that is cultivated, together with that of the ideal that is proposed, define between them the special course to be adopted by individuals under whatever circumstances may arise in practice.

Society has a right to control the conduct of its members, and the habitual conduct reacts upon the character, though the conduct is the result of the original nature as well as of the controlling circumstances. What we call the "formed character" is, in fact, the second nature begotten by social conditions out of the first, in which capabilities reappear as ability, or, to borrow the more exact German idiom, in which *Fähigkeiten* are transformed into *Fertigkeiten;* and the course of life, on which it becomes possible to pass judgment, is the virtually spontaneous fruit of the second nature. Very few talents are absolutely irresistible, and nearly every choice power that ripens into choice performance has been deliberately cherished and developed by careful nourishment and exercise. And, at the same time, it may be noted that nearly all the possessors of exceptional power in any one special direction also possess more than the average of miscellaneous ability, so that it really lies within their own power to elect their own social *rôle*. But if such a special ability is once allowed to enter on the course of production, the impetus becomes uncontrollable, and the future of the whole man becomes immediately dependent on the fortunes of his genius. And in processes that are partly deliberate and partly the necessary consequences of voluntary acts, the moment to which responsibility attaches is that of self-committal to a line which, once taken, can never be altogether abandoned.

The born painter cannot but draw, the born musician cannot but compose, the born mechanic invents, the born mathematician works problems; but men of genius, at least, have a choice between the *rôle* of artist and of amateur, and it is a question open for discussion whether they are morally bound to prefer the former. The object in view is to attain the *maximum* specialisation of active ability without narrowing the range of personal consciousness. We have no sense of incompleteness in the life of Socrates or Spinoza, or of Sir James Brooke or Garibaldi, because the discharge of the predestined function seems to include a provision for all the personal impulses and moral inclinations. On the other hand, in the case of such men as Goethe or Humboldt, we have an almost oppressive sense of personal completeness, mixed with a vague impression of something wanting, as if their very completeness isolated them from complete contact on any one side with the ordinary world; and to measure their objective eminence we have to regard Humboldt as the successful explorer and geognostic, and Goethe as the friend of Schiller and the author of "Faust," or both as types and models of the possible range of human accomplishment—sinking the relations in which they could effect no more than ordinary men, or even less than ordinary men with narrower faculties but more intense power of self-abandonment to the exercise of faculty.

Apart from such exceptional cases as that of universal genius, or of a talent as minutely defined as that of a grammarian or a decipherer of hieroglyphics, human aptitudes class themselves generally in the same lines as the various leading objects of ambition and aspiration. A special susceptibility to one form or another of natural good inspires the work of a Mozart, a Newton, a Titian, or a Keats; and hardly less special, in its way, is the vocation to seek not this good or that, but every possible good for all the world; or since that ambition is really too high for human powers, to seek every possible means for facilitating the life and development of all possible good. And for those who understand by morality the conscientious pursuit of the rationally chosen Best, it is an interesting practical question whether the philanthropist's life is essentially better than that of other specialists, and whether every form of natural good ought to (*i.e.*, had better) be cultivated in conscious subordination to a more comprehensive ideal, or whether, to realise the

SOCIAL AND INDIVIDUAL PERFECTION. 331

most comprehensive ideal possible, we require the maximum of self-assertion in every special normal tendency? The case might be stated in this way: are all normal pursuits good in themselves, or only good for the sake of the abstract goodness made up by their combination? Or again: is it a higher function to organise and arrange the contributions of natural force than to contribute fresh force to the development of social life?

To this it may be replied, that natural morality conceives every special form of natural good as indispensable to the whole result of perfection, and that there are not degrees of indispensableness, and, generally speaking, we have no moral ground for exalting one form of natural good, one phase of social service, above another, or one above all the rest. It is only when the imperfections of our actual systems, social, religious, and political, obtrude on our consciousness, that we feel as if the one thing needful to all of us were right guidance towards a better state, and that the best leaders of men are those who can supply this, our chief and most urgent want. We are not blind to the sublimity of mathematical truth, or callous to the emotions vibrating in the voice of poetic passion, only while men and women are starving round us in brutal misery, or battening in brutal ease, the problem and the poem seem far away from half our life, and we become unwilling accomplices in the indifference of our age to some of the noblest works of man. We are called away from the peaceful life of intellectual perception, and many of us are fain to turn reformers in despair, not because we have the reformer's talent or the reformer's taste, but because the world needs so much reform that it has failed to give us any narrower task more in keeping with our modest powers and private inclinations.

Still there is a distinction, of which we may as well recognise the full significance, between action which has its motive in the agent's personal impulse to do that act rather than another, and action which has its motive in the agent's desire that such a thing be done, whatever the doing may cost him, and however little personal concern he may have in the result accomplished. For the reason just suggested, we are more ready to give the name of moral effort to the latter class of doing; but at the same time we may admit that, in an ideal state of things, with the social mechanism duly adjusted, and only needing to be kept in repair, the distinction would disappear, and the professional curators of the machine, finding their task no harder or more painful than that of other craftsmen, would cease to receive additional regard, or perhaps rather, the class would disappear altogether, like armies from a Quaker continent, when every special form of energy had learnt to exercise itself in conscious subjection to the claims of other forms, and in conscious devotion to the best general result.

We are inconsistent because the world is inconsistent, and at one moment cry out for the help of moral virtue and disinterested self-sacrifice, while at the next we grow impatient of the imperfection that makes the sacrifices needed, and we challenge the saints to complete their work by giving us a world where there shall be no place for saintliness. It is not absolutely good that the best men and the best deeds should be swallowed up in the painful resistance of evil; only now, and as far in front as we can see, there is evil enough to occupy whole armies of reformers, though we may dream if we please of a millenium when the armies shall disband because all the world has joined them, and the reformers find their occupation gone because at last every man has found a work to do and has learnt to do it faithfully. And, partly for the sake of that distant day, it behoves us not to lose sight of the fact that natural good is older than human crime or folly, and may be young yet when many of our virtues, like many of our pleasures, are shelved in the museum of unconsciousness.

There is something abnormal in a life all spent in pleasureless resistance to what is. To do good by wholesale is the hardest of arts; it requires a talent that is rare, and only those who possess it feel bound in conscience to the self-denial required for its exercise. But it is inaccurate to say that a perfectly virtuous man *likes* (or ought to like) doing good to his unfortunate fellow-mortals, or that he does what is right because he finds it pleasant, and that it is a part of virtue to like doing whatever it is best to do; because to like a thing, to find it pleasant, is to accept its existence as a whole unreservedly, to have no fault to find with it; and no one has this feeling in righting a wrong, at least no clear-headed person who would unfeignedly rather not have had it to right. There may be a transient satisfaction when the remedy applied is found complete and effectual, but with the true philanthropist this half personal feeling is almost merged in sympathy with the relief of those who are benefited, and promptly superseded by compassion for those still unsuccoured. It is not so easy as it looks to add to the happiness of mankind; good-will goes but a little way, and the modern stoic has no sooner accommodated himself with resignation to his own share of the objective ills of life, than the harder, or at least more interminable task confronts him of acquiescing in all the present irremediable suffering of others. He is the servant of the servants of men, and his task is to guide and harmonise the action of all who work without thinking for all who enjoy without thinking; to teach them how to compass the ends they desire when they have not learnt to will the means that lead to them. Even in the work of reform there can be no self-assertion, for the world, as it is, is made and animated by wills that it is the altruist's endeavour to enlighten and content, not to alter by constraint: there is much suffering in the world, and the reason of the suffering of those who suffer remediably is that they do not at this present moment will the first step towards the improvement of their condition. There is no one so badly off that perfect wisdom would not mend his case, but with the best will in the world, perfect wisdom cannot be imparted wholesale, only by degrees and as the patient is able to bear it; people cannot be helped to their own good by force, and it is only when good-will is wanting, when men are content that others should suffer for their profit, or at least by their connivance, that altruism becomes for the moment militant, but it has no satisfaction in the fray, for cruelty is the *summum malum*, an absolute evil, the perception of which is unmitigatedly painful, even though we do not suppose all who have the misfortune to be criminal to be condemned to an eternity of remorse.

Certainly no one is virtuous for amusement; but if the altruists' concern for the misfortunes of others prevents their life from being happier than the egotists', it is also certain that they would not consent to wish away the power of sympathy, which, though a source of suffering to themselves, is the condition of their practical usefulness. They must endure the consciousness of evil, moral and material, as a step toward amending it, just as a man must be tormented with ambitious desires before he can imagine happiness to consist in moulding other men to his will. The few fine souls called to this tragic fate do not ask or need our pity; the vocation is irresistible; and as experience abundantly proves that society does not subsist by a series of equitable exchanges, it is to the superogatory virtue of these lovers of their kind that the human race must look for its redemption from the curse of natural imperfection. Certainly exchanges should be equitable, and objective rights may be maintained by law; but the moral, the religious attitude of mind, recognises only duties, and those in whom it is most perfect argue, with sweet unreasonableness, that the less the past and the present have done for them, the more must they needs do for the present and the future. We poor sinners, who are far from that holy state, can at least almost understand why the will of those who can lead such a life is good to do it, and how a peace which passeth understanding follows from the perfect unity of will and deed only attainable by those who have known and conquered every human pain, and turned their knowledge and their victory into a force working for the good of all mankind.

We are not all born saints, and the counsels of perfect self-devotion must be left for those who can receive them; but in a world of saints there would be no room for that saintly grace, and in the world that now is there are many whose natural appetites make no damaging or unreasonable demands upon their fellows. The arts and sciences are naturally good and morally innocent, and we can more easily imagine a society got beyond the need for reform than one able to dispense with the cultus of truth and beauty. The chief moral good is perhaps to have learnt from nature to know, and feel, and desire the truth and beauty of the world that might be, but it is something to possess the best of that which is, to perceive and represent even if we cannot create. We have an impersonal ideal of beauty and truth, which we venerate as something outside ourselves, and a life spent in such worship has an ideal end, though that end is not the happiness of other sentient beings. Artists and men of science are the high-priests of this worship, and it is for them to throw open its temples to the many; but no true worshipper believes himself to be the final cause of his God; if such a connection is dreamt of at all, it must lie the other way, and we count men to be of worth as they struggle into an apprehension of the divine.

The difference between this conception and the view of art as ministering to enjoyment, and of culture as serving only to quicken and stimulate the taste, is, that, in the one case, the man aspires to master his inspiration, to possess the vision, to enjoy the revelation, in a word, to subordinate art to the artist; and that, in the other, the whole consciousness is abandoned to the impression that is given, desire is swallowed up in disinterested apprehension, even the will is suspended, and the personal exercise of a faculty by which the vision is embodied and the revelation declared, seems only present to the individual as an act of more complete self-identification with the influences that are his inspiration. This is doubtless what is meant by the often-repeated phrase that all true art must be religious, which sounds like a paradox when religion is confounded with belief in the established theology of the age. During the last three hundred years there have been painters who were good Christians enough, but no sacred picture has been produced to compare for devout religious insight into the glories of natural form with the turn of a horse's head in the Elgin Marbles, carved by men who, whether they believed in the divine lineage of Athene and said their prayers to Poseidon or not, had seen in their own Attica blue skies, grey olive boughs, curling waves, and prancing war-horses, and had absorbed all the lessons of divine truth lurking in such sights for the sons of men. It is hard to formulate all the difference between the true artist and the mechanician, but perhaps it lies chiefly in the refinement of spiritual candour that is able to receive general intellectual, as well as merely sensible impressions from external forms : if Turner was a true painter, it was because he knew how to paraphrase sight in shapes and colours that are emotional.

But to see, or to feel what is seen, is not everything. To make a fine art of passion or attachment to the beautiful in nature, art, or human life requires the abandonment of all the faculties, and is so absorbing as to leave the mind no leisure for other claims; pleasurable emotions, however rich and variously modulated, do not occupy the whole of man, and life becomes one-sided if exclusive importance is attributed to their cultivation. Of course, any one with a rooted habit of referring every point of conduct to a supposed external rule of right will say, Why should we not, if it pleases us, take the part, the side of life that we like best, and let the remainder go ? But if it is admitted that there can be no reason for anything except the nature of things and of men, it is a simple answer that the whole is larger than its parts, and that, even if we believe ourselves to be naturally one-sided, we may acknowledge the quality to be a defect, though the acknowledgment might prove our nature less one-sided than we thought. If the object is to make life rich and full, each individual must have wealth and variety in himself, not merely by contrast to a too monotonous level in the men around him; it is a parasitic originality that only becomes conscious of itself in opposition, for it takes little wisdom to differ from a fool, while much learning is needed to agree with some of the wise. The truest intuitions are detached, and though the creations of art are immortal, and each moment of æsthetic consciousness complete in itself, they add nothing to each other, they do not weave themselves into a continuous, progressive, organic whole.

Emotions spend themselves and leave a fading memory, but all true knowledge, which is the perception of constant relations and necessary fact, hangs together, as the world does, so that none of it can quite cease out of being. The enjoyment that comes to us from without is ours for a moment and ends; the force that we expend is ours and remains, but only on condition that we give away its fruits; but knowledge both lasts and grows and stays with us; we possess it even to that last refinement upon the rights of property, it is ours to bequeath; of all our best spiritual treasures, that alone can be left behind us unimpaired. Our happiness dies with us, or rather, it dies daily, if it is born so often; our actions live in their fruit, which might set our teeth on edge if we lived to taste it; only the truths we knew, the scraps of scientific certitude which we rescued from the dark abysses of unknown existence, are altogether ours, with a possession the more absolute that it can be shared, ours and our children's after us, as long as we and they live in a world more constant than man. It is an old complaint against Providence that virtue is monotonous, that there are many ways of sinning, and that men are fond of novelty; but science at least is as various as vice, and if we consider that knowledge grows by being shared, that the interest of all who seek knowledge is one, that the end which many conspire to seek will be reached in part, and that to reach a desired end is pleasant, and chiefly that the pleasure of success in a pursuit only disappoints us when we fail to gratify the one desire that is stronger—for a sympathy to multiply the pleasure to infinity—then without any unphilosophical optimism it may perhaps be hoped that even if the world were peopled, as we hardly think it ever will be, exclusively with scientific atheists, a considerable proportion of them might still find it possible to rise above the resignation to their earthly condition which is enjoined by morality to the contentment which is a counsel of religious perfection.

But although a special interest attaches to the problems of morality, in consequence of their bearing on the concerns of human life and the responsibilities of choice, this very fact lends a degree of embarrassment to their discussion, and tempts us to rank them amongst matters of too deep and intimate concern for it to be exactly decorous to speak freely of them in public. The feeling may be called either spiritual modesty or *mauvaise honte* as we please, but there certainly is a general disposition to feel that conscience is a thing about which the less said the better in civilised society: certain forms of ignorance or vice are spontaneously condemned as radically unattractive and in bad taste, but the worst taste of all is to plead guilty to the inheritance of a worse and a better nature, with the attendant doom of struggle, failure, and aspiration. We are impatient of many of the coarser necessities of our being, and since the religious formula has ceased to be generally received, popular philosophy has given no reason why men should be cursed with a divided will, and they try to hide the infirmity as they would hide an hereditary malformation of body. And it is in this way only that the relaxation of religious faith can fairly be said to threaten the foundations of morality; for men who have strength and rectitude enough to make a sacrifice of inclination which their judgment enjoins, will follow inclination on the easier road if their judgment speaks only to condemn the feebleness of a divided purpose. Since we have ceased to lay the blame of our own shortcomings on the devil, our self-respect impels us rather to profess that we don't care about being any better than we are, than to resolve against continuing so much worse than in our secret hearts we should like to be.

Closely connected with this mixture of pride and cowardice, which paralyses more human effort than we perhaps suspect, is an intellectual fastidiousness that forbids the mind to supplement the irresolution of the will. We are on our guard against "the solemn folly of taking ourselves too seriously;" and because we have critical acumen enough to know that the most fortunate result of our best efforts will be objectively insignificant, we try despairingly to escape from the limitations of incompetence by the self-imposed limitation—of indolence—which, unluckily for our sagacity, turns out, of course, to be objectively narrower even than the one by which we scorned to be confined. And yet there is a ground of reasonableness in our dread of overstrained pretensions and moral priggishness. If we are in the habit of feeling as strongly as we can feel about small interests, without noting their comparative smallness, it becomes easy to infer circuitously that they cannot be so small after all, since they excite the same feelings as objects of unimpeachable grandeur, which is as false as the first impressions of Cheselden's patient, that all objects were the size they appeared on the plane of vision.

The ironical modesty of the present day is, in part at least, a reaction from the rather boisterous insistence of the "broad" or "muscular" school of twenty or thirty years ago, on the doctrine that "life is real, life is earnest," and earnest souls a commodity over which heaven and earth can hardly make too much ado. And it might even be said that the critics, who make no moral effort at all, because they think the best efforts in their power would fall disgustingly short of the sublime, may yet retain a clearer sense of what constitutes moral sublimity than worthy and conscientious people whose vision of the ideal is obscured by too near and absorbing contemplation of the duty of the moment. Of course there is no necessary connection between fastidiousness and inertia, or between good intentions and a defective sense of moral proportion, but this happens to be the present relation between the defects and qualities of actually opposing schools, and to each school the defect of the other is in a way a sign of the quality most needed by itself. A degree of ease and spontaneity in well-doing is fairly included in our ideal of character, and what we object to as priggishness is not really overweening ambition or exaggerated idealism, but in practice always some real fault of taste or obtuseness to the effects of mental perspective — invoking motives on too large a scale in proportion to the end proposed, or magnifying the end to correspond to the—subjective —magnitude of the considerations which led to its proposal. It is the duty of the poorest creatures amongst us, no less than of saints and heroes, to strive after the realisation of their own best self, but we object instinctively to a confusion of the tone proper to struggles in which the interests of humanity are concerned with that appropriated to merely private vicissitudes. Ingenuous boys and intelligent girls by the half million may think quite as much and as conscientiously about the duty of self-culture and the ways and means of self-development as Goethe, but outside sympathy with their mental history will be proportioned, not to the depth and sincerity of their feeling, but to the value of the objective result.

Nor is this all: we have a right to demand, as a part of the many-sided ideal of human culture, that though the will continues rigidly faithful to the line of action accepted as the best possible, it shall do so without prejudice to the right and duty of the mind to prefer a conceivable better. As in the Platonic allegory, the steeds and the charioteer are both included in the same spiritual being, and the steeds have to bear the lash and goad of their own better half; while, on the other hand, the charioteer must have steeds and a roadway—a will to guide subject to real conditions—or there is no entering upon the arena at all. The triumph of spiritual discipline is to keep the relation between the soul and the ideal unalterably close through all the varied functions of life, of which perhaps a material majority have by rights no conscious bearing on the ideal. As a matter of judgment, we admire those persons who keep a firm and constant hold on the duties that are accepted, but, as a matter of taste, we require the hold to be light and flexible, for even our judgment rejects the idea of a wooden fixity about the human copy of the illimitable divine idea. It is one of the points of sympathy between art and religion that both are haunted by an impression that "the fashion of this world passeth away," and that, therefore, the becoming temper for man—who passes away still more surely and swiftly—is in all things to live as one not bound to the life he leads, to "weep as though he wept not, to rejoice as though he rejoiced not, to buy as though he possessed not;" but this "detachment," which is carried by asceticism so far as to bid those who live be as though they lived not, branches off also into a kind of secular antinomianism which it is curious to compare with the more orthodox sentiment. The life of unrestrained passion shares with the life of absolute self-repression an impatience, which natural morality is obliged to condemn, of the real conditions of human existence. The attempt to avoid sin by avoiding action, and pain by crushing sensibility, is near akin to the attempt to avoid failure by abstaining from effort, and self-denial by abstaining from moral relations. And just as Christians and Buddhists have sought to renounce all bondage to the objective world, the ideal of æsthetic lawlessness requires its votaries to refuse obedience to the subjective constraint of conscience or principle.

One theoretical attraction of the "Vie de Bohême" is that just because it is not approved by the reason, criticism and enjoyment of it are more absolutely free, that is to say, the enjoyment is tempered by self-criticism, and the criticism is not exposed to mortification by practical tests. Like sectarian religions, its popularity depends on the supposed antagonism of an unenlightened world; hence a comfortable sense of latent rationalism and potential superiority is fostered in the minds of those who seem bent on travestying the work of conscience by their almost comic efforts not to fall by accident into the practice of any of the prosaic virtues that might frequently be of use in their case. The situation lends itself to epigram, and to carry off its inconsistency, the professional child of impulse exhausts himself in ironical contempt for the state of things in which he is entangled. But satire becomes wearisome at last, when the satirist is always his own butt, and the listener learns to distrust the reality of impulses that give themselves up to ridicule so easily, or the sincerity of the ridicule poured on impulses that have so little self-assertion, and yet are allowed to rule. It is impossible for those who abandon themselves to the habitual performance of "actions of a class"—good or bad —to regard all actions with the disengaged indifference of the critic, who makes a rule of universal abstention, and in spite of his more or less witty protestations that the world's work is vanity and its pleasures vexation, the votary of pleasure, as of any other kind of toil, finds himself at last acting—with the regular constancy of a Philistine—as if he believed that his own special form of vanity and vexation were the only one to be desired or endured. Only a few, of the more intellectual sort of libertine, attain to a *quasi* religious detachment and do really solve the problem of desiring as not desiring, enjoying as not enjoying, and, in fact, starting from a scruple of taste or understanding, end by emancipating themselves from the thraldom of passion as completely as other men do at the call of prudence or moral sympathies. Christianity in its prime was prompt to welcome such repentant sinners, who had learnt in the world the asceticism they came to practise in the cloister when their last personal illusion had given way; and it is perhaps a sectarian prejudice that leads moral philosophers of the present day to look askance at such allies. All roads lead to Rome, and the cultivation of every normal faculty to conclusions in harmony with human nature and human fate. But to make the adoption of the true scientific faith easy to these devotees of carnal perfection, and for the sake of those natural truths to which they remain faithful through all their indolent fallacies, it is especially necessary for the morality of the future to be on its guard against æsthetic stupidity and intellectual exaggeration, as well as against moral blemishes of a deeper dye. The Encyclopedist's charge against Robespierre — " Avec ton Etre Suprême tu commences à m'embêter "—would be really damaging to the votaries of natural perfection, because their cultus is self-contradictory, *i.e.*, naturally imperfect, if it is preached with an insistence that becomes tiresome. The object of their worship is infinite, but human powers of adoration are limited, and it is not a religious duty to chafe against immovable restraints, but, on the contrary, to submit to them freely, so that no natural force may be wasted by a gratuitous collision with their reality. If the reverential impulse is intermittent, that too is the work of nature, and man may not be wise above what is given him.

We come back, then, to our starting-point, that no rational rule of life is to be found for individuals out of relation to their real place in a faulty but improvable society. At the same time, we cannot agree with those moralists who deny the existence of self-regarding duties, because the greater part of our obligations are to society and owe their recognition to the force of social feelings. It is true that the opposition between duty and interest is, in their case, less apparent, for self-interest, rightly understood, means good, and self-regarding good is never painful in its results (as a personal contribution towards social good may be), but it is often difficult in performance, so as to be attended with the same inward sense of constraint and moral pressure as other duties. Indeed there are some characters who seem to own no obligation except to their own opinion, and find the decisive motive for self-devoted action rather in the impulse to be what they think right themselves than to do what they imagine to be beneficial to others. But this distinction is only psychological; there is no objective antagonism between the claims of personal perfection and social duty, because the rejection of a real and valid external claim is one of those misdeeds which injure the character, even though it may be a misfortune to the character that the claim should exist. But under any conceivable circumstances one course of conduct will be the most right, and the course which is right from one point of view is right from all. We can imagine, say, a politician or a writer of genius compelled to choose between the duty of providing for his family and the duty of giving his best—and least saleable—work to the world; *noblesse oblige*, and the great man owes himself to the larger claim; but if he does the best he can for his own household, he does it no wrong, even though he may have sons or daughters for whom the best life would have been one of ease and luxury. No man is bound to impossibilities, and the sacrifices that are imposed by circumstances cannot be laid to the charge of individual consciences. But according to the strict unbending rule of perfect morals, the only personal sacrifices that men have always a moral right to refuse are those which would detract from their efficiency as a social instrument, or foster imperfection in the person for whom the sacrifice is to be made. The loyalty of chivalrous nobles to a bad king, of faithful servants to selfish masters, of good women to brutal men, are examples of the latter kind; for though devotion rising to the most complete self-sacrifice is a fine and beautiful thing if the cause or the person is worthy, if they are not worthy, the devotion may be even worse than thrown away. The devotion of the good to the bad may, really or apparently, serve to make the best of things for the moment, but even so the devotion is only morally, not naturally or æsthetically, beautiful; and if we look beyond the special case to its place in the general stream of tendency, we see that its only final justification must lie in the conversion of its recipient to a temper less exacting of sacrifice. Even then it would have been better if the occasion for the first self-devotion had not arisen, for the same amount of virtue, instead of neutralising vice or maleficent weakness, would have been left available for the positive service of mankind against unavoidable impersonal evils.

The very extension which we are prepared to give to the range of social claims makes it the more necessary to insist on the fact that "otherness" or "not-selfishness" by itself does not make a claim valid, any more than egotism or self-regardingness by itself makes a desire wrong. No moral problem is harder than that of holding the balance even between the just claim of the self and its surroundings; and as there is something radically unamiable in juridical quibbling about personal rights in moral relations, we feel the more need of cultivated and responsive consciences, whose intuitions may sum up at once the tacit pleadings on both sides, and carry conviction with their verdict, unembittered by dispute. But it is neither natural nor healthy to conceive the welfare of society as depending, like the stability of a child's house of cards, upon the mutual support given to each other by units who have no power of standing erect by themselves. Ends that a man does not value enough to seek for his own sake will not seem better worth seeking for the sake of some one else, and ends that he feels to be worth attaining will be sought on their own merits, and not because others may share his opinion of their desirability.

The self-regarding duty of cultivating all the natural powers and sensibilities cannot be derived from the social duty of exercising all the acquired ability in conscious deference to the coequal rights and duties of other members of the community; but we are certainly bound to consider the relation between the two ideals of natural morality, the personal completeness of the individual, and his complete adaptation to the discharge of given social functions. In the present state of things, specialisation of function may seem more valuable than versatility of power, because the greater part of the life of individuals is taken up with various social relations; they cannot aim merely at being good specimens of their kind, or rather, it becomes a part of specific excellence to fulfil the demands of given relations with ideal completeness, even if, in so doing, some possibilities of personal accomplishment remain unrealised. For the individual it is not an end to act, or to feel, or to know, the inner life craves breadth, while the outer action gains in force by circumscription, and the ideal combination—or compromise—is to feel and understand in the midst of serviceable action, or to act and feel sanely while making a business of rational apprehension.

There can hardly be a more dangerous mistake made in good faith than that of assuming that the division of labour, which is socially convenient, must be mimicked by a subdivision or scattering of mental and moral qualities among different individuals or classes, restricting intelligence to an aristocracy of birth or wealth, making industry the prerogative of a proletariate, sensibility the speciality of women, and full human life the affair of no one, except perhaps a few doctrinaire Hedonists. This is one of the weakest points of the positivist ideal, which, even if in itself desirable, is too much at variance with psychological possibilities to be thought of as attainable. Just as in society the complete and highest development of every class presupposes equal proportionate development of the others, so in individuals it is impossible to separate the healthy growth of energy, affection, and intelligence, since feeling is the echo of action, and thought the summary of feeling. The seclusion of a class, a sex, or a profession from all active interests, that it may devote itself without distraction to the cultivation of the emotions, would defeat its own purpose, for the emotions must have *de quoi vivre*, they cannot stir without stimulus in an artificial vacuum, and their natural food is drawn from the conditions under which personal impulses and desires assert their instinctive vitality. It is not necessary to force the character into a narrow and mechanical formalism; passions controlled but not repressed may be trusted to break out with all desirable strength when the fitting occasion offers itself, unless such occasions are deliberately shunned; and passion for its own sake, indulged *coûte qui coûte* under the least ideal conditions, is not a product to be seriously desired or cultivated upon principle. And though action and passion seem to culminate in the perceptions of reason, we cannot make even rationality stand for the whole of manly excellence. The reason is the last word of the achieved; but the man who is all reason has done his do, there is no further spring of original power in his soul, he has come to the end of himself and his possibilities, and is but, as it were, a register or commentary on the outer world, a knowing machine, adding nothing to the sum of being. Hence we cannot take the "man of science" for the ideal hero of the future, nor find the key to our difficulties in the spread of devotion to positive knowledge. We are little the better for knowing about things not worth doing or experiencing; and that which is still being done or felt is a contribution to the stores of consciousness, which may be digested by and bye into new forms of doctrine, such as present knowledge is unable to forestall, and yet cannot afford to exclude. Human beings contribute to society such material services as they can, and receive in return the suggestive impressions without which further action would be unmotived, and continued life a blank. And the condition of the harmony between man and nature, of which the moral law is the formula, is only the existence of such a real congruity between the inner and the outer tendency as makes the human best compatible with the mixed realities of the world which is not human, and still less divine.

VIII.

CONCLUSIONS.

"Aud I turned myself to behold wisdom, and madness, and folly: for what can the man do that cometh after the king? even that which hath been already done.

"Then I saw that wisdom excelleth folly, as far as light excelleth darkness."—ECCLESIASTES.

If science is an art of naming, every name is a generalisation, and to call Nature names implies a reference to more than one experience, however real, intimate, and infelicitous; the appropriate name will characterise the universal experience, which is mixed.

VIII.

CONCLUSIONS.

IT is a common mistake, born of the close and normal connection between thought and feeling, to suppose that every one who takes the trouble to state a proposition must be personally attached to the facts he formulates. Yet we may apprehend a truth without being in love with it, and we may be in love with truth without being in love with all the facts which we learn to know for true.

If the outline of belief sketched in the preceding pages is approximately in accordance with facts, it is of little moment whether writer or reader is glad or sorry that the facts are thus, and not otherwise. We have endeavoured to reproduce faithfully the best and the worst of the truth as it is, leaving—as it must be left—to personal moods and feelings to pronounce sentence of love or aversion for the final result. On the whole, we believe broad possibilities of good to stretch beyond the narrow certainties of private ill; but it is a question for each man's conscience, judgment, or taste, whether the one is a sufficient compensation or atonement for the other.

The best we can say is, that the world does not appear to be under the government of a bad God. The natural laws which the mind recognises as irresistible are not such as the soul need refuse to obey. Speaking in the first person, it cannot be said that we feel a compulsion which our inmost conscience rejects. When men bring an indictment against Providence, it is because they see that the allotment of natural good and evil in the world is not proportioned to the moral deserts of individuals; and they say in their haste, The ruler of the world is unjust. And if we reply that, on the contrary, the world has no ruler, and that its vicissitudes follow each other in a fixed course, determined by the natures of co-existing things, they repeat the charge with a difference, and say, Then the laws of the world are unjust. The above pages have been written in vain unless we have shown that just laws do not exclude unequal fortunes; that the constancies of relation prevailing among the heterogeneous facts of nature are the condition not only of natural stability, but of all natural life, growth and enjoyment; that the law may be "holy and just and good," while the imperfection of the things subject to the law may—by virtue of the general laws, which it were a loss to repeal—work pain and evil, not only to the imperfect thing itself, but to its unoffending fellow-creatures. The laws of human life are not unjust to individual men, though the administration of the law in an imperfect world may bear with unequal severity upon some; and though nature, as a whole, does not acknowledge a responsibility towards the human species in the matter of rewards and punishments, it cannot be said that man, in his merely human relations, is the subject of unjust laws because obedience to the just laws to which he is subject is not always for his temporal advantage. We are no more subject to unjust laws than to an unjust lawgiver; we are free to do or be the best we can, for anything the universe cares to the contrary; all the natural laws of which we own the sway are on the side of reason, justice, progress, and perfection, and we distinctly do not feel a permanent pressure from the nature of things urging us to dishonesty, cruelty, or misconception; our will is not irreconcilable to the strongest tendencies of nature, which we feel to be towards natural and spiritual good; they leave us free to see and tell the truth, to love peace, and follow after righteousness— whether we do so or not is another matter, but the charter under which we hold our life from the universe secures us in these good and sufficient liberties.

But here, mayhap, some gloomy young agnostic interrupts: Out on all these canting, conceited sycophants of creation! Have we not read the sober Mill, the cynic Schopenhauer, the refined Renan? What of the sufferings of man and beast, rampant brutality, abject fear, remorseless crime, and incurable pain? Shall we praise a natural law which brings forth all these fruits of hell? Humanity forbid! We had no thought of praising nature, though few of these miseries are the work of her laws; they come from the natural imperfection of things, which is such that if we had the choice of being unborn, not a few of us, perhaps, might be glad to seize it. But what, pray you, brothers malcontent, does it prove against the morality of the laws by which moral agents live, that you or I or the raw-boned donkey of an ill-conditioned costermonger, are not providentially supplied with the means of gratifying our most lawful appetites, nor even with opportunities for displaying our specific excellences and developing our specific gifts? Is the good of life less good because it is unequally distributed? Do those pleasures cease to be desirable which you or I desire in vain, or those powers cease to be admirable which we find no pretext for admiring in ourselves?

Shall I blaspheme reason because I am no Spinoza, art because I cannot draw, music because I have no ear for it, the beauties of nature because I am shortsighted, the charms of society because I stammer, athletic sports if— like Hamlet—I am "scant of breath"? Shall I disparage political liberty because I have no vote, political power because my constituents preferred the local brewer, the delights of friendship because he thinks me a bore, the sweetness of love because she married somebody else, the glory of success because you do not read my book? Though I am poor and dyspeptic, shall there not be cakes and ale for the well-to-do with an appetite? The law of love is good and joy-giving, yet I may waste my life in mad dependence on a Delilah's face; truth is good, yet there are scientific bats who, in the name of truth, banish love and beauty from their lives because they cannot be prepared for the microscope; strength is good, though when we set the wheel of action rolling, it may break from our grasp or drag us with it whither we did not mean to go. But it is not law, only awkward fact that determines our concrete ill-luck; the laws are good laws to live by, and we owe them no grudge because you or I may fail to live fortunately. The strongest forces in nature are those which struggle towards unseen heights of natural good, and I may own as much, though my own short life be irretrievably spoilt because I have not found a place to suit me in the service of the forces; there were round holes and square on the board, but if I was born a scalene triangle, what does it prove against the rules of the game?

Say I have set my ambition too high, sought a field for potent action and to act worthily of the field, and fell back into heartbroken discontent because the field itself had to be fought for through ignoble chicane, and by the time it was almost won, the power—if I ever had it—to act effectively was lost:—what then? If the field is cleared, some one else will have a better chance than I, and some of those who have a better chance may be better able to use their chance. I have failed, and that is ill, so far as it goes; others may succeed, and that will be well, by comparison; and "in the name of all that's relative," why should we torment ourselves because there is no place for terms of absolute eulogium in the history of our experience? After all, it is almost a law, a very wide generalisation indeed, that we all get, on the whole and in the long run, whatever we want most, for if we only want hard enough, circumstances give in to us at last. If I wanted truth more than happiness and innocence more than enjoyment, nature and her laws have done me no wrong: they that seek find, and to him that knocketh shall be opened—at least the gate of content and resignation, if that is what he wants most.

This is the best and worst of it as regards the single soul: righteousness is possible, and so is misfortune, spiritual as well as temporal. But for that immaterial body that we call society, there is no worse evil than the misfortune of its members, and the best that we can say is, that such misfortune may be brought to a minimum by the intelligent action of society in all its parts. Natural evil will probably last as long as natural life; when men have done their best for themselves and for each other, pain and loss and benefits out of place will still keep human hearts versed in the art of aching. There is little to choose in the matter of happiness between the pain of bereavement and of unsatisfied craving; but though the object of our effort is to make possession the rule, and either kind of painful exception as rare as possible, while human life continues as we know it, so long happiness will be, as it were, the narrow line—as hard to tread as Mahomet's bridge—separating the two boundless deserts of want and misery. But still men find their way across the desert now, with all the chances of ill-luck, ill-will, and stupidity against them, and the aim of society is to put the chances on their side. It has been said: The dice of God are always loaded; and it rests with men to load the dice in their own favour, to multiply the influences tending in favour of good fortune, so as to allow the possibilities of good to encroach upon the region of blind, impartial chance, and cause an increasing part of human life to be determined by conscious will, and less and less by the mechanical sequences of unfeeling, unintelligent nature.

The supreme power, named by Spinoza *Deus sive Natura*, owns no duties to the human race, and though man has owned duties to the Supreme—and why not if their discharge be natural and good?—our concern is with the duties of men to each other, and it is still a new and somewhat startling conception that the claims from this quarter may be as infinite as the demands of any imaginary creator. On the one hand, we seek for a sufficient reason for the incessant exercise of each and all of our vital powers; on the other, we are half afraid of acknowledging the force of the one omnipotent and omnipresent motive which presents itself. We own a duty to our neighbours, and the good Samaritan still stands high in our esteem, but popular ethics avowedly shrink from the admission, which would stamp our living practice with condemnation, that our duty to our neighbour is—we hardly dare to write it—to do *all* that in us lies to enable those with whom we are in constant relationship to live the best life they can, and to live meanwhile the best life *we* can, as a duty, first indeed to ourselves, but then also to those with whom we are in contact, and lastly to society in general, or the unknown members of its mass whom our actions and being may indirectly influence. It is a tremendous proposition that we are bound to do all the good that we conceivably can, that every misfortune which we can in any way alleviate has a claim on us for help, and that the life of every man is to be held under conditions imposed by the needs of his fellows, that, in fact, there are no degrees of obligation, and that the same reasons which would seem now sufficient to make it right to render a cheap and easy service to a friend, also make it right in case of need to render arduous and self-denying services to the stranger that is within our gates; that duty is co-extensive with ability; and that, while the distinction may be maintained between sins of omission and sins of commission, all deliberate omission of a possible act clearly seen and believed to be good is to be classed, and reprobated, and avoided as a sin.

It has been said that this is too hard for flesh and blood, and that we are dishonest in continuing to accept the tradition of an obligation which we do not seriously think of satisfying. Secular morality, it is urged, must moderate its demands to suit the moderate limits of human virtue and capacity; and since there is no *deus ex machina* to enforce devotion to a divine ideal, men must be left to the sway of personal human motives, which only exact a finite and tolerable measure of self-denial. But, on the other hand, though we say that the God in whose name men have clung to an ideal of perfection is but a dream of the mind, a shadow of the will, giving them no real help in their endeavour, the fact remains that men have owned the infinity of duty, not as a dream or shadow, but in living truth, and if men have sought perfection before now without receiving superhuman help in their search, shall they in these latter days turn with open eyes to a less worthy goal? To say they must, is indeed a godless—say rather a soulless creed; to say they will, is false and faithless.

And when it is accepted, the tremendous burden of social obligation lightens itself at once, for it is borne in common. If, indeed, the duty of every man and woman be as full and searching as we tremble to think it, the future before them may be happier than we ever dared to hope; for the law that is binding on one is binding on all; every small service that is rendered, every small obligation that is fulfilled, may be repaid a thousand-fold. While the one owns duty and service to the many, the many can give still more potent help and guidance to the one, not only lightening the objective difficulty of his tasks, but reconciling the spirit to his obligations by the flow of unselfish sympathy. The one renders to society such small services as he can, and all society in return is at the bidding of his wants; and in truth, society has less to gain by the perfect life of its several members than they have to gain by a social order which would let them live perfectly. for human opinion is the atmosphere breathed by human agents, and as the air they breathe, so their health and strength of limb. Perhaps, after all, society asks no more from its members than to make a wholesome atmosphere for each other—not one breeding agues of indecision, fevers of envious discontent, and epidemics of quarrelsome greed. No one doubts his own power to live innocently and wisely, if all his neighbours would show him how, and a sanitary reform in the region of thought and feeling modifies conduct for the better, even without consciousness of effort.

But though the discharge of social services may profit alike the givers and receivers, the services on both sides must be a gift, and not a matter of sale and purchase; for a rigid counting of the cost is fatal to the moral life, as the lack of intellectual daring and generosity is fatal to all natural energy. It is true, though the fact proves nothing against the supreme naturalness of virtue, that there is no certain assurance that he who does most for his kind will receive most help from them in his need—only a general certainty that the harvest is according to the seed, and that each addition to the number of those who have done what they can lessens the gross weight of evil and mishap which prevents even the best of men from doing all that they would.

But there is one last objection to be met: If earth is turned to heaven by the reciprocal good offices of mankind, who will be content to leave it? and is it not a cruel mercy to reconcile men to a life they must quit so soon? We are no optimists, and our wildest dreams do not go beyond a hope of making untimely death once more the worst enemy of the living. Persons who have only lived out half their natural life on earth look to another world for compensation, but it may be that those who, while it was time, have filled their consciousness to overflowing with the experiences of a sympathetic energy, satiate themselves with existence so, and have no desire left for immortality. Those whose energy has been productive, who have lived much, and over-lived much, who have tested the limits of their powers, and see to the end of the work which it is possible for them to do, they, in the fulness of years and attainment, sing, we may conjecture, their *Nunc Dimittis* to the Universum with at least as much feeling of relief as of reluctance.

If people could think of themselves as immortal with the immaterial eternity of geometrical truths, they would have no reason either to desire or to dread a posthumous existence. But, in fact, of all our acquired tastes, the taste for living for ever is the one which will be found least deeply rooted amongst men, if for no other reason, because it has never been strengthened by indulgence. No mortal knows whether a resurrection to eternal life would answer his expectation or not, but many good people are at pains to explain that they could not take their own souls *au sérieux*, unless they believed them to be immortal, and we have no wish to cavil at the means by which so necessary a result may be obtained; only, looking at things dispassionately from without, the misgiving arises, whether our own respect for the human soul would stand the strain of seeing our good neighbours produced to infinity. If man's duration were not as finite as his good qualities, he would need infinite tolerance to endure his own presence through the ages.

The kind of immortality that may be certainly anticipated, and that influences the present action of living men, is not personal but material. The desire for fame, subjective immortality, is reasoned away as easily as that half of ambition which consists in the desire to be thought of as great, powerful, or in any way illustrious; no one on reflection cares to be admired by fools, and the admiration of the few competent judges whom a candidate for greatness finds among his contemporaries is exactly proportioned to his real merits; but though it follows from the nature of the case that good work is appreciated by those who know what is good, the least part of the motive that actuates those who are able to do good work is the knowledge that it will be appraised at its true value by a few. The sufficient reason for any act is a clear and adequate apprehension of the act as good to do, which makes the doing of it appear as an end in itself, whether the deed is applauded and the doer remembered or not, for these are accidents lying beyond the power of the individual will to control, and wise men do not place their happiness at the mercy of contingencies. To be remembered is not an end. We are not the better now for what generations still unborn will think of us, if we have the power to make them think at all; it is they who will be the better for our thought of them. Our present desire is not for an idle fame, but for the triumph of the truths and tendencies which have been the guides of our action—not the less so because the triumph of a cause is followed by the dawn of new truths and tendencies, whose champions will then have more right than our ghosts or tombstones to honour and praise among the living. It is enough for us to know that what we have done, be it less or more, will in any case live in its natural effects, and that, whether it knows the fact or not, the future will be, within approximately calculable limits, as much the better as we may have chosen to make it for our action on the present.

Life and death are equally natural, and neither is a pure good, neither an unmixed evil. The Stoics asked, " What good is it to the bubble while it holds together, and what harm when it is burst?" and we can only answer, that to live according to nature, and to die a natural death, is the sum of all the natural good we know or can think of as attainable by man. " Things without life, and things without reason, and things that have rambled and know not the way," have less of natural excellence in them than the man of strenuous and temperate virtue, who is constantly faithful to his true self and to the impressions of the Not-self by which his inner life and being are conditioned. More than this the resources of thought and language do not allow us to maintain or suppose. If it is asked what healthy, vigorously-minded men, with plenty of desires of their own, riding rough-shod over weaker tendencies, have to do with the doctrine of natural necessity and the praises of universal perfection, the answer is easy, for they have not much. Men who are swayed by simple personal desires, untroubled by religious doubts and moral perplexities, live almost automatically the less complex, we do not presume to say the lower,—perhaps the happier—life of irrational nature, of roses, brambles, turtle-doves, or tigers, as the case may be; they are under the law of the land and of opinion, but they have naturally little concern with the gospel of religious morality. If they, too, are moderately good of their kind, it is not from the vague hope they sometimes believe themselves to entertain of being by and bye transformed, by a power not themselves, into beings of another (how can we say a better?) kind. Such hope is not, in most cases, lively enough to be efficient as a motive, but if it were so, then certainly the fact that men can live well and cheerfully by the help of anything so immaterial as hope deferred, proves that not much immaterial help is needed to carry the majority of them through the material troubles of life. Of its immaterial troubles, two of the most intolerable, fear and disappointment, have no power over the enlightened reason and the chastened will. We do not fear what is certain; we succumb or endure. Disappointment only comes to those whose hopes have been unreasonably high or unreasonably confident, and to lose a false hope of the future does not make men less able to face a present reality.

Heaven and hell are names or visions; the earth is ours—here a hell of sensuality and hardened cruelty, there a heaven of love and beauty and wisdom, with a tender smile upon her gracious lips, and yearning prophecy in the melting depths of her unfathomable eyes.

www.ingramcontent.com/pod-product-compliance
Lightning Source LLC
Chambersburg PA
CBHW020310240426
43673CB00039B/761